THE HANDY BUG ANSWER BOOK

Also from Visible Ink Press

The Handy Science Answer Book, 2nd edition

Can any bird fly upside down? Is white gold really gold? Compiled from the ready-reference files of the Science and Technology Department of the Carnegie Library of Pittsburgh, this best seller answers 1,400 questions about the inner workings of the human body and outer space, about math and computers, and about planes, trains, and automobiles. By the Science and Technology Department of the Carnegie Library of Pittsburgh, 7.25" x 9.25", 598 pages, 100 illustrations, dozens of tables, $16.95, ISBN 0-7876-1013-5.

The Handy Weather Answer Book

What's the difference between sleet and freezing rain? Do mobile homes attract tornadoes? What exactly is wind chill and how is it figured out? How can the temperature be determined from the frequency of cricket chirps? You'll find clear-cut answers to these and more than 1,000 other frequently asked questions in *The Handy Weather Answer Book.* By Walter A. Lyons, 7.25" x 9.25", 398 pages, 75 illustrations, $16.95, ISBN 0-7876-1034-8.

The Handy Space Answer Book

Is there life on Mars? Did an asteroid cause the extinction of dinosaurs? Find answers to these and 1,200 other questions in *The Handy Space Answer Book.* It tackles hundreds of technical concepts–quasars, black holes, NASA missions and the possibility of alien life–in everday language. With vivid photos, thorough indexing and an appealing format, it's as fun to read as it is informative for space lovers and curious readers of all ages. By Phillis Engelbert and Diane L. Dupuis, 7.25" x 9.25", 590 pages, $17.95, ISBN 1-57859-017-5.

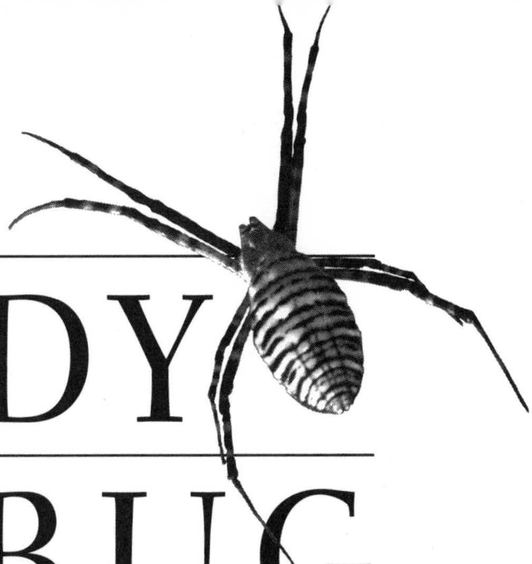

THE HANDY BUG ANSWER BOOK™

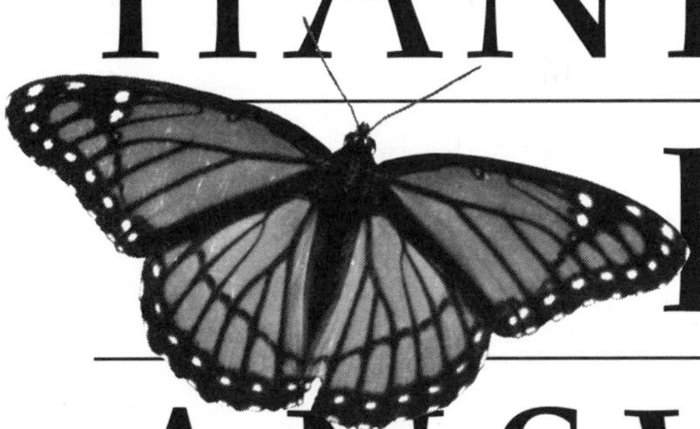

Dr. Gilbert Waldbauer
Professor Emeritus, Department of Entomology • University of Illinois at Urbana-Champaign

Foreword by Dr. May R. Berenbaum
Professor and Head, Department of Entomology • University of Illinois at Urbana-Champaign

Detroit • New York • London

THE HANDY BUG ANSWER BOOK™

Published by Visible Ink Press™
a division of Gale Research
835 Penobscot Bldg.
Detroit, MI 48226-4094

Visible Ink Press and The Handy Bug Answer Book are trademarks of Gale Research.

Most Visible Ink Press™ books are available at special quantity discounts when purchased in bulk by corporations, organizations, or groups. Customized printings, special imprints, messages, and excerpts can be produced to meet your needs. For more information, contact Special Markets Manager, Gale Research, 835 Penobscot Bldg., Detroit, MI 48226-4094.

Art Director: Michelle DiMercurio
Typesetting: Graphix Group
Cover Photos: Robert J. Huffman

Library of Congress Cataloging-in-Publication Data

Waldbauer, Gilbert.
The handy bug answer book / Gilbert Waldbauer ; foreword by May R. Berenbaum.
p. cm.
Includes bibliographical references and index.
ISBN 1-57859-049-3
1. Insects—Miscellanea. 2. Arthropoda—Miscellanea I. Title.
QL467.W25 1998
595.7—dc21 98-21694
CIP

Printed in the United States of America

10 9 8 7 6 5 4 3 2 1

Contents

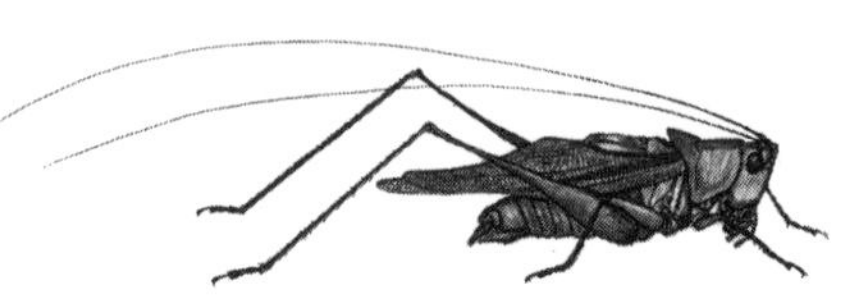

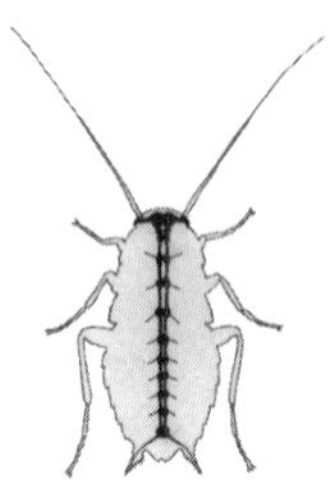

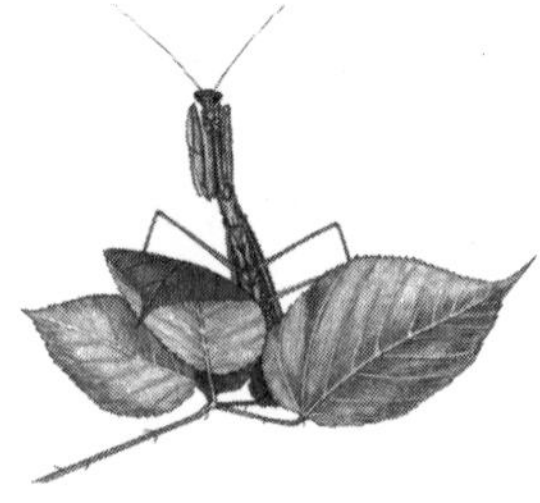

Foreword

A Wonderful World at Your Fingertips—and Under Your Feet

Insects are not exactly user-friendly organisms. There's the size thing—most of them are too small to examine closely, and a good number of them move so quickly that, even if they are readily visible without magnification, it's difficult to get more than a general impression of legged-ness as they scurry past. There's also the fact that they're outwardly so different from what we're accustomed to. With skeletons on the outside, an embarrassment of legs, and various appurtenances resembling household appliances more than appendages sprouting from various and sundry body regions, they are, to say the least, difficult to relate to. Their astonishing abundance adds to the confusion. With over 750,000 described species, there are more species of insects (and their other jointed-legged relatives in the phylum Arthropoda) than there are any other kind of animal. Their sheer number makes them impossible to ignore; both the number of individuals and the biomass they make up are staggering. The biomass of ants alone dwarfs the biomass of humans on the planet.

Questions inevitably arise about insects because, difficult as they may be to understand, they are simply impossible to avoid. Insects are in more different places in the world than virtually any other organism, in habitats ranging from the high Arctic to tropical rainforests to petroleum pools to glaciers to mines a mile below the Earth's surface. Their tendency to turn up where they are not welcome has meant that knowing about insects has a direct and economic impact on human lives. In the U.S., insects cause an estimated five-billion-dollar loss to staple crops alone each year. They also exact their toll in the form of destruction of fruit crops, greenhouse and nursery products, forest products, livestock, stored grain and packaged food, and household goods and furniture. As vectors, or carriers, of human diseases, they cause incalculable losses in the form of illness or death due to malaria, yellow fever, typhus, plague, dengue, and innumerable other diseases.

But insects defy easy generalization or stereotyping. While some insects cause massive economic loss, other species contribute economic benefits in a magnitude unequalled by most invertebrates. Insect-pollinated crops exceed in value nine billion dollars annually, and insect products, including honey, wax, lacquer, silk, and so on, contribute billions. Biological control of both insect and weed pests is worth additional millions in reclaimed land and crop production, and even insect disposal of dung is economically significant in pasturelands throughout the country. So, economic incentives alone provide reasons to wonder about insects. Add to that economic incentive the inescapability of insects in human lives and questions multiply.

Up until now, finding the answers to those questions has been a challenge. Among other things, much of the information available about insects is far more than most people want to know; entomologists write tomes for other entomologists, which are specialized, jargon filled, and alarmingly illustrated with, among other things, detailed diagrams of insect genitalia. That's all changed, thanks to Gil Waldbauer's effort in *The Handy Bug Answer Book*. Now, for the curious or even reluctant inquirer, answers to 800 questions about insects are provided in a single volume, the manifestation of Dr. Waldbauer's half-century of experience of being up close and personal with insects of all descriptions. These answers are written in an engaging manner and are refreshingly free of unapproachable technical language. Learning the answers to so many questions about insects is probably the best way for people to cope with these unavoidable cohabitants of Planet Earth—to satisfy curiosity, solve insect-related problems, and even, possibly, to replace fear and loathing with grudging admiration for one of the most remarkable success stories on the planet.

Dr. May R. Berenbaum
Professor and Head, Department of Entomology,
University of Illinois at Urbana-Champaign
Author of Bugs in the System: Insects and Their Impact on Human Affairs

Introduction

Why write a book about insects and other bugs intended for nonspecialists rather than professional entomologists? Why should a nonspecialist read such a book? These questions are two faces of the same coin and have the same answers.

First, insects are just plain fascinating! I took much joy in writing *The Handy Bug Answer Book,* because I find insects to be the most interesting of all the animals on Earth. I hope that you will feel the same way after reading this book. They are endlessly intriguing because they do fascinating things. For example: Honey bees have a language. Ants keep aphids as domestic animals. Certain flies secrete milk and have an analogue of a uterus. Monarch butterflies, not to be outdone by birds, make a migration of over 2,000 miles. Many plant-feeding insects are infallible botanists that can, at a taste or a sniff, recognize plants that belong to the botanical group on which they specialize.

For more than 40 years, I have been a professional entomologist, a professor of entomology at the University of Illinois in Urbana-Champaign. Teaching about insects and doing research on them in the field and in the laboratory has been a great joy. It is as if I were being paid to pursue my hobby.

Most of the animals on Earth are insects. According to recent estimates, about 1,200,000 species of animals are known to science, and about 900,000 (75 percent!) of them are insects. The beetles alone number about 350,000 species, about 30 percent of the known animals. How many species of insects remain to be discovered? The estimates vary from a conservative nine million to a high of 30 million. Not only are there a lot of different kinds of insects, but they are exceedingly numerous. A swarm of migratory locusts in North Africa was estimated to consist of about eight billion individuals and to weigh about 20,000 tons. Such population outbreaks are out of the ordinary, but insects are surprisingly numerous under normal circumstances. A square yard of forest soil may contain almost 30,000 of them, and a hive of bees may be populated by over 50,000 individuals. Insects are abundant virtually everywhere except in the oceans and on the polar ice caps.

As a group, the insects are necessary to the survival of the human race, because they are essential components of virtually all terrestrial and fresh water ecosystems, including those in which we live and those that provide us with food, fiber, timber, and most of the other organic necessities of life. The ecological roles of insects are many and varied. Most ecosystems could not function without the scavenging insects—second only to bacteria and fungi as decomposers of feces and dead animals and plants—that recycle nitrogen, carbon, and the other elements necessary to life. Without insect predators and parasites, ecosystems—including our orchards and crop fields—would be disrupted by uncontrolled and disastrous population outbreaks of insects, other animals, and plants. About 80 percent of the world's plants are more or less dependent upon insects for pollination. Without pollinating insects, many plants would become extinct, and the human diet would become monotonous. The grains and other grasses, which are wind-pollinated, would survive, but the great majority of other fruits and vegetables would not, nor would many of the forage plants that feed milk cows and beef cattle.

Although insects in the aggregate are a blessing, pest insects are our most numerous and consuming competitors for the world's supply of food, fiber, and timber. In 1988, pest insects cost the American economy well over $14 billion, more than enough to command our interest and more than enough to justify more research on insects than is being done now. Furthermore, a few insects are a threat to the health of humans. Take, for example, the anopheline mosquitoes that transmit malaria. In 1970 there were about 270 million cases of malaria and about two million deaths, mostly in the tropics and especially in Africa.

The Handy Bug Answer Book considers the structure of insects, how their bodies function, their growth and metamorphosis, their behavior, and their place in the ecological and economic scheme of things. I have tried to write in a friendly, nontechnical style that I hope will suit the great majority of readers. The many photos and illustrations enhance the descriptions, and I hope you find the color photos in the center of the book particularly stunning. The index is detailed and central to using this book. If a subject piques your interest, the index will lead you to the other pages on which it is considered. If you come upon a word that you don't know, the index will lead you to an explanation in the text, which is usually on the first page listed. In this way, the index serves in lieu of a glossary.

Acknowledgments

Many people contributed to the completion of this book, and I am greatly indebted to them all. Several of my professional colleagues gave generously of their advice and wisdom: May Berenbaum, John Bouseman, Fred Delcomyn, Susan Fahrbach, Larry Hanks, James Nardi, Phil Nixon, Tom Phillips, and James Sternburg. Thanks are also due to Dorothy Houchens, who did an expert job of typing the various versions of the manuscript.

My wife, Stephanie Waldbauer, read an early version of the manuscript and offered a great deal of constructive criticism that greatly improved the book.

The book benefitted tremendously from the efforts of my editor at Visible Ink Press, Jeff Hermann, and from the input and encouragement of Julia Furtaw and Christa Brelin. Additional 'thank yous' go to Michelle Banks for her editorial assistance, Bob Huffman for the cover photos and for his copywriting efforts, Michelle DiMercurio for her artistic expertise, Pam Reed and Randy Bassett for photo cropping and scanning, Sarah Chesney for her permissions work, Jeff Muhr for everything technical, Barbara Cohen for the indexing, and Marco Di Vita of the Graphix Group for his typesetting skills.

Gil Waldbauer

BUG BASICS

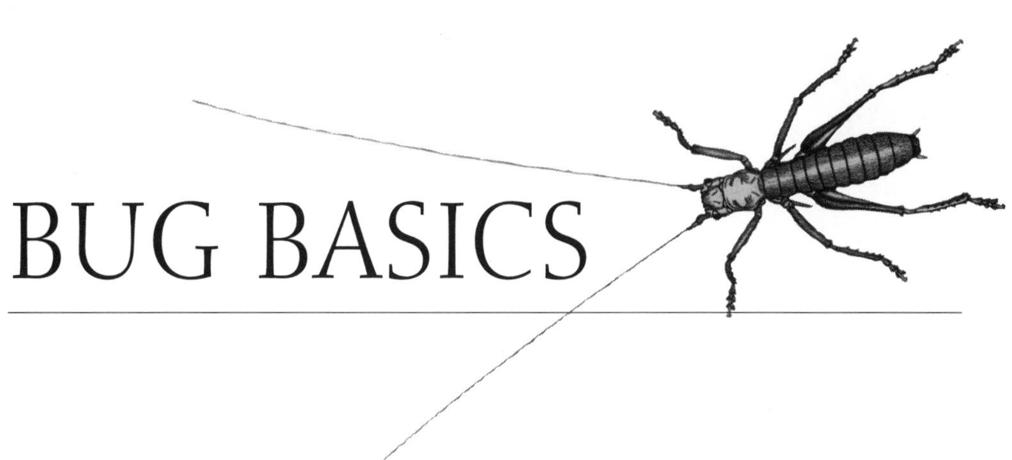

What is a **bug**?

This word is used loosely and means different things to different people. When entomologists are being hard-nosed, they insist that "bug" can be used only to designate insects of the order Hemiptera, sometimes known as the "true bugs." Physicians and bacteriologists have been known to call disease-causing germs bugs. But when most people use this word, they have in mind multi-legged creatures such as beetles, moths, cockroaches, spiders, and millipedes; in other words, just about any one of the hundreds of thousand of species in the phylum Arthropoda.

Are there bugs that **do not have legs**?

Most people use the word "bug" to refer to creepy-crawly creatures with many legs. Bug is, admittedly, a nonscientific and loosely used word, but including legless creatures such as worms, slugs, and snails among the bugs stretches the word too much. Maggots, some beetles, and other immature insects such as larval bees and wasps do not have legs, although they do have legs when they become adults.

What is an **arthropod**?

The Arthropoda, by far the largest of all the phyla, includes all of the animals that have an exoskeleton, or hard outer shell; a body that is made up of a series of segments; and six or more pairs of jointed legs. The phylum Arthropoda is generally divided into nine classes, five of which are familiar to almost everyone, and include virtually all of the arthropoda that most people are likely to see: the centipedes, the millipedes, the arachnids, the crustaceans, and the insects.

Entomologist Edward S. Ross collects termites from a termite mound. (Photo by Edward S. Ross.)

How many insects and other **arthropods remain unknown**?

The arthropods that remain to be discovered, mainly insects, greatly outnumber those that are already known to science. While hundreds of thousands of arthropods other than insects, mostly mites, are still unknown, the insects that have yet to be discovered and named number in the millions, about nine million according to a recent conservative estimate and perhaps as many as 30 million according to a more daring estimate.

Broadly speaking, **where on the earth** can insects and other arthropods be found?

Virtually everywhere! Centipedes, millipedes, arachnids, and insects live mainly on the continents and islands. Centipedes and millipedes are strictly land-dwellers. Most arachnids are terrestrial, but a few live in or on fresh water, and a very few live along the coasts of the seas and can tolerate being covered by the tide. Most insects live on land, but a sizable number live in fresh water, and a few even live in the seas. Crustaceans live mainly in salt water, but some live in fresh water, and a few even live on land.

How many of the world's insects have been **discovered and named**?

No one has counted them all, and the estimates vary. About 900,000 species is close to the truth, about 75 percent of all the known animals.

How many different kinds of arthropods are there?

There are several reasonably reliable estimates of the number of arthropods that are currently known to science. Different authorities arrive at somewhat different estimates, but most of them are in tolerably close agreement with each other. A more or less typical estimate is that, of the approximately 1,200,000 known species of animals, about 980,000, or 82 percent, are arthropods.

What is an **entomologist**?

My *Oxford English Dictionary* defines entomology as the branch of zoology concerned with insects. Thus, an entomologist is a person who studies insects. In actual practice, entomology departments in universities also house people who study arachnids, particularly ticks and mites, centipedes, millipedes, and even annelid and nematode worms. People who study crustaceans, however, have traditionally been housed in zoology rather than entomology departments.

BUGS THAT ARE NOT INSECTS

CENTIPEDES

What is a **centipede**?

Centipedes belong to the class Chilopoda. In the members of this class, the segments of the body have come together to form two body regions, a head that bears chewing mouthparts and a single pair of long antennae, and a long and slender trunk consisting of a variable number of similar segments, each of which bears one pair of legs.

Are centipedes **venomous**?

Yes, they are, but they rarely bite people. They use the venom to subdue their prey. The venom is injected by a pincer-like pair of "poison fangs" that are located beneath the head and are actually the greatly modified legs of the first body segment behind the head.

Do centipedes really have a **hundred legs**?

The literal meaning of the name centipede is one hundred legs. It is formed from two Latin root words: *centi*, a hundred, and *ped*, a foot. Some of these animals have as few as 30 legs, while others have as many as 346 legs.

Where do centipedes live?

Most centipedes live in the tropics, but they are well represented in temperate regions. By day they hide in sheltered places, often under rocks or logs, but at night they come out to hunt for their prey.

What do centipedes **eat**?

All centipedes are predators that eat small animals, usually earthworms or insects, but some of the tropical species are large enough to capture and eat small lizards or mice.

Are centipedes ever found in our **homes**?

Centipedes that normally live outdoors occasionally wander into houses or, more often, are brought in with wood for the fireplace. But one species, the house centipede, is a regular occupant of homes and other buildings. It prefers damp areas and most often lives in cellars, bathrooms, or closets, where it is sometimes seen running about at night on the floor or walls as it hunts for flies, cockroaches, or other insects. Full-grown house centipedes may be from two to three inches long and are easily recognized by their exceptionally long and slender legs and antennae. If you see one of these creatures in your home try to keep yourself from squashing it. House centipedes do no harm, but are really beneficial because they eat cockroaches and other less welcome bugs that invade our homes.

Do centipedes ever **attack people**?

No, but if a centipede is picked up and handled, it may try to defend itself by biting with its poison fangs. On rare occasions people have been bitten by house centipedes that they have picked up.

How many different kinds of centipedes can be **found in America north of Mexico**?

Although most of them are tropical, about 100 species occur in America north of Mexico.

MILLIPEDES

What is a **millipede**?

Millipedes belong to the class Diplopoda, a name that means double legs, from the Greek *diplo*, double, and *poda*, a foot. Like centipedes, they have long, slender bodies that consist of a head with chewing mouthparts and one pair of antennae, which are much shorter than those of centipedes, and a trunk that consists of many segments. Each segment bears one pair of legs. A single hard shield covers two segments, and thus it looks as if there are two pairs of legs per segment.

How big are the biggest centipedes?

Some centipedes, especially certain tropical species, are among the largest of the arthropods. In the United States, the biggest ones, essentially tropical species, live in the southeastern states and may be as much as ten inches long.

Do millipedes really have a **thousand legs**?

The literal meaning of the word millipede—a compound of two Latin root words: *mill,* one thousand, and *pod,* a foot—is, of course, a thousand legs. Millipedes do have a great many legs, but none of them has as many as a thousand. Some have as few as 80 legs, and others have as many as 400 legs.

Where do millipedes live?

Most of them live in the tropics, usually in damp places: in the soil or rotting wood; in clumps of moss; under rocks, logs, or fallen leaves; or in other protected sites.

How many different kinds of millipedes occur in America north of Mexico?

As with the centipedes, most millipedes live in the tropics, but about 100 species can be found in the United States and Canada.

What do millipedes **eat**?

Most of them eat dead leaves or other decaying plant material, but a few feed on living plants and sometimes injure garden and greenhouse plants. A very few prey on small insects and other arthropods.

Are millipedes **good and caring parents**?

Most are not. They just drop their eggs on the ground and abandon them. But some of them spin a protective silken cocoon around their egg mass or dig an underground chamber in which they hide their eggs. A few species of millipedes are attentive parents that care for their offspring much as birds care for their eggs and nestlings. The females prepare an underground nest in which they lay their eggs, brood the eggs until they hatch, and then guard their young until they are capable of surviving on their own.

How do millipedes **defend themselves** against birds, mice, and other animals that might try to eat them?

Some species curl themselves up into tight balls, thus exposing only their armored upper sides to the predator. Many millipedes—but not all of them—have a series of stink glands that open along the sides of the body and that, if the millipede is attacked, emit a fluid or a vapor with an offensive smell. In at least some species, this fluid contains hydrogen cyanide and is sometimes strong enough to kill insects that are confined in a closed jar with an individual of one of these species.

Do millipedes ever **attack people**?

No, but if a millipede is handled, the defensive fluid that oozes from its body may irritate the skin.

ARACHNIDS

What is an **arachnid**?

An arachnid is, not surprisingly, a member of the class Arachnida, which consists of many sorts of creatures that are quite different from each other, including, among others, spiders, scorpions, harvestmen (daddy long legs), mites, and ticks. The segments of an arachnid's body are grouped as two regions, the cephalothorax, a combination of head (cephalon) and thorax, and an abdomen that bears no appendages. The cephalothorax has four pairs of walking legs plus one more pair of legs, called the pedipalps, that are near the mouth and have been greatly modified to serve as antennae, or feelers.

What is the **etymology** (not entomology) of the name Arachnida?

Arachna, a Greek word that means spider, also appears in the context of Greek mythology. As the myth tells us, Arachne of Lydia was a Greek woman who became such a skilled weaver that she ventured to challenge the goddess Athena, who was also a great weaver, to a contest. The goddess wove a tapestry that portrayed the gods as majestic beings. Arachne wove an even more beautiful tapestry that showed the gods enjoying their amorous adventures. Enraged at the perfection her rival's creation, Athena tore it to pieces. Arachne hanged herself in despair. But the goddess took pity on her and turned the rope into a cobweb and Arachne into a spider.

What is a **spider**?

Most people know what spiders look like and most spiders are easily recognized—among the exceptions are some small spiders that are very deceptive mimics of ants. Speaking more technically, spiders are arachnids that have an unsegmented abdomen that is attached to the cephalothorax by a slender stem. You may have to look closely to see this stem.

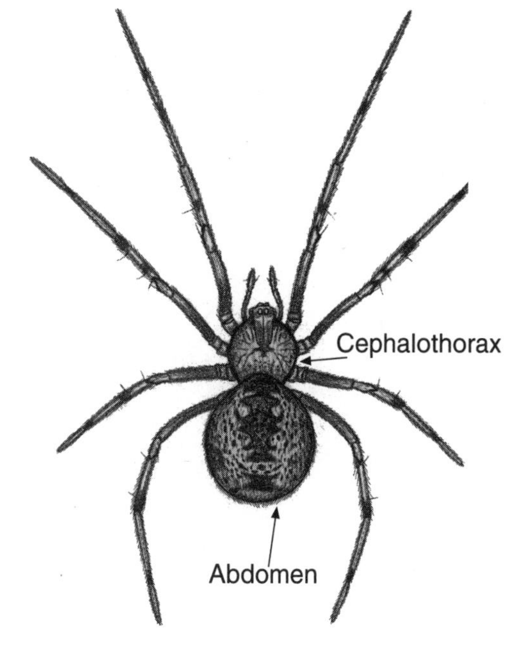

(Illustration by James B. Nardi. Courtesy of Iowa State University Press.)

How many **different kinds** of spiders can be found in North America?

About 2,500 out of a world total of about 30,000 known species. But many spiders, probably including quite a few North American species, have yet to be discovered and named.

What do spiders **eat**?

All spiders are predators that eat other animals, usually insects but also other arthropods. A few of the larger spiders eat small vertebrates, including birds.

How do spiders eat?

Many spiders first inject the intact body of the prey with digestive enzymes that liquefy its tissues. This liquid is then sucked up, and the spider discards the more or less intact outer shell of the prey. Other spiders crunch up the prey to expose its soft inner tissues and then flood them with digestive enzymes. After sucking up their meal, they discard a shapeless mass of chewed-up outer shell.

An orb-weaving spider's web covered with dew. (Photo by Edward S. Ross.)

Are spiders venomous, and what do they use the venom for?

All spiders are venomous and use the venom to subdue their prey. The venom is injected by a pair of fangs that grasp and pierce the prey animal. Each fang is traversed by a duct, a narrow tunnel, that carries the venom from a poison gland near its base to an opening at the tip of the fang.

How do spiders **catch their prey**?

Some spiders lie in ambush and snatch any insect that comes too close. Other spiders hunt for the insects and other arthropods that they eat, then pounce on them as a cat pounces on a mouse. But most spiders, which happen to be those that are most familiar to people, trap their prey in silken webs.

What are the different **kinds of spider's webs**?

Webs that are most commonly seen are the radial and usually geometrically regular orb webs that we see hanging vertically between two plants or the branches of a tree or shrub; the close-woven horizontal sheet webs that are sometimes scattered over our lawns and are conspicuous early in the morning when the dew that clings to them glistens in the sun; and, finally, the irregular webs spun by house spiders, the cobwebs that are so unsightly when they are covered with dust.

How is an **orb-weaving** spider's web constructed?

A web is always constructed between two firm supports, such as adjacent twigs of a tree. It is anchored at its top to a sturdy line of silk, the first part of the web that the spider spins, that bridges the gap between the supports. When people build a suspension bridge, the span may begin with a fine line carried by an arrow shot from a bow. In a similar way, some spiders get a line across the gap between supports by clinging to one support as they release from their spinnerets a fine strand of silk that is wafted over to the other support by the breeze. Once fastened, this "bridge line" is pulled tight and reinforced with additional strands of silk. The spider next spins a drooping loop that is anchored at the two ends of the bridge line. The spider then drops down from the center of this loop on a thread that it anchors to some support below, thus creating a Y-shaped structure that is the foundation for the rest of the web. It then spins a 360-degree array of radial threads that run from the crotch of the Y to various points on the surrounding vegetation. These radii support the spiral of sticky silk that will trap insects that blunder into the web.

How does an orb-weaver know that an insect is **trapped in its web**?

Since it sits somewhere on the web, it feels the vibrations caused by the struggling insect. Guillame de Salluste du Barta, the 16th-century French Huguenot poet, wrote:

> Or almost like a spider, who, confined in her web's center, shakt with every wind, moves in an instant if the buzzing fly stir but a string of her lawn canapie.

Do **drugs** affect a spider's ability to spin its web?

Yes, they certainly do. Spiders induced to ingest mescaline, a hallucinogen from the peyote cactus, built orb webs that were smaller than normal and that had abnormally variable angles between the radial lines of the web. Spiders on a high dose of caffeine seemed to have "coffee nerves"; their webs were barely recognizable, no more than an irregular tangle of threads that would catch no insects. Another hallucinogen, LSD (lysergic acid), induced spiders to waste extra time and energy on building abnormally neat and regular webs that would catch no more insects than the usual webs.

How do spiders **"fly" without wings**?

They don't really fly; they "balloon" through the air on a long, fine strand of silk. Young, newly hatched spiders, surrounded by scores or even hundreds of their brothers and sisters that hatched from the same egg mass, must disperse in order to avoid overcrowding. Spiders of some species disperse by ballooning. A spider that is about to balloon climbs to some high point, perhaps the tip of a blade of grass, faces into the breeze, and pays out a long strand of silk from the spinnerets at the tip of its abdomen. This strand of gossamer is wafted upward by the breeze like a kite. Eventually the pull on this strand of silk is sufficient to lift the spider into the air. Ballooning spiders may drift with the breeze for distances from a few yards to hundreds of miles. They can rise high into the air. One was caught at an altitude of 15,000 feet in a trap mounted on an airplane.

What is a **web-casting spider**?

These nocturnal spiders catch insects much as a fisherman catches fish with a cast net. They spin a web so small that they can pick it up and hold it with their four front legs. A hunting web-caster hangs upside down from its hind legs, the elastic net small and in its contracted state, as it waits for a meal to appear. When an insect comes close, the spider spreads the sticky web wide and catches the insect in it. If the insect is caught, the spider bundles it up in the net and sucks it dry through the mesh.

What is a **bolas spider**?

Bolas spiders are aggressive mimics. That is, they attract their prey, exclusively night-flying male moths, by mimicking a female moth of the prey species by emitting odors that are chemically identical to certain components of her sex attractant pheromone. When a male moth bent on sex, lured in by the false pheromone, flies close enough, the spider "lassoes" it with a sticky glob of glue at the end of a long strand of silk. This device is really more like the bolas used by Argentine gauchos than the lasso used by cowboys.

Can spiders **change color**, and why do they do so?

Crab spiders, which do not spin webs, are ambushers that seize their prey when it comes close. Some species wait in ambush on blossoms to catch such nectar-seeking insects as bees and butterflies that land on the blossom. A well-camouflaged ambusher is likely to be more successful than a conspicuous one that is easily noticed by an approaching insect. Not surprisingly, some species of crab spiders that habitually lurk on flowers have evolved the capacity to change their color like chameleons so as to match the color of the different kinds of blossoms on which they wait. For example, one species can change from yellow to white and back again, and another can switch back and forth between pink and yellow.

What is a **wolf spider**?

Wolf spiders are hunters that search for their prey rather than waiting for the prey to come to them. They are loners, never running in packs like their namesakes. These large, long-legged spiders hunt in daylight, using their vision to spot prey. Their eight eyes, very keen at perceiving movement, are arranged so that the spider can see to the front, to the sides, and, to some extent, to the rear. When a wolf spider spots a victim, it stalks it much as a lion stalks an antelope, creeping stealthily towards it, and, when it has come close enough, putting on a burst of speed and leaping onto the victim. Wolf spiders hunt mainly on the ground but will occasionally climb up onto vegetation.

What are **trapdoor spiders**?

These nocturnal ambushers spend their whole life in a silk-lined burrow in the ground that is covered by a hinged trapdoor made of silk. There they are fairly safe from their own predators but can rush out to seize such insects as grasshoppers, beetles, or ants

Wolf spider with young. (Photo by Edward S. Ross.)

that pass nearby. Some trapdoor spiders are alerted to passing insects by vision or touch, but others deploy a "high-tech" alarm system, silken threads that radiate outward from the burrow. Insects or other small animals that contact these "tripwires" immediately alert the waiting spider, which rushes out of the burrow to catch the unfortunate animal.

What is a **water spider**?

This European species spends its life beneath the surface of a still pond or lake living in an air-filled "diving bell" of its own making. It begins the construction of the diving bell by weaving a small sheet of silk that it anchors in a horizontal position to a submerged water plant. It then swims to the surface, traps a large bubble of air between its abdomen and hind legs, and returns to the silken sheet to release the bubble beneath it. The bubble floats up and is trapped beneath the sheet. Several such trips fill the diving bell. It then sits in the bell with its legs, which are very sensitive to vibrations, extended out into the water. When it detects vibrations from a swimming insect or even one struggling on the surface, it rushes out to catch it and then returns to its diving bell to eat it.

Do spiders **care for their young**?

All spiders, to varying degrees, cover their eggs with silk, a few primitive species with just a few strands and others with a dense layer of silk in the form of a discrete egg sac. Many female spiders carry their egg sacs with them or guard them in other ways. These behaviors are, of course, elementary forms of parental care. Some spiders give more elaborate care to their young. Female wolf spiders carry their egg sacs with them everywhere, and when the eggs are ready to hatch, the mother tears the tough egg sac open so that her babies can make their way out. They immediately scuttle up onto her abdomen and ride there until they are ready to begin feeding, at which time they drop to the ground. A European spider, *Theridion,* provides a far more advanced form of parental care. The female closely guards her egg sac, which hangs in a protective tent in the upper part of her web. For several days, the newly-hatched spiderlings feed on a liquid that oozes from the mother's mouth. They share the mother's food, eating liquids that ooze from wounds that she makes in the tough outer shell of the prey. Eventually, the young grow large enough to help their mother make captures by throwing strands of their own silk over the struggling insect. When the mother ultimately dies, her offspring eat her body, her last contribution to the welfare of her babies.

How big is the world's **biggest spider**?

Big enough to cover a dinner plate! The largest known spiders are the Goliath bird-eating spiders of the coastal rain forests of northeastern South America. The largest one known, a male collected by a scientific expedition in Venezuela, had, according to the *Guinness Book of Records*, a leg span of over 11 inches. According to the same source, the heaviest bird-eating spider known, a female captured in Surinam in 1986, weighed a colossal 4.3 ounces. That big a spider could easily subdue a bird. Most birds are much smaller. Wood warblers generally weigh only about 0.35 ounces, a scarlet tanger about one ounce, and a bird as large as a bluejay only about 3.5 ounces.

How do male spiders avoid being **eaten by their mates**?

Approaching a female is a very risky business for a male spider. He is much smaller then she is and cannot very well defend himself against her. She may mistake him for a prey animal and kill him before he can so much as touch her. Spiders have evolved two main ways of placating females during courtship: visual signals and telegraphic signals. Visual signals are used by hunting spiders, spiders that do not spin webs, and are at their epitome in the little jumping spiders, which have very large eyes and apparently considerable visual acuity. The males are very conspicuous in appearance and movement, so as to better let the female know that they are a potential mate and not a meal. A male jumping spider is likely to be gaudier than the female, to have colorful, swollen pedipalps, to have his face adorned with tufts of hair, and to have long front legs that are gaudily ornamented with spots of bright color, spines, and fringes of colored hair. The male approaches a female in a ritualized dance, moving forward a step at a time with his front legs raised as he jerks his body and waves his pedipalps. If

Which North American spiders are likely to bite people?

Only the black widow and the brown recluse. The black widow occurs in southern Canada and every state of the continental United States except Alaska. The brown recluse occurs in the central region of the United States from Indiana, Illinois, and Iowa south to the Gulf states, and also in Arizona and California. The female black widow, the dangerous sex, is shiny black with red markings, usually in the shape of an hour glass on the underside of her abdomen. She is about one-half inch long. The brown recluse female is as much as one-half inch long, has very long legs, and is brown in color with a dark violin-shaped marking on the cephalothorax.

she is receptive, she will let the male crawl on her body, otherwise, she signals rejection by jerking her body up and down.

Male web-spinning spiders must cross the female's web to mate with her. This puts them in great danger. When a female feels her web twitch, she rushes across it, hurls herself on the entrapped prey, and quickly injects it with venom before it can break away. She could easily mistake an approaching male for a meal. Consequently, a male forewarns the female of his presence by plucking a strand of her web in a code that she will innately recognize. He moves towards her cautiously and will soothingly stroke her body. Nevertheless, if the male does not hurry away after inseminating the female, he is likely to be eaten.

A particular wolf spider from Europe, *Pisaura,* placates the female in an altogether different way than do jumping spiders and web spinners. Before looking for a female, he catches a fly or some other insect, and instead of eating it, wraps it in silk. When he finds a female, he offers her this "sac lunch." If she accepts it, he inseminates her as she eats.

How do spiders **copulate**?

In a very unusual way. They have evolved the nicety of internal fertilization, but since the males don't have a penis, they use their pedipalps, the arm-like "feelers" adjacent to the mouth, to place their sperm into the body of the female. The tip of the pedipalp, which works like a rubber-bulb syringe, is the intromittent organ. Before a male seeks out a female, he sucks his pedipalps full of semen that he has deposited from the true genital opening at the base of his abdomen onto a small silken web that he has spun ahead of time. If he survives the courtship, he thrusts a pedipalp into one of the female's two genital openings and squirts in his semen.

What are the **symptoms of spider bites**?

The bite of the black widow may cause severe muscular pain, a boardlike rigidity of the abdomen, tightness in the chest, difficulty in breathing, and profuse sweating and nausea. Death occurs rarely. In the case of the brown recluse, a local necrosis, an area of dead tissue, forms at the site of the bite. Other symptoms occurs only rarely and fatalities are extremely rare.

Under what circumstances are people most often **bitten by black widow spiders**?

The majority of bites are inflicted on men or boys sitting in an outdoor privy, or pit toilet. Black widows sometimes spin their web just beneath the hole in the seat, often a good place to catch flies. If the unfortunate person's penis dangles in the web, the female spider rushes to attack; presumably in defense of her egg sacs, which are attached to the web.

Under what circumstances are people **bitten by brown recluse spiders**?

The brown recluse occurs outdoors and a person could be bitten while working in the garden or turning over a rock. But this spider is more likely to occur indoors than is the black widow. It might hide in piles of paper, clothing, bedding, or a shoe. People have been bitten when they roll over onto a brown recluse in bed.

What is **arachnophobia**?

Arachnophobia is a morbid and abnormal fear of spiders. Among the animal phobias, it is second in frequency of occurrence only to the fear of snakes.

What is a **tarantula**?

Many large, hairy spiders of the tropics and subtropics are called tarantulas. But this name, derived from the city of Taranto in southern Italy, was originally applied only to a European spider, not related to the big, hairy "tarantulas." The bite of the European tarantula was believed to cause a disease, known as tarantism, that caused people to break into a frenzied dance. There is no truth in this, but during the 15th to 17th centuries, tarantism hysteria led people who imagined that they had been bitten by a tarantula to dance to exhaustion as they did the tarantella, a frenetic dance that they believed to be both a symptom of and a cure for tarantism.

Daddy Longlegs

Are **daddy longlegs** related to spiders?

Like the spiders, daddy longlegs are arachnids. They look a bit like spindly spiders but are instantly recognizable by their ridiculously long legs. A closer look shows that there is no narrow waist as in spiders and that cephalothorax and abdomen are broadly joined. A really close look reveals that the abdomen is segmented. Daddy longlegs have stink glands, but you have to get close to smell them.

Do daddy longlegs **bite**?

No, they do not. They are inoffensive creatures that are of some benefit to humans because some species eat insects and because others are scavengers that help to decompose dead organic matter.

Scorpions

How can **scorpions** be recognized?

Scorpions are very different in appearance from other arachnids and are easy to recognize. They vary in size and color, but all species are otherwise pretty much alike. The segmented body bears four pairs of legs and a pair of large crab-like pincers. The long and thin segmented tail (abdomen) has a bulbous, thorn-like stinger at its end.

Where in North America do scorpions exist?

Scorpions are found in warm climates, often in arid areas. In the United States they are found in the southwestern and the southeastern states. In the east, one species gets as far north as the southern tip of Illinois.

What do scorpions **eat**?

All scorpions are predators, and between them they eat an astonishing variety of small animals, most often arthropods such as insects, spiders, millipedes, centipedes, and others. Some of the larger scorpions are known to eat small lizards, snakes, and even rodents.

How do scorpions catch and **subdue their prey**?

Some scorpions are ambushers that sit and wait for prey to come to them, while others are active hunters, foragers that move about in search of prey. The prey animal is seized with the pincers. If it is small, it is usually eaten without being stung. If it is large or unwieldy, it is first subdued by stinging. The stinger, which is at the tip of the long and slender abdomen, can be brought to bear only if the abdomen is arched forward and downward over the body so as to bring the stinger in contact with the prey, which is held by the pincers at the front end of the scorpion's body.

Do scorpions **sting** in defense?

They sting as they attempt to defend themselves against the many predators that view scorpions as potential meals. Among the invertebrates that eat scorpions are centipedes, spiders, and some insects, especially ants. But the worst invertebrate predators of scorpions are other scorpions. Among the vertebrates that eat scorpions are frogs and toads, lizards, birds, and mammals. If a human disturbs a scorpion, perhaps by turning over a rock or sticking a foot into a shoe or boot occupied by a scorpion, the scorpion reacts as it would to any other attacker—by stinging.

Just **how dangerous are scorpion stings** to people?

All scorpions are venomous and sting with a bulbous, thorn-like structure at the end of the tail (abdomen). But the toxicity of the venom to humans varies with the species of scorpion. The sting of most scorpions is painful and causes swelling and discoloration at the site of the sting but is not dangerous. A few scorpions are very dangerous and cause fatalities. Of the 40 or so species of scorpions that occur in the United States, only one, a 2.5-inch-long yellow or yellow and brown species that is found only in Arizona, causes death. A related species that occurs in Mexico, known as the Durango scorpion, is especially dangerous. During a 39-year period, it was responsible for 1,665 deaths, mostly of children, and mostly in the city of Durango, which at that time had a population of only 50,000.

How are scorpion stings **treated**?

Today antisera for the venoms of most dangerous scorpions are available and often save lives if they are administered soon enough and in the right quantity. There are also some useless folk remedies. In parts of the Sudan, the site of a scorpion sting is smeared with sesame oil in which scorpions have died and disintegrated. In other parts of the Sudan, the site of a sting is rubbed with the charred toenail of a baboon.

Scorpion with stinger poised. (Photo by Edward S. Ross.)

How do scorpions **mate**?

The male, smaller than the female, grasps his mate's pincers with his pincers and leads her in a mating dance, the *promenade a deux*, that may last as much as an hour. The promenading couple eventually comes to a suitable hard surface where fertilization can take place. Scorpions, unlike spiders and almost all insects, practice indirect internal fertilization. That is, although the sperm ends up in the body of the female, the male does not insert them with a penis or some other appendage. When the couple finally finds a suitable place, the male deposits a compact packet of sperm on the ground and, still holding her by the pincers, helps the female to position herself so that her genital opening is directly over the packet of sperm. She then takes the sperm up into her body.

Does a male scorpion **sting his intended** during the courtship?

Yes, usually several times. The male penetrates a membranous area of the female's body with his sting and may leave it embedded there for several minutes. It is not known whether or not the male actually injects venom into the female. The effect of the mating sting on the female is not known, but it is tempting to think that it functions like a love bite.

Scorpion with young. (Photo by Edward S. Ross.)

Do scorpions **lay eggs**?

No, they do not. They are truly viviparous, that is, they give live birth to their young. A female that is ready to give birth goes to some protected place, sometimes under a rock or in a burrow. When the young are ready to come out she raises up on her legs and arches her abdomen over her cephalothorax. The tiny young drop to the ground one at a time and soon make their way to the top of the mother's cephalothorax by climbing up her legs. There they remain until they disperse just after their first molt, three days to two weeks later, depending on the species. A single litter may consist of somewhat over 100 young in some species and far fewer in others. The average litter size for scorpions as a group is somewhere between 20 and 30.

Mites

What is a **mite**?

The mites are the tiniest of the arachnids. For that matter, they are among the tiniest of all the animals. If you look at a mite under magnification, you will see that, generally speaking, its body consists of two discernible parts: a small head-like structure, which bears the mouthparts and the feeler-like pedipalps, and the main part of the body, which is not segmented and in adults bears four pairs of legs. The mites are easily recognized because they are the only arachnids in which the mouthparts and legs are on separate parts of the body.

Where do mites occur?

Mites are essentially ubiquitous. That is, they can be found almost everywhere on land, in fresh water, and even in the seas. They live high in the Arctic and are among the few arthropods that can be found in Antarctica; they occur on tidal flats and sandy beaches of the seas; and they occupy almost every other habitat imaginable, far too many to list here. Among the arachnids, only mites feed on plants or live as parasites in or on the bodies of other animals. They live in the soil and up to the tops of trees, in galls that they form on plants, in birds' nests, and in or on the bodies of insects, reptiles, birds, mammals, and other animals. Mites live in dried fruits, cheese, and other stored foods. They live in the dust in our homes and even in beds and upholstered couches and chairs, their food the dander from human bodies.

How many **different kinds** of mites exist?

There are a great many, and we have only begun to know them. So far, about 30,000 species are known, but it is likely that about a half million more remain to be discovered.

Are mites **important** to people?

Very much so. Before we consider how they affect us adversely, we should recognize that the good that they do as a group far outweighs the harm that they do to us. On the plus side, mites are important and often essential components of the ecosystems that are important to people. For example, some of them are important decomposers that help to return dead organisms to the soil, and predatory mites help to keep populations of pestiferous mites and insects in check. On the negative side, they themselves may be parasites of humans and our domestic animals; some of them transmit human diseases; others attack our crop plants; and some damage grain and other stored products.

What are **spider mites**?

They are plant feeders that, despite their small size, are often conspicuous because they are very numerous, web over leaves with myriads of thin silken threads, and cause leaves to turn yellow by sucking their sap. Spider mites attack many different kinds of plants, among them greenhouse plants, orchard trees, and field crops.

Are you likely to have mites living in your skin at this very moment?

It is very likely. Most people, about 75 percent of those checked, have minute—almost microscopic—mites living in their hair follicles and sebaceous pores, particularly those of the eyelids, eyebrows, and nose. These mites, which belong to the genus *Demodex,* seldom do any harm, although in rare cases they may cause an acne-like condition.

Which mites live in the **ears of moths**?

Several species of mites live in no other place than the ears of adult moths of the family Noctuidae, a family that has no generally applicable common name but includes, among others, such well-known species as the armyworms and cutworms. One of the mites in question infests only one of the moth's two ears, but others often occupy both ears.

Why do some ear mites occupy only **one of a moth's ears**?

These mites, which deafen the ear in which they live, would endanger themselves by occupying both ears. This is because the moths use their ears to listen for moth-eating bats and take appropriate evasive action when they hear the call that a bat makes when it uses echo-location to find its prey. A moth that is deaf in one ear is hampered, but a moth that is deaf in both ears is helpless and is likely to be devoured, along with its mite passengers, by a hungry bat. Since several mites may board the same moth at different times, mites that come along after the first mite to come on board must have some way of avoiding the unoccupied ear and finding their way to the one that is already occupied. No one has demonstrated just how they accomplish this, but it is known that late arrivals follow the same, often circuitous, route that the first mite followed as it searched for an ear. Thus, it is almost a certainty that the first mite to arrive marked its path with a chemical, a pheromone, that marks the trail for later arrivals.

Why can some mites occupy **both of a moth's ears**?

Because they live only in the outer part of the ear and do not deafen it by destroying its sensory structures. Sometimes these mites occupy only one of the moth's ears, often because only one mite boarded the moth.

Do mites live in the **nests of birds**?

The nests of most species of birds are occupied by mites. Some of these mites are a benign presence, scavengers that eat only organic debris in the nest, but others are parasites that suck blood from the occupants of the nest. The nest of a starling may harbor as many as 80,000 tiny, blood-sucking mites.

CHIGGERS

What are **chiggers**?

This is a large group of very tiny, almost microscopic mites that, among them, parasitize all classes of vertebrates except fish. They are all ectoparasites, that is, they live on the outside of the host's body, as opposed to *endoparasites,* which live inside the host's body. Chiggers are parasitic only as very young immatures just hatched from the egg. Later in life, they are probably predators, possibly feeding on the eggs of small insects such as springtails.

How do chiggers **affect people**?

They cause a rash known as chigger dermatitis; the skin, especially of the legs and waist, is speckled with rather large, raised, red spots that itch ferociously and are caused by the feeding activity of those tiny mites. Chiggers do not suck blood and, contrary to popular belief, they do not burrow in the skin. They inject an enzyme that digests skin cells and thus eats a long narrow tunnel down into the skin. The tunnel is lined by hardened secretions that are a part of the skin's defensive response. The chigger sits at the upper end of the tunnel and ingests the partly digested skin cells that are within it.

How do chiggers get on a **person's body**?

Groups of newly-hatched chiggers lurk near the tops of plants in berry brambles or in areas overgrown with tall grass, weeds, or shrubby plants. There they wait quietly until they are alerted to the approach of a person or some other vertebrate by a waft of carbon dioxide that emanates from its body. If the animal comes close enough, they climb on board.

What can a person **do about** chigger bites?

The best thing is to avoid chiggers in the first place. Stay out of the weedy areas in which they are found, but if you must enter such places, you can keep most of them off your body by tucking your pants into your socks and spraying your ankles, belt line, and fly with a repellent. If you do get some bites, try not to scratch them. They go away faster if you leave them alone. There are many reputed remedies for chigger bites, but the only one that works for me is to apply *Lanacane* or some other over-the-counter cream that contains a contact anesthetic such as benzocaine. This relieves the itching and curtails the urge to scratch.

What is **tsutsugamushi disease**?

This debilitating and sometimes deadly disease, also known as scrub typhus or Japanese river fever, is caused by a microorganism, a *Rickettsia,* that is transmitted from rodents to humans by a chigger known as the akamushi (dangerous bug in Japanese). During the Asian and Pacific campaigns of World War II, tsutsugamushi was second only to malaria as a cause of medical casualties.

Ticks

What is a **tick**?

We often speak of ticks and mites as if they were two separate groups of arachnids, but ticks are really nothing more than very large, blood-sucking mites that take their meals from reptiles, birds, or mammals. In North America, there are only two families of ticks: the hard ticks, which have the body more or less covered on top by a hard, patterned shield; and the soft ticks, which are leathery and relatively soft-bodied everywhere. Soft ticks live in the nest or sleeping place of their host: in burrows, caves, cracks, and crevices. They parasitize snakes, birds, bats, and several other mammals including humans, visiting the host frequently to take many small blood meals of short duration. They lay their eggs, usually a thousand or less, in the nest of the host. Like the soft ticks, hard ticks, as a group, take blood from various reptiles, birds, and mammals, but they do not live in the nest of the host. The eggs, usually several thousand of them, are laid on the ground and the young ticks must climb onto a passing animal for a blood meal. They climb to some high point such as the tip of a leaf or a blade of grass and grab onto passing animals with their front legs. Some hard ticks must board and feed from as many three different host animals before they grow to adulthood and lay eggs, and they may have to stay on the same host for several days before they can fully engorge themselves.

Are ticks **detrimental to people** and other animals?

Some are just an annoyance, but others transmit diseases of domestic animals and people. Ticks are second only to mosquitoes in their importance as transmitters of human diseases.

What is Lyme disease?

Named for Old Lyme, Connecticut, where it was first found in North America in 1975, this is the most prevalent tick-borne disease of humans in the United States. It is caused by a spirochete, a kind of bacterium, that is transmitted from small mammals and birds to people by the bite of the deer tick, a hard tick. Deaths due to Lyme disease are rare. In its early stage it causes a ring-shaped rash, fatigue, and joint pains. In its later stage, which may come years later, it may cause chronic arthritis and neurological and cardiac problems.

Do **deer** have a role in the transmission of Lyme disease?

Deer have an indirect but very important role. Since the bacteria that cause Lyme disease do not survive in the bodies of deer, these animals are not a part of the wild reservoir of this disease. However, although immature deer ticks prefer to take blood from birds and small mammals, adult deer ticks prefer to feed on large mammals. Deer, the only large wild mammal present in many parts of the United States, are often virtually the only source of blood for adult deer ticks. Thus, for all practical purposes, a large population of deer ticks can exist only where deer are present and plentiful. The rapid increase in the incidence of Lyme disease in the United States is tied to a concomitant explosion of the population of white-tailed deer. In Connecticut, for example, deer had been all but wiped out by the end of the 19th century. In 1896, the Connecticut Commission of Fisheries and Game found only one or two dozen deer in the state, but by 1988, the population had soared to 31,000 and by 1996 to over 52,000.

Where in North America is Lyme disease most prevalent?

It has been reported from all of the states except Hawaii, Alaska, Montana, and New Mexico, but is most prevalent in the eastern states. Over 90 percent of the cases have been reported from the states along the Atlantic Coast from Massachusetts south to Virginia. Connecticut is a hotbed of Lyme disease. In 1991, the highest incidence in the nation was in this state, a rate of 37.4 known cases per 100,000 people.

What is **Rocky Mountain spotted fever**?

This rather uncommon bacterial disease is transmitted from rodents or rabbits to humans by the bite of a hard tick, the Rocky Mountain wood tick in western North America and the American dog tick in the East. Despite its name, Rocky Mountain spotted fever occurs throughout much of the United States, in parts of Canada, and from Mexico to South America. The mortality rate of this disease is fairly high, between 5 and 10 percent, but fewer than a thousand cases are reported from the United States each year.

CRUSTACEANS

What are **crustaceans**?

The crustaceans, members of the class Crustacea, are mostly sea-going arthropods, including such gastronomic delights as crabs, lobsters, shrimps, and prawns, and also barnacles, hermit crabs, and the planktonic krill that are a mainstay in the diet of baleen whales. Some crustaceans, among them crayfish and many much smaller species, live in fresh water. Among the very few terrestrial species are the sowbugs and pillbugs that we find when we turn over a rock or a log on the ground. Except for sowbugs and pillbugs, people usually do not think of crustaceans as being bugs.

FOSSILIZED INSECTS

What is a **fossil** and what do fossils tell us?

An insect fossil, or any other fossil, is the remains or impression of a prehistoric plant or animal, usually petrified and embedded in amber or rock. Fossils are usually found in specific strata, the consecutive layers that make up the earth's rocks. The fossils in the strata reveal the history of life on earth. Unless the strata are tilted or otherwise disturbed by some geological upheaval, the oldest fossils, often of organisms that became extinct hundreds of millions of years ago, are in the lower layers, and the more recent fossils, sometimes of organisms that are identical or similar to organisms that still exist today, are in the upper layers. Strata can be seen where roads cut through rock formations or where rivers have eroded their way down through the rocks. In the Grand Canyon, for example, the Colorado River has exposed strata that were laid down throughout the approximately 300 million years of the Paleozoic Era—from the Cambrian Period, which ended over 500 million years ago, during which the long extinct trilobites swam the seas, to the Permian Period, which ended about 240 million years ago and saw the appearance of the dinosaurs and the evolution of many insects. The strata in the Grand Canyon are readily visible since the walls of the canyon are almost vertical, the river having cut down into the rock rapidly while the sides of the canyon have eroded slowly because there is so little rain in this area. Eastern river valleys, on the other hand, have gently sloping sides because heavy rains erode the sides of the valley about as quickly as the river scours its bed and thus cuts down into the rock.

How **old** are fossils?

The oldest known insect fossils were formed about 400 million years ago, but the fossil record of life goes back much farther than that. Fossils of single-celled creatures, probably bacteria, found in Australia are 3.5 billion years old. The first fossils of mul-

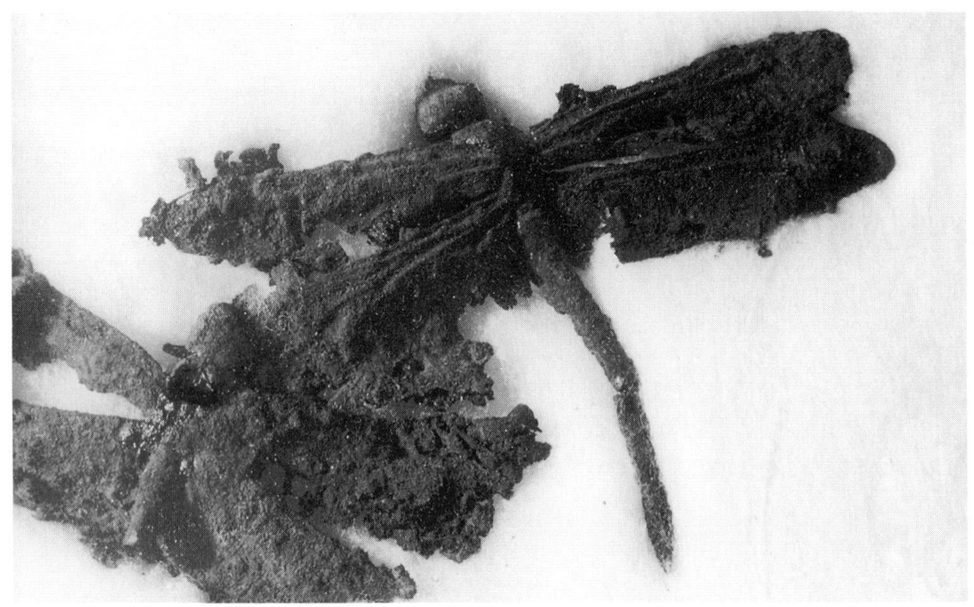

Fossil of dragonflies taken from the LaBrea Tar Pits. (Photo by Tom McHugh. Courtesy of Photo Researchers, Inc.)

ticellular creatures are found in rocks that are about 700 million years old. Very recent fossils, some of them the well-preserved wing covers of species of beetles that still exist today, are found in peat that was deposited only 15 to 20 thousand years ago. The beginnings of fossil formation are going on even today. For example, an insect that falls into a lake is buried by silt that is carried in by a stream; or when a volcano erupts, insect and other organisms are buried in volcanic ash and may be preserved as fossils that will survive into the distant future.

Where are insect fossils found?

Insect fossils have been found in at least 150 sites around the world, in strata that date from 400 million years ago to the recent past. There are, however, many gaps in the fossil record of the insects. As mainly land animals, they are less likely to be buried in deposits of sediment, which eventually become sedimentary rocks, than are invertebrates that live in the sea. Several important deposits of insect fossils exist in the United States. At Mazon Creek in Illinois, they are found in ironstone concretions from the 300-million-year-old coal beds. The other well-known sites in the United States are of much more recent origin, and produce fossil insects that are very similar to insects that are with us today. The Florissant shales of Colorado contain fossils of insects, many beautifully preserved, that fell into an ancient lake about 25 million years ago and were covered by fine silt, much of it of volcanic origin, that settled to the bottom of the lake and formed the shale. Limestone deposits in northeastern

Oklahoma and at Elmo in central Kansas are somewhat older than the Florissant shales but contain similar insects. Beautifully preserved insects are found in amber, the fossilized resin of ancient trees. Amber can be found embedded in many places throughout the world.

When did the **first insects** appear?

They must, of course, have appeared some time, perhaps millions of years, before the earliest known insect fossils were formed. Springtails from Scotland, which occur in rocks about 400 million years old, are the oldest known insect fossils. Springtails are tiny, primitive creatures that belong to the order Collembola. But some authorities don't consider springtails to be insects. Fossils that everyone agrees are insects were formed as much as 300 million years ago. They are mostly isolated wings.

How many ancient insects are now **extinct**?

There were many, but no one knows how many. We do know that at least fourteen ancient orders of insects have disappeared, and each order may have had thousands of member species. Orders are the major subdivisions of a class. For example, the beetles, moths and butterflies, and wasps and bees constitute three separate orders of the Class Insecta, the insects.

Are the **cockroaches really the most ancient** of the insect groups that still exist today?

The cockroaches go back a long way, at least 300 million years, but even so, they are not the most ancient of the insects. Mayflies and relatives of the grasshoppers are equally ancient, and the springtails and insects similar to modern silverfish are even more ancient.

Did **giant insects** exist in the ancient past?

Yes, they did. Certain fossilized ancestors of the dragonflies, some with a wingspan of 28 inches, are the largest insects that have ever been discovered. In their day, the Carboniferous Period, the age of coal formation that extended from about 360 million years ago to about 290 million years ago, they were the largest flying creatures in existence. At that time, the birds and the flying reptiles had not yet evolved. These giant dragonflies were, like their smaller modern descendants, predators that probably caught their prey on the wing, perhaps by darting out from a perch on a giant tree fern to snatch an insect from the air.

How old is the **most ancient of the ant fossils**?

The oldest known ant fossil, beautifully preserved in amber from New Jersey, is about 80 million years old. It is a primitive ant that proved to be a missing link between the ants and the wasps that entomologists had all along thought to be the ancestor of the ants. It was found below a seaside bluff at Cliffwood Beach, a residential area just south of Newark.

FOSSILS IN AMBER

What is **amber**?

Amber, familiar to us as a semi-precious stone used in jewelry, is the fossilized resin of ancient trees of several different species, among them one related to the *Araucaria,* or Norfolk Island pine (pine is a misnomer), that is grown as a house plant. Some pieces of amber contain beautifully preserved insects and other organisms—easily visible through the transparent amber—that were trapped in the sticky resin as it oozed from the tree.

What **kinds of organisms** are found in amber?

Among the inclusions in amber are bacteria, fungi, and fragments of many plants. Animals, other than arthropods, found in amber range from worms and mollusks to frogs, lizards, the feathers of birds, and the hair of mammals. Arthropods in amber include millipedes, centipedes, arachnids of many sorts, crustaceans, and insects of 25 different orders, all of which still exist.

Where is amber found?

Deposits of amber are found all over the world. Well-known deposits of fossil-containing amber are in Burma, China, Siberia, Lebanon, Sicily, Romania, on the shores of the Baltic Sea, the Dominican Republic, Mexico, New Jersey, Canada, and Alaska.

How old is amber?

Since amber is fossilized plant resin, it can, of course, be no older than the earliest resin-producing plants. These are probably the seed ferns, which are now extinct but occurred during the Carboniferous Period, the age of coal formation, from 360 to 290 million years ago. The earliest known amber dates from that period but is found only as small fragments and is poorly known. The major, well-studied amber deposits are anywhere from about 25 million to somewhat over 130 million years old.

What is **Baltic amber**?

Baltic amber, which sometimes contains beautifully preserved insects, is found along the shores of the Baltic Sea in Europe. It was formed from the resin of trees in an extensive forest that covered the region about 40 million years ago. Some of this ancient forest is under the water of the Baltic Sea, whence come the pieces of amber that wash up on the shore during storms. At one time, it was thought that the resin came from a species of pine, but recent evidence indicates that it came from a tree related to the *Araucaria* that we grow as a house plant. Baltic amber, the most famous of the world's ambers, has been used in jewelry for millennia and has been treasured by Europeans since the Stone Age.

How can I tell if the Baltic amber in my jewelry is the **real thing**?

You can be sure that it is the real thing if it contains a visible fossil of an insect or some other creature. Although your Baltic amber is not likely to contain a visible fossil, it is almost bound to contain numerous tiny plant hairs that will be visible through a low-power microscope. The most commonly seen plant hairs, often called oak hairs, are shaped something like a sparse tuft of minute threads. If your amber does not contain oak hairs it probably is not the real thing.

INSECT BODIES: THE OUTSIDE

What is an **insect**?

An insect is an arthropod that has the segments of the body fused or grouped to form three body regions: head, thorax, and abdomen. The head bears the eyes, the mouthparts, and one pair of antennae; the thorax bears three pairs of legs and, in most insects, one or two pairs of wings; with the exception of a very few primitive insects, the legs of the abdominal segments have been completely lost except for some at the tip of the abdomen that have been modified as genital structures.

What is an **exoskeleton**?

While fish, birds, people, and other vertebrates have an *endoskeleton,* a supporting framework that is inside the body, insects and the other arthropods have an *exoskeleton,* a supporting framework that covers the outside of the body. The body wall of an insect consists of two parts: a living inner cellular layer and a more or less hard outer layer, called the cuticle, that is secreted by the cellular layer. The cuticle, which consists of a tough and durable mixture of chitin and protein, is lifeless, just as are the hairs of our head. But, unlike hair, it cannot grow once it has been laid down. The cuticle, the supporting skeleton of the insects, consists of three layers: a thick inner layer that is usually quite flexible, above that another thick layer that is usually rigid, and on the very top a microscopically thin layer that is known as the epicuticle.

What does the exoskeleton do?

The exoskeleton is, of course, the framework of the body, the place to which the muscles attach. It is also the outer covering of the insect's body, just as the skin is the covering of your body. Thus the exoskeleton helps to regulate the exchange of water and

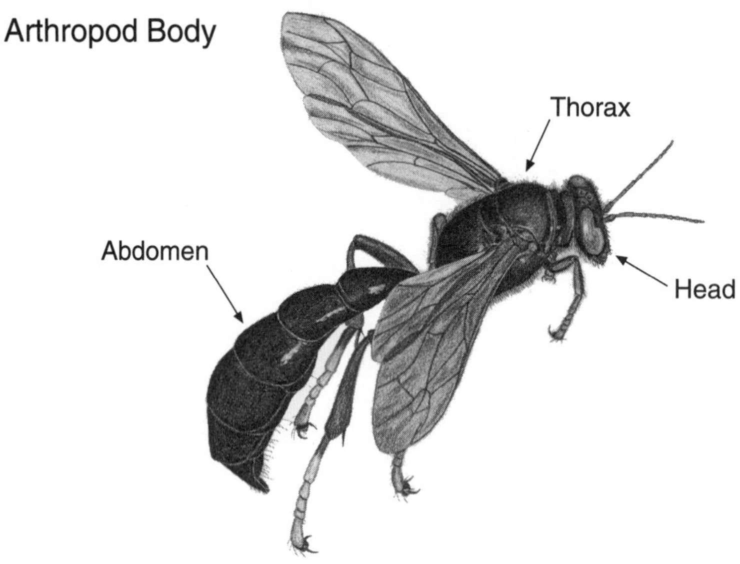

(Illustration by James B. Nardi. Courtesy of Iowa State University Press.)

gasses, such as oxygen and carbon dioxide, between the insect and the atmosphere. It also physically protects internal organs from injury, in many insects as armor plating that protects against attacks from predators or parasites.

Do insects have **internal skeletal** structures?

Although the exoskeleton is the framework of an insect's body, there are some internal skeletal structures to which muscles attach or that brace the exoskeleton. These structures are actually a part of the exoskeleton, invaginations of the body wall, something like the tube that you can form by poking a finger into an inflated rubber balloon.

Does the cuticle **extend into the body**?

Cuticle lines the front and hind sections of the digestive canal, and it lines the entire tracheal system, the air-filled tubes through which oxygen enters the body.

Can insects **really get as big** as the gigantic moths and cockroaches that threaten humans in movies?

They cannot. One reason is that the exoskeleton cannot possibly be strong enough to support the weight of an insect of that size. Exoskeletons are very strong when they

How does an insect covered by a rigid exoskeleton manage to walk and make other movements?

The answer is that the exoskeleton is not entirely rigid. In critical places where flexibility is required to permit bending, as at the leg joints, or where expansion must occur, as between the segments of the abdomen, the body wall is membranous rather than rigid. Where it is membranous, the flexible inner layer of the cuticle predominates over the rigid outer layer.

are small, but relatively much less strong when they are large. The part of the exoskeleton that covers the body itself is essentially a hollow cylinder, and it is in the nature of hollow cylinders to become weaker as they become larger.

What does the **epicuticle** do for an insect?

The most important function of the epicuticle is to minimize the loss of water from the insect's body. A waxy, waterproof layer of the epicuticle covers the body like a raincoat, but its purpose is to keep water from getting out rather than to keep it from getting in. The waxy layer is covered by a thin protective covering, known as the cement layer, that keeps the wax layer from being abraded. The wax layer is essential, most obviously to insects that do not have ready access to water, such as those that live in and eat dry substances such as wood or stored grain.

How do we know that the **wax layer** is essential to an insect?

In one experiment, blood-sucking true bugs that drag their abdomens on the ground as they walk were confined on a piece of paper dusted with alumina, an abrasive. A day later, they died after having lost almost 50 percent of their body weight, obviously as water that was lost through the parts of the cuticle from which the cement and wax layers had been abraded. Bugs confined on alumina-free paper lost very little weight and survived. Bugs whose abdomens were raised above the surface were not abraded when they walked on paper dusted with alumina. They lost very little weight and survived, showing that the alumina had not affected the bugs in some way other than by abrading the cuticle.

What causes the **iridescent colors** that shine from the cuticles of some insects?

These are "physical colors" that are not due to a pigment. They are almost always interference colors, produced by a laminated surface, a surface covered with closely packed microscopic plates, or laminae, that are parallel to each other. Such a surface can reflect different colors, depending upon the distance between successive laminae. For example, blue light will be reflected if the distance between laminae is about the same as the wave length of blue. Yellow light will be reflected if the wave length is about the same as the wavelength of yellow. Tilting the surface or viewing it from a different angle is equivalent to changing the distance between laminae, thus producing a rainbow of iridescent colors by changing the color reflected as the angle is changed.

How does an insect covered with a lifeless cuticle **sense light, odors, or other stimuli**?

Light passes through transparent areas of the cuticle. The cuticle over an eye is not only transparent, it also forms the lenses of the eye. A transparent area of the cuticle directly over the brain of the polyphemus moth cannot resolve images or otherwise function as an eye, but it does let light fall directly on the brain, thus giving the pupa the ability to sense the length of the day. Touch and the chemical senses are served by living hairs that penetrate the cuticle. If something touches the insect's body, one or more hairs will be deflected, thus stimulating a nerve at the base of the hair. Branches of nerves that are sensitive to odors or tastes go out into hairs, pegs, or other structures that penetrate the cuticle. Their tiny nerve endings extend into minute pores in the cuticle of the hair and are thus accessible to molecules of the substances that the insect must smell or taste.

How **strong** are insects?

They are much stronger than humans. A bee, for example, hauled a burden on wheels that was 300 times its own body weight. An ant can pick up a pebble that is about 50 times its own weight. In the 1940s there was a flea circus on 42nd Street near Times Square in New York City—probably the last of the flea circuses in North America. There you could see fleas pulling tiny chariots that were enormous in comparison to the size of the flea. At the end of the 19th century, Charles Rothschild, one of the great authorities on fleas, watched a "circus flea" pull a huge object and estimated the feat to be equivalent to "a man dragging two full-sized elephants round a cricket ground." The comparison between insects and humans is not really fair. Insects have the tremendous advantage of small size. Relatively speaking, small animals are generally stronger than large animals. This is due to differences in the surface area to volume ratio. As size increases, the surface area, which is measured in only two dimensions, increases in proportion to the square of its length; but the volume, which is measured in three dimensions, increases in proportion to the cube of its length. Thus, the larger an animal is, the larger is its volume relative to its surface area. Insects can thus perform feats that are impossible for larger animals because their muscles, whose strength is proportional to the area of their cross section, need move a volume, a mass, of muscle that is relatively small compared to the area of its cross section.

THE HEAD

Why does the **head capsule** of an insect look like a little skull?

Because the several segments that have combined to form the head are so completely and indistinguishably fused that the lines of segmentation are not visible, giving the head the appearance of a single, skull-like unit. Although the separate segments cannot be distinguished in the head of a post-embryonic insect, they are separate and apparent in a developing embryo. The number of segments that are in the head is still being debated by students of insect anatomy. The number proposed by various authorities ranges from three to seven.

What kinds of **sense organs** are found on an insect's head?

Generally speaking, insects, like most other animals, meet the environment head-on. Thus, the insect is well-served by the concentration of sense organs on the head: the eyes, the antennae, and the antenna-like palpi of the maxillae and the labium. Between them, these organs are sensitive to light, odors, tastes, touch, wind currents, heat, and moisture, but not all insects have all of these senses.

What is the **function of the antenna-like palpi** of the maxillae and the labium?

They bear taste receptors, and many insects use them to identify their food and to monitor it as they eat. For example, when a grasshopper or some other plant-feeding insect encounters a leaf, it palpates, or touches, it with its palpi to determine if it tastes like food. Even as it eats, each palpus is constantly on the move as it monitors what is being ingested.

Does the **surgical removal of the palpi** affect the insect's feeding behavior?

Experiments of this sort have been done with certain caterpillars that, like many other plant-feeding insects, are host specific. That is, they will eat only certain species of plants. Tobacco hornworms, the caterpillar stage of a hawk moth, normally refuse to eat anything other than the leaves of tobacco, tomato, or closely related plants. After their palpi were removed, they ate and prospered on the leaves of dandelion and other plants that they would otherwise have refused to so much as nibble. It seems that with their palpi excised they could no longer taste substances that would have deterred them from eating dandelion and other plants that they would normally have rejected.

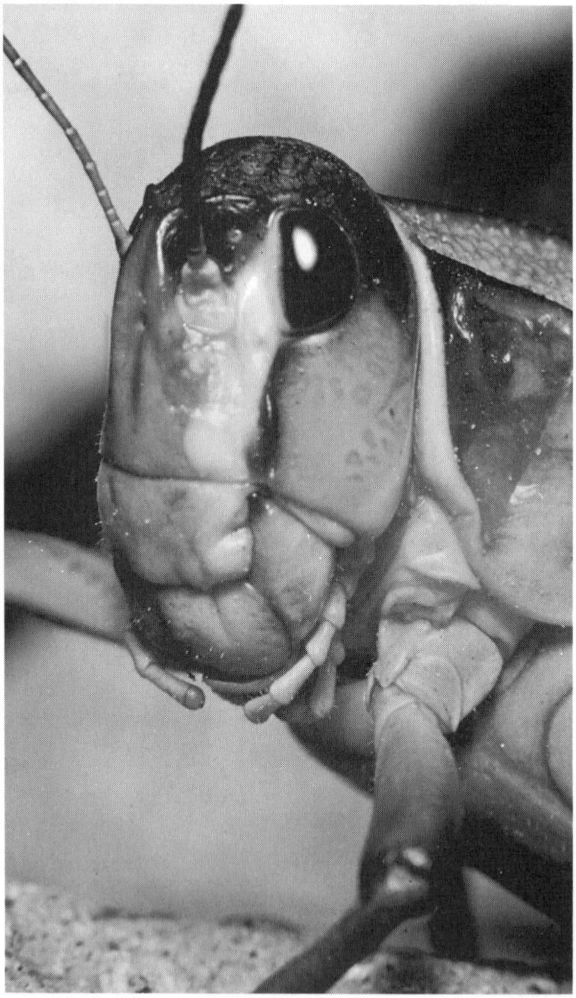

The Mouth

Close-up of grasshopper mouth. (Photo by Edward S. Ross.)

How do the **mouthparts** of an insect differ from those of a vertebrate such as a person?

An insect's mouthparts are responsible for the ingestion of food, just as are the teeth and tongue, the mouthparts, of a human. There the similarity ends. While teeth and tongue are inside of the mouth opening, an insect's mouthparts are outside of the mouth opening. Furthermore, the paired mouthparts of an insect are derived from legs of its ancestors that became grouped around the mouth opening when several segments of the body came together and fused to form the head. In insects that eat solid food, such as grasshoppers, beetles, and caterpillars, one pair of these modified legs, the stout and unsegmented mandibles, do the snipping and chewing. Another pair, the segmented maxillae, the second jaws, are behind the mandibles; and the third pair, which are behind the maxillae, have fused to form the labium, the lower lip. The maxillae and the labium bear antenna-like structures known as palpi. An unpaired flap of the head capsule, the labrum, serves as the upper lip, and another unpaired structure, the hypopharynx, is between the paired mouthparts and functions much like our own tongue, shifting food about between the jaws and pushing it back through the mouth opening so that it can begin its peristaltic trip through the digestive system. This basic design, the chewing mouthparts, has been modified in various ways to accommodate the ingestion of different foods, notably liquids such as plant sap, nectar, or blood.

How does a female mosquito **ingest the blood** of a vertebrate?

The first problem is to pierce the skin to get at the blood. To this end, all of the mouthparts except the labium have been converted to long, slender stylets that fit together to form a long tube that is as slender as a needle and that pierces the skin by gently and almost painlessly slicing through it. The blood is then sucked up through a channel formed by the greatly elongated labrum and the mandibles. The labium, which is also lengthened but does not pierce, serves as a scabbard that holds and protects the stylets when they are not in use.

Are the **piercing-sucking mouthparts** of true bugs (Hemiptera) the same as those of mosquitoes?

The mouthparts of blood-sucking true bugs are quite different in structure from those of mosquitoes, although they serve the same end. As in a mosquito, the bug's labium has become a scabbard that protects the piercing and sucking apparatus. But unlike a mosquito, the bug's labrum is short and is not one of the piercing stylets—its hypopharynx has been lost—and the piercing-sucking tube is formed from only the maxillae and the mandibles. This is just one of many instances in which unrelated animals have evolved different ways of accomplishing the same thing.

What are **siphoning mouthparts**?

Moths and butterflies have greatly lengthened siphoning mouthparts that, like a soda straw, can be inserted deep into a blossom to suck up nectar. Siphoning mouthparts are greatly simplified. They are made up of only one part of each maxilla, the two parts fitting together to form the long sucking tube. Since the sucking tube is always long, often nearly as long as the body and sometimes much longer, it must be gotten out of the way when the moth or butterfly is not sipping nectar or some other liquid. In its resting position, the tube is neatly coiled beneath the head like a watch spring. When the moth or butterfly prepares to drink, the sucking tube is uncoiled and extended straight out by the pressure of blood that is pumped into its hollow walls—much like one of those paper-tube party favors that uncoils when you blow into it.

How do flies, which cannot chew or bite, manage to **eat solid sugar**?

Flies have sponging mouthparts. A rather thick and stubby proboscis ends in a pair of bulbous pads, actually an extreme modification of a part of the labium, that can mop up liquids like sponges. A sucking tube composed of the labrum and the hypopharynx extends down the proboscis to a point between the sponge-like pads. When a fly feeds on solid sugar, it holds the pads against the sugar, salivates onto the sugar, and contains the saliva between the sponge-like pads. When enough sugar has dissolved in

Butterfly Mouthparts

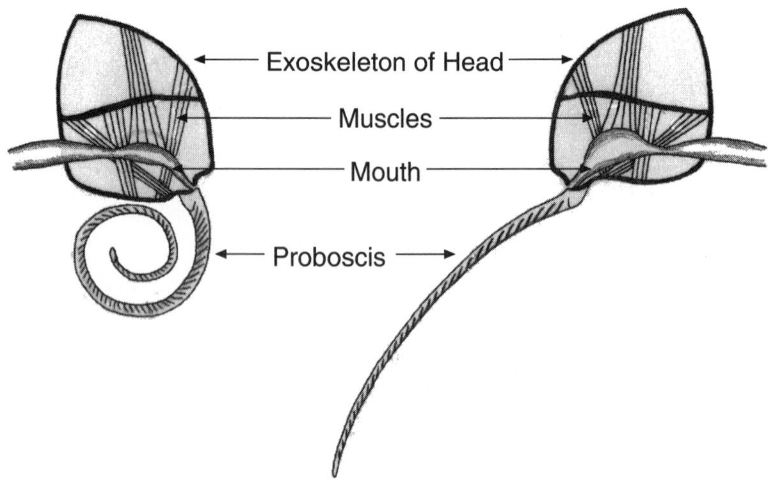

(Illustration by James B. Nardi. Courtesy of Iowa State University Press.)

the saliva, the fly sucks it back up through its sucking tube. In a similar way, flies drink thin films of liquid by mopping them up and gathering the liquid together with their sponging pads.

How do the **aquatic diving beetles**, known as water tigers, eat their prey?

The mandibles of these beetles, but not of all beetles, are used to grasp the prey and to suck out the contents of its body. The mandibles are long, sickle-shaped, and come to a fine point. After they pierce the prey, digestive juices are injected into its body through channels that run the length of the mandible from its base next to the mouth opening to its tip. What happens next is known as extra-intestinal digestion. Enzymes in the digestive juices digest and liquefy the muscles and other internal organs of the prey. The beetle then sucks up its predigested meal through the channels in its mandibles.

The Eyes

Do flies have **eyes**?

I was asked this question by an English major in one of my classes. Ever the teacher, I tried to drive home a lesson by telling the student that he already knew the answer if he had ever swatted flies. The fly's almost instantaneous response to the wave of a swatter shows that it sees quite well, at least as far as the detection of motion is concerned. If you are wondering if the fly might have been spooked by air currents caused by the moving swatter, note that controlled experiments showed that the escape response can be elicited by the sight of movement alone. Flies actually have five eyes. Like almost all insects, they have a pair of compound eyes, one on each side of the head. Like many insects, but far from all of them, they also have three simple eyes arranged as a triangle on the front of the head between the compound eyes.

Close-up of robber fly eye. (Photo by Edward S. Ross.)

Why are **compound eyes** called compound eyes?

When seen with a bit of magnification, a compound eye looks like a mosaic of hexagonal facets. Each facet is the lens of a separate light-sensitive unit known as an ommatidium. A compound eye is composed of many ommatidia, usually hundreds and sometimes many thousands of them.

How does a compound eye **work**?

According to the mosaic theory of insect vision, each ommatidium contributes its little bit to the whole picture. An ommatidium has a very narrow field of vision and is stimulated mostly by the light that shines directly into its lens. Thus, each ommatidium contributes a dot of light of a certain intensity and color, and all of the dots together form a picture much as a mosaic of tiles forms a picture.

Do any insects have **more than two** compound eyes?

Whirligig beetles appear to have four because each eye is divided into two parts by a band of cuticle. You have probably seen these predaceous, streamlined, black beetles—groups of them swimming at the water's surface as they gyrate in tight loops or circles. Their divided eye, the lower part beneath the surface and the upper part above the surface, enables them to simultaneously look for prey on the surface film or in the water beneath the surface film.

Do insects have **good vision**?

They are generally very good at detecting movement as the light from a moving object sweeps over the field of ommatidia. But the compound eye is rather poor at resolving images. Visual acuity depends upon the number of ommatidia in the compound eye—the more of them, the better the eye is at resolving images, just as the sharpness of a picture printed in a newspaper improves as the number of dots that make up the picture increases. As is to be expected, insects that rely mainly on their chemical senses have relatively few ommatidia, while those to whom vision is important have many. Worker ants, which do not fly and live in a universe of tastes and odors, generally make few demands of their eyes. While there are some species that have a few hundred ommatidia in each compound eye, a few worker ants are blind, and others have no more than a few dozen ommatidia. House flies, which make somewhat greater demands on their eyes, have about 4,000 ommatidia in each compound eye. They fly rapidly and must see to avoid obstacles and to make a landing. Dragonflies may have as many as 28,000 ommatidia in each compound eye. They require great visual acuity as they fly in pursuit of their prey, sometimes insects as small as mosquitoes.

Do insects have **stereoscopic vision**?

Some do and some do not. Most insects do not have stereoscopic vision because the visual fields of the two compound eyes do not overlap. Their eyes are likely to be widely separated, useful for spotting prey or approaching predators, because they encompass a wide field of view, sometimes close to 360 degrees. But the compound eyes of some insects—the aquatic nymphs of dragonflies, for example—have overlapping visual fields, making stereoscopic vision and depth perception possible. If a dragonfly nymph is blinded in one eye, it often misses prey that it strikes at, presumably because it no longer sees stereoscopically and cannot judge the position of the prey accurately.

How do we know that insects actually see and respond to colors?

We know this from the results of many behavioral experiments. The first conclusive experiment to show that insects respond to colors was done by Karl von Frisch, later to share the Nobel Prize for his work on insect behavior. He trained honey bees to come to a small dish of sugar water placed on a square of blue paper interspersed among similar gray papers of various brightnesses. Bees that had been trained to come to a dish of sugar water on a slip of blue paper came to a clean blue paper even when its position in the array of gray papers was changed. They found the blue paper even though the whole array had been covered with a glass plate and a clean and empty feeding dish had been placed over each square of paper. The bees were able to distinguish blue from various shades of gray, even grays that matched the blue in brightness. In this way, von Frisch showed that honey bees can distinguish yellow, blue-green, blue, ultraviolet, and "bee's purple," a mixture of ultraviolet and orange.

Do insects see colors?

Yes. They can see some colors that we cannot see, but we can see some colors that they cannot see. The portion of the spectrum that is visible to humans extends from violet (a wavelength of 400 millimicra) to red (a wavelength of 750 millimicra). Generally speaking, insects are sensitive to a spectrum of wavelengths that extend from the near-ultraviolet (300 to 400 millimicra), which is invisible to us, to orange (606 to 650 millimicra) but cannot see red, which is visible to us.

When he tested honey bees that had been trained to a red paper, they confused red with black and dark gray, showing that they are red-blind.

Is their ability to perceive the **near-ultraviolet** useful to insects in nature?

Definitely. A honey bee, for example, can orient to certain flowers that reflect in the near-ultraviolet but that look red to us, a color to which the bees are not sensitive. Furthermore, nectar guides, sign posts that direct bees and other insects to the part of the blossom where the nectar is located, are sometimes visible only in the near-ultraviolet. Some nectar guides consist of patches of color at the bases of the petals or of a pattern of radiating lines on the petals that converge at the opening of the nectary. Nectar guides that reflect only light in the near-ultraviolet are invisible to us, but we can see them if we photograph blossoms through a special lens filter that passes near-ultraviolet but blocks other colors.

What are the **simple eyes**?

Many insects lack simple eyes, but many others have either a pair or a triangle of three of them on the front of the head between the compound eyes. Each simple eye, or ocellus, consists of one large lens with a layer of many light-sensitive elements beneath it. The ocelli cannot possibly perceive a sharp image, because the focal point of the lens is far behind the light-sensitive elements.

Of what use is a simple eye if it cannot focus on an image?

The simple eyes are far more sensitive to light than are the compound eyes. In terms familiar to photographers, the simple eyes of some insects have an aperture of *f* 1.8 to *f* 1.5 while the compound eyes have an aperture of only *f* 2.5 to *f* 4.5. We are far from knowing all of the functions of the simple eyes, but it is clear that, at least in some insects, they are involved in perceiving light from dark, the cue that controls the daily activity rhythms of some insects.

The Antennae

Are the **antennae** a pair of modified legs?

This is a reasonable question. After all, the antennae are segmented, as are legs, and they are located on the head along with mouthparts that are without doubt modified legs. But the evidence, particularly that from the embryonic development of insects, indicates that the antennae are definitely not modified legs, and that they had an independent origin in some far-distant ancestor of the insects. They were probably present on the first segment of the ancestor's body, even before that segment had combined with leg-bearing segments behind it to form the definitive insect head.

Are antennae always thread-like, as are those of crickets and cockroaches?

Definitely not. Antennae are variable in structure; most entomology texts list 14 or 15 different types. Each different type probably serves some special sensory function, but what that function may be is known for only a few of the many types. Among the various types are those that are *filiform,* thread-like; setaceous, bristle-like; *capitate,* with a club-like head; *serrate,* saw toothed; *pectinate,* comb-like; and *plumose,* feather-like.

What **sensory capabilities** do antennae have?

No one species of insect has antennae that serve all of the functions listed below, but considering the insects as a group, antennae may be sensitive to odors, tastes, touch, heat, moisture, and wind currents. The antennae of a few insects even perform non-sensory functions.

Why do some male American silk moths have such **large antennae**?

Both sexes of American silk moths such as cecropia, luna, and polyphemus have comb-like antennae with "branches" on both sides, but the male's are much more broadly widened than are the female's. A male finds a female by following a stream of scent (a sex attractant pheromone) that she releases and that drifts downwind from where she sits. The greater his distance from the female, the lower the concentration of scent that reaches him, but his broad antennae accommodate thousands of tiny scent receptors, thereby increasing his ability to perceive low concentrations of the female's pheromone.

The *plumose* (feather-like) antennae of the luna moth. (Photo by Edward S. Ross.)

Why are the antennae of a **male mosquito** so huge and feather-like?

His antennae are his ears. The plumose antenna, with its very fine branches, is sensitive to sound waves in the air. The sound waves cause the antenna to vibrate just a bit, and these vibrations are perceived by a sense organ in the base of each antenna.

What do male mosquitoes **listen for**?

They find their mates by using their "ears" to listen for the high-pitched hum of a flying female mosquito. Sex-deprived male mosquitoes got so excited at the sound of a tuning fork that rang at the same pitch as a female that they tried to copulate with each other and even with a cloth that shielded the tuning fork.

What is the special function of the **antennae of a house fly**?

The antennae of house flies, blow flies, stable flies, and related species are wind speed indicators. The bulbous terminal segment of these three-segmented antennae bears a small feather-like projection that catches the wind like a sail, thus causing the whole segment to twist slightly. The degree of twist is transmitted to the central nervous system, where it is translated into wind speed or, in the case of a flying individual, into air speed.

Are insects sensitive to high temperatures?

They are, and in many insects this sensitivity is more or less localized on the antennae, although it is not confined to the antennae. The ability to sense differences in temperature is important to insects for at least two reasons. First, they must avoid places that are damagingly hot or above the optimum temperature at which their bodies work most efficiently. Second, for insects that take blood meals from birds or mammals, the warmth of the victim's body is an important factor in locating the victim. A blood-sucking insect from South America is exceedingly sensitive to temperature differences and can orient to an object that is less than two degrees Fahrenheit above the temperature of its surroundings. This ability is abolished by cutting off the antennae. The ability of certain insects to avoid high temperatures was greatly disrupted when only the last segment of their antennae was surgically removed.

Are the antennae used to **locate food**?

Many insects orient to food from short or even fairly long distances by their sense of smell, and in insects the odor receptors are located chiefly on the antennae. Honey bees, for example, use their sense of smell to help home in on nearby blossoms as they seek nectar and pollen. An experiment showed that the two antennae perceive an odor separately, thus enabling the bee to localize the odor by comparing the strength of its effect on the two antennae. Bees trained to turn toward the source of an odor made the wrong choice and turned away from the odor when their antennae were crossed and fixed in place. For example, if the bee's left antenna was now on its right side, it moved toward the left although the odor came from the right.

What is an **electroantennogram**?

Just as an electrocardiogram (EKG) is a record of the electrical currents generated by a beating heart, an electroantennogram (EAG) is a record of the electrical impulses that pass along the antennal nerves when an antenna is stimulated by an odor. An EAG recorded from the antenna of a male silk moth stimulated by the sex attractant pheromone of a female has a characteristic form that can be distinguished from an EAG taken from the same antenna when it was later stimulated by some other odorous substance.

Are the antennae **sensitive to humidity**?

Insects have special humidity receptors that are usually located on the antennae but in some species are located elsewhere on the body. The ability to distinguish between dry air and the humid air that they prefer is important to the many insects whose survival depends on how well they can conserve the water in their bodies. The humidity sense can be very keen. Certain beetle larvae can, under experimental conditions, respond to differences in relative humidity of only 0.5 percent.

What function do the **antennae of phantom midges** serve?

The phantom midges, so called because the aquatic larvae are largely transparent and difficult to see, have antennae that are modified for grasping and holding their prey, various small aquatic creatures including mosquito larvae.

THE THORAX

What is the structure of the **thorax**?

The thorax, the body region immediately behind the head, is a union of three segments, which in most insects are immovably fused to each other so as to form a firm base for the attachment of the legs and the wings. At least in some stage of the life cycle, the thorax bears three pairs of legs, one pair on each segment. The legs may be modified in various ways: for walking, jumping, swimming, digging, or grasping. In most insects the second and third thoracic segments each bear a pair of wings. In the main, the wings are used for flying but in some insects they are modified to serve other functions.

The Legs

Are the **legs** of insects composed of separate segments?

A leg is composed of five segments. The basal segment, which articulates with the body and is generally short, is the *coxa*. Articulating on the coxa is another short segment, the *trochanter,* which is fused to the basal end of the *femur.* The femur is generally long and rather thick to accommodate the powerful muscles that move the next segment, the *tibia,* on the femur. The tibia is usually long and thin, often the longest segment of the leg. The insect's foot, the *tarsus,* articulates on the end of the tibia. It is divided into as many as five subsegments, almost always bears a pair of claws, and generally has one or more membranous sacs between the claws.

What is the function of the **membranous sacs between the claws** of an insect's leg?

In some insects they are very sticky, allowing the insect to cling to smooth surfaces. Honey bees hang on with their claws when they are on a rough surface but hang on with these sticky sacs when they are on a smooth surface. We have all seen house flies use these sticky sacs as they crawl up a pane of glass or hang upside down from the ceiling.

Are there **legless insects**?

Some insects are legless during one or more stages of the life cycle, but all insects have legs at some time during their lives. Otherwise, it would be impossible for them to disperse, and no species of animal or plant can long survive if it cannot disperse. Take scale insects as an example. The tiny legless and wingless oyster shell scales that often encrust the stems or twigs of a lilac do have legs and move about actively when they first hatch from the egg. But they soon settle down on a plant and secrete a hard waxen scale that covers the body. When they molt, they retain their piercing-sucking mouthparts, which suck sap from the plant, but lose their legs, eyes, and antennae. And so they remain, essentially parasites of the plant, until they molt to the adult stage. The adult males have legs and wings and are quite mobile. But the adult females remain eyeless, antennaless, and legless. They stay under the scale, attract a male by means of a sex attractant pheromone, lay a mass of eggs under the scale, and then shrivel up and die.

What do legs used for **walking and running** look like?

They are slender and have no noticeably swollen segments. They are usually of medium length, especially in fast-moving insects such as cockroaches and certain beetles. Most insects with very long legs, such as the walkingsticks and water scorpions, move slowly and deliberately.

How does a **six-legged animal** walk?

By using the alternating tripod gait. The front and rear legs of one side of the body and the middle leg of the opposite side of the body form a tripod and move as a unit. The two tripods that are thus formed alternate with each other as the insect walks. This gait provides far more stability than does the two-legged gait of a person or the four-legged gait of a horse or any other quadruped. When an insect walks or runs, its center of gravity is always within the legs of one or the other of the tripods. For this reason, a running insect such as a cockroach can suddenly "turn on a dime," making a much tighter turn than would be possible for a person or a quadruped.

How far can fleas jump?

Fleas have been known to make leaps of thirteen inches, about 200 times the length of their own bodies. This has been said to equal a 900-foot jump by a six-foot man.

How **fast** can insects run?

One of the fastest running insects is the American cockroach, which sometimes infests warehouses or the basements of homes. It has been clocked running at a rate of about 32 inches per second, or about 1.8 miles per hour. This seems slow, but when scaled up for size, it is the equivalent of an animal about the size of a lion running at a speed of about 70 miles per hour. Among the slow-moving insects, ants have been clocked walking at a speed of about 0.64 inches per second, or about 0.04 miles per hour.

How are the legs of a **grasshopper modified for jumping**?

The first two pairs of a grasshopper's legs are of the walking type, but the hind legs are very evidently modified for jumping. They are longer than the others, and the femur is greatly swollen to accommodate the powerful muscles that move the tibia. When a grasshopper prepares to jump, it raises the front part of its body on its walking legs and flexes the joint between the femur and the tibia. When it actually jumps, the tibiae of both legs are suddenly extended, straightening the legs as the tibiae push against the ground and propel the grasshopper into the air.

How far can a grasshopper jump?

In a single leap, a two-inch grasshopper frightened by a bird or some other predator can cover a distance of about 30 inches, about 15 times the length of its own body. If a human athlete could jump as far as a grasshopper, he or she could leap a distance of about 100 feet, one-third the length of a football field.

How are the legs of a **flea modified for jumping**?

The hind legs of the flea are of the jumping type. As in the grasshopper, they are longer than the others and the femur is packed with the muscles that power the jump. Unlike grasshoppers and other jumping insects, however, a jumping flea turns head over heels in mid-air and lands facing in the direction from which it came. Fleas jump in order to board the host from which they will suck blood—a bird or a mammal of some sort, perhaps a bank swallow, a dog, or even a human. They also leap to get away from their worst enemy, the host, which bites or scratches to get rid of them.

What is unusual about the **legs of a thrips**?

The tarsus of a thrips has only one or two segments and there are usually no claws on the tarsus. Thrips are the only insects that lack claws. The terminal segment of the tarsus is hoof-like in shape and houses a sticky membranous bladder that the thrips can protrude or withdraw at will. The sticky bladder helps in negotiating slippery surfaces, such as the petals of the blossoms in which many thrips live. (Thrips is one of those peculiar English words that ends with an "S" in both the singular and the plural.)

Can insects jump **without using their legs**?

Springtails, cheese skippers, and click beetles can propel themselves high into the air without using their legs.

How do **springtails** jump without using their legs?

Near the end of the abdomen of a springtail, there is a fork-shaped— really "Y"-shaped—appendage called the furca. The furca can be swung forward under the abdomen and held flexed against the undersurface of the abdomen by a catch known as the retinaculum. The furca can be put under quite a bit of tension, and when it is suddenly released by the retinaculum, it swings down and backward quickly and with considerable force, propelling the little springtail high into the air.

How do **legless cheese skippers jump** into the air?

Cheese skippers, legless maggots that actually do live in cheese, prepare to leap by bending the body into a loop. The loop is formed when the maggot bends its head back under its body to grip the posterior end of the abdomen with its mouth hooks. The longitudinal muscles of the abdomen contract and put the arching larva's body under tension. When the larva releases its grip, the body suddenly straightens, strikes the surface of cheese or table, and thus throws the maggot two or three inches, or even more, up into the air.

How do **click beetles leap** into the air without using their legs?

In his pioneering textbook, *An Introduction to Entomology,* John Henry Comstock of Cornell University, the first great teacher of entomology in the United States, wrote as follows:

> There is hardly a country child that has not been entertained by the acrobatic performances of the long, tidy-appearing beetles called snapping-bugs, click-beetles, or skip-jacks. Touch one of them and it at once curls up its legs, and

> drops as if shot, it usually lands on its back, and lies there for a time as if dead. Suddenly there is a click, and the insect pops up into the air several inches. If it comes down on its back, it tries again and again until it succeeds in striking on its feet, and then it runs off.

As it lies on its back, the beetle arches its body so that it is supported at only two points, one at its front end and another at its hind end. The beetle then tenses the muscles that straighten its body. When this tension is suddenly released by the trigger-like click mechanism, the body straightens and the beetle is catapulted several inches up into the air.

What is a **mole cricket**?

Mole crickets, compactly built insects that resemble moles, use their front legs to burrow in the soil, usually near water and as much as six to eight inches below the surface. Each of its front legs is stout and sturdy, the shovel-like tibia broadened for moving soil, and the coxa and femur greatly enlarged to hold the powerful muscles that drive the tibia. Mole crickets eat plant roots, earthworms, and other insects.

How are the front legs and the thorax of a **praying mantis** modified for catching prey?

A praying mantis is an ambusher of prey that sits and waits for its next meal to come near. Its grasping, raptorial front legs are held up and forward in the seemingly prayerful attitude that gave this insect its common name. The mantis is an efficient ambusher, beautifully adapted for the task. The femur and the tibia, designed for grasping the prey, are toothed and oppose each other like the two "jaws" of a pliers. The mantis's reach is greatly extended by the elongated coxa, which— although short and stubby in most insects—is as long as the femur in the mantis. Its reach is even farther extended by the attachment of the front legs to the end of what appears to be a long giraffe-like neck but is actually the greatly lengthened first segment of the thorax. Unlike the situation in almost all other insects, this segment is not immovably fused to the second segment, but is, rather, freely moveable. Thus, the mantis can swing this segment with its grasping legs to one side or the other so as to capture prey that would otherwise be out of reach.

How are the **legs of hangingflies** modified for grasping prey?

Oddly enough, the elongated tarsi of their hind legs are raptorial, that is, modified for grasping. This arrangement seems less odd when we consider how hangingflies catch their prey. Like mantises, they are ambushers that wait for their prey to come within reach, but there the resemblance stops. Although hangingflies are so long-legged and spindly that they resemble crane flies, they are not true flies and have two pairs of wings rather than the one pair that is characteristic of the true flies. As its name indicates, a hangingfly spends most of its time hanging by its front legs from a leaf or a stem, usually in the undergrowth of a shady place. The long hind legs hang straight down, and the raptorial tarsi grab insects as they fly by.

Katydid Leg and Ear

Katydid leg

Cross section of katydid ear

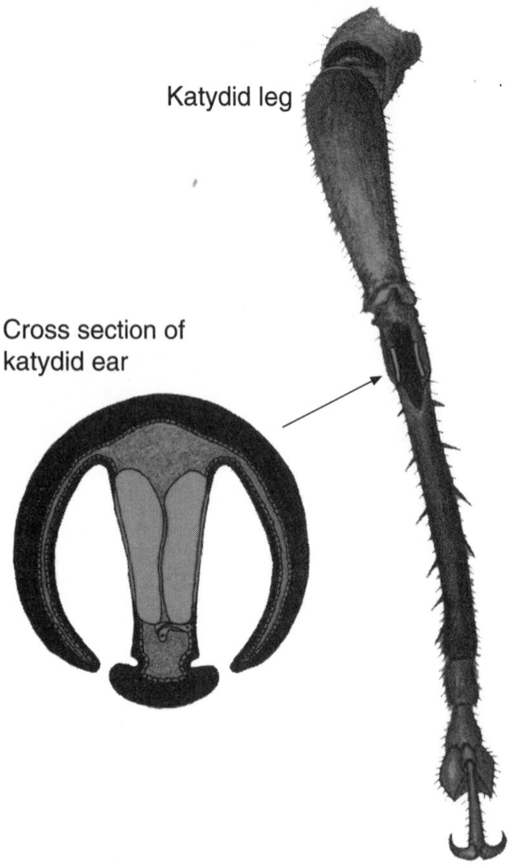

(Illustration by James B. Nardi. Courtesy of Iowa State University Press.)

What purpose do the **grasping legs of a louse serve**?

Piercing-sucking lice, which are all parasites that live amongst the hairs of a mammal, have the tarsus and tibia modified for grasping a single hair. The tarsus is one-segmented and bears a single claw that opposes a thumb-like projection of the tibia much as a person's thumb opposes the forefinger. The louse, wary of falling off its host or being scratched off, flattens itself against the skin and holds onto the base of a hair with each of its grasping legs, the middle and hind legs in the case of the crab louse of humans. The socket formed by the tarsus and the tibial thumb is a close fit for the thickness of the hair.

How does a **male diving beetle** use its grasping front legs?

It uses them to hold onto the smooth and slippery body of the female during mating. The male's legs do not grasp in the usual way, like pliers or tweezers. Instead, the flattened tarsi bear adhesive cups, or suckers, that adhere to the slick body of the female.

Are the legs of insects modified for **functions other than locomotion and grasping**?

There are many such modifications. Among them is the "pollen basket" of the honey bees, a basket-like arrangement of stiff hairs on the hind tibia that can hold a large ball of pollen. In some insects, including the honey bees, the front legs bear brush-like "toilet organs" that are used to clean the antennae. Grasshoppers produce sound by rubbing the tibia of the hind leg against a wing. The ears of crickets and katydids are on the tibiae of the front legs.

SWIMMING

Do insects **swim**?

Some terrestrial insects can swim rather feebly if they fall into the water. But the champion swimmers are aquatic species that live in puddles, ponds, lakes, and streams. A few aquatic species crawl on water plants and have no special adaptations for swimming, but many aquatic insects have legs that are modified to function as fins or paddles. Mosquito larvae are legless, but, nevertheless, they manage to swim quite well by undulating their bodies.

How do **immature dragonflies** swim?

Young dragonflies propel themselves through the water by forcefully ejecting a stream of water from the anus. This has been incorrectly referred to as "jet propulsion." But the dragonfly's system actually works like a rocket, by expelling a limited supply of propellant. Jet engines continuously take in air at the front and forcefully expel it at the back by heating it.

How are the legs of insects **modified for swimming**?

With the exception of larval mosquitoes and some of their relatives, most, but not all, of the insects that swim are true bugs or beetles. Most of them swim with the hind legs, sometimes in conjunction with the middle legs. Generally speaking, the tibia and the tarsus are broadened to form paddles whose area is often increased by a fringe of stiff hairs. Most swimming insects are streamlined, so as to offer as little resistance to the water as possible. Many of them are also flattened from top to bottom to make them more stable.

Mosquito larva hanging below the water surface. (Photo by Edward S. Ross.)

How **fast** can insects swim?

One of the fastest swimmers, the whirligig beetle, can swim on the surface in short bursts of up to 40 inches per second (2.3 miles per hour) as its hind leg makes from 50 to 60 strokes per second. It is much slower under water, moving at speeds of only about 4 inches per second (0.2 miles per hour).

How do **mosquito larvae** swim?

When a legless mosquito larva that is hanging just below the surface film of the water is frightened, perhaps by a passing shadow, it makes a dash for the bottom as it swims by rapidly undulating the body from side to side. When at the surface or browsing for food on the bottom, it can glide along slowly as its mouth brushes vibrate rapidly, creating a current that brings in particles of food.

How do tiny **parasitic wasps** lay their eggs in the eggs of diving beetles?

Diving beetles lay their eggs under water, and these parasitic wasps swim to them by rowing with their wings at a rate of about two strokes per second.

What makes it possible for **water striders** to skate on the surface film of the water?

Water striders are light enough so that they can be supported by the surface film. The surface film is stronger than you might think. You can, for example, get a slightly oily sewing needle to sit on top of the surface film if you place it there with care. The water strider's feet are covered with a waxy secretion that, like the oil on the needle, repels water and thus prevents the feet from breaking through the surface film. Since this waxy secretion lubricates the feet, it could make it difficult for the water strider to gain purchase against the surface film as it skates along. In many species, this problem is solved by allowing the claws or other structures of the tarsus to minimally penetrate the surface film.

What do water striders do on the surface film of the water?

They eat insects that fall onto the water. The surface film is their feeding niche. Sensory hairs on the legs perceive the ripples that spread in circles from an object that has fallen onto the surface of the water. Alerted to a possible meal, the water strider skates to the fallen object and sucks the juices from its body if it turns out to be an edible insect. You can check this out by dropping some tiny object that will float onto the surface film near a water strider. An insect or even a small bit of a twig will do. The water strider will approach the object and may even feed if the object is an insect.

THE WINGS

Were insects the **first animals** to conquer the air?

They certainly were, and they are the only invertebrates, animals without backbones, that ever evolved the power of flight. The earliest known fossil insect with wings lived about 350 million years ago, long before any other flying animal, mammal, bird, or reptile, had evolved. The first pterosaur, a flying reptile, appeared about 90 million years later, the first bird about 200 million years later, and the first bat not until 300 million years later.

Are the wings of insects **modified legs**?

They are not. The wings of flying reptiles, birds, and bats are all modified legs—obvious to you if you have ever eaten a chicken wing. The wings of insects are flattened outgrowths of the body wall of the upper portions of the second and the rearmost segments of the three segments of the thorax.

How did the wings of insects **evolve**?

They originated as flattened flanges of the thorax that could be used for gliding. There are two main hypotheses that seek to explain the origin of these gliding surfaces and their conversion to wings: according to the "flying fish" hypothesis, the gliding surfaces were originally gill plates of an aquatic insect that often left the water to sit on the stem of a plant, perhaps to escape enemies, and that used its broadened gill plates to glide back down to the water. The "flying squirrel" hypothesis postulates a tree-dwelling insect that developed gliding surfaces to glide from tree to tree or down to the ground. (This hypothesis is often used to explain the origin of flight in birds.) Both hypotheses agree that flight began with a gliding insect that ultimately developed the wing hinges and muscles that make powered flight possible.

Dragonfly with wings displayed. (Photo by Edward S. Ross.)

What are the "**veins**" of the wing?

The veins are narrow channels in the wings through which blood flows and that are traversed by nerves and thin air tubes that carry oxygen. The pattern of the venation of the wings is an important taxonomic character that distinguishes species, genera, families, and even orders of insects.

What kinds of **muscles** control and drive the wings of insects?

In most insects, indirect wing muscles cause the wings to beat. In an arrangement unique to the insects, the indirect muscles attach not to the wing but, rather, to the springy walls of the thoracic segments that bear the wings. They are powerful muscles that make the wings beat by moving the thoracic walls to which the wings attach. Direct wing muscles attach to the base of the wing. In all insects, the direct muscles are responsible for folding the wings and for controlling the attitude of the wings in flight. In a few insects, cockroaches and dragonflies among them, they also help to drive the downstroke of the wing in flight.

How **rapidly** do insects beat their wings?

The rate varies from insect to insect. A large-winged butterfly may flap its wings at a frequency as low as 8 to 12 beats per second. A mosquito may beat its wings at a rate of 600 beats per second, rapidly enough to produce a high-pitched sound that is audible to the human ear.

How **fast** do insects fly?

Flying is much faster than walking. A horse fly has been clocked at 15 miles per hour and a dragonfly at 36 miles per hour. Charles Henry Tyler Townsend, a controversial and sometimes unreliable student of the Diptera (flies, mosquitoes, and their relatives), is notorious for his estimate that bot flies can fly at speeds of 1,200 feet per second, or 818 miles per hour— considerably faster than the speed of sound, which is about 742 miles per hour. Townsend did not report little sonic booms caused by the passage of this bot fly. He was, of course, wrong: no animal is known to fly at such high speeds—not even a peregrine falcon making a power dive to intercept another bird. His estimate was not based on measurements of any sort. It was just a wild guess.

Do **all insects** have wings?

Quite a few insects have no wings. Insects are wingless for two reasons. Some, which never evolved wings, are said to be *primitively wingless.* Others, said to be *secondarily wingless,* are descended from winged ancestors but lost the wings as an adaptation to their particular life-style. Only the most primitive of the insects, about 7,500 species worldwide, are primitively wingless. Among them are the springtails and the silverfish that sometimes live in our homes. Secondarily wingless insects are better off without wings than they would be with them. For example, insects that live on small, windswept islands may be wingless although they have close relatives that do have wings. On such islands a flightless individual is more likely to survive to reproduce itself than a flying individual that may well be blown out to sea. Winglessness is also an advantage for parasites, such as lice and fleas, that live amongst the hairs of a mammal or the feathers of a bird. Wings would be in the way as a louse or a flea moves through a jungle of hair or feathers, and, besides, the wings would soon become so worn and frayed as to be useless.

Do all winged insects have **two pairs** of wings?

Quite a few insects have only one pair of wings that can be used for flying. The other pair, usually the hind wings, has either been lost, as in some mayflies, or converted to some other use, as in beetles and flies.

Is there an **advantage to having only one pair** of wings?

The major advantage seems to be that it is aerodynamically more efficient to be two-winged rather than four-winged. Some insects that have not lost their hind wings have, for all practical purposes, become functionally two-winged by evolving mecha-

What has become of the front wings of beetles?

They have become wing covers, a part of the body armor. They are called elytra. The elytra have lost their veins, are hard and rigid rather than membranous, and are opaque rather than transparent. The elytra typically cover the entire abdomen and all but the first segment of the thorax, but in a few beetles, notably the rove beetles, they are short and leave most of the abdomen uncovered. Generally speaking, the elytra are held out of the way above the thorax while the membranous hind wings do the flying.

nisms that link together the fore and hind wings on the same side of the body. Wasps and bees, for example, couple the small hind wing to the large forewing by means of a zipper-like device, a row of hooks on the trailing edge of the front wing that catches on a ridge at the leading edge of the hind wing. Moths have a different way of coupling the wings. In females, the frenulum, a tuft of stiff bristles on the hind wing, locks into the retinaculum, a tuft of bristles on the front wing. In males, the frenulum is a single stiff spine that is caught in a single hook-like projection, the retinaculum, of one of the veins of the front wing.

Are insects equipped with **gyroscopes**?

Mosquitoes and all of the other flies have sense organs that work on the same principle as the gyroscope. They are greatly modified hind wings. Known as halteres, they are tiny club-shaped organs. The head of the club is swollen and heavy with blood, and the thin shaft bears at its base sense organs that perceive the slightest bending of the cuticle of the shaft. As the insect flies, the halteres beat in unison with the front wings, at the same frequency and in the vertical plane. They are organs of balance that monitor the attitude of the flying insect's body. Just as centripetal force tends to keep the wheel of a gyroscope spinning in the same plane, the haltere tends to keep beating in the same plane. Any deviation in the attitude of the insect's body— yawing, pitching, or rolling—tends to force the heavy head of the haltere out of the plane in which it is beating, thus causing a slight bending of the shaft of the haltere. This bending is perceived by the sense organs at the base of the shaft and communicated to the central nervous system, which interprets it and signals a suitable correction to the wings.

Do insects other than mosquitoes and flies have **halteres**?

The hind wings of male scale insects are halteres that function much like the halteres of mosquitoes and flies. Female scale insects, which never acquire legs, antennae, or wings, also lack halteres.

Why does the **color of a butterfly's wing** rub off on your fingers?

The wing membrane of a butterfly or moth is colorless and transparent. The color is in very small scales that cover the wing, overlapping like the shingles on a roof. If you touch a moth or a butterfly, some of these colored scales come off on your fingers, "rubbing off" the color. The scales are so tiny that their shape is not apparent. To the naked eye they look like nothing more than tiny particles of colored dust.

THE ABDOMEN

How is an insect's **abdomen** built?

The segmented structure of an insect's body is most clearly visible in the abdomen. Basically, the abdomen consists of 11 segments, but all of them are visible in only a few primitive insects, such as bristletails (silverfish and related species) and jumping bristletails (a family related to the bristletails). In most other insects not so many segments are visible. Ten abdominal segments are visible in quite a few insects, but some insects show even fewer. In flies, for example, only four segments are visible, but four others are telescoped within them. Many insects have genital appendages at the end of the abdomen that are actually highly modified legs, claspers in males and an ovipositor (egg laying organ) in females. Otherwise, no vestige of the abdominal legs of the ancestor of the insects remains except in the same primitive species that have 11 visible abdominal segments.

How can the abdomen of a mosquito **bloated with blood** swell to several times its usual size?

The abdominal segments of mosquitoes and most other insects are joined to each other by ample membranes that let each segment telescope into the preceding segment, and in many insects including mosquitoes, the hard upper and lower walls of each segment are joined by membranous side walls. Under most circumstances, these membranes are folded away out of sight between telescoped segments or between the hard upper and lower walls of a segment. When a mosquito bloats itself with blood, the membranes unfold and allow the abdomen to expand both in length, as the segments untelescope, and in width, as each segment expands. This ability is useful not only to insects that bloat themselves with blood or other food but also to gravid female insects, whose ovaries often swell enormously.

What are **abdominal styli**?

Styli are vestiges of abdominal legs and are found on only the most primitive insects. Bristletails and jumping bristletails have paired styli on most of their abdominal segments. Although styli are one-segmented, they are usually quite long and easily seen.

Laying Eggs

How do insects **lay their eggs**?

Some insects have no special egg-laying organ and simply place their eggs on some appropriate surface such as the underside of a leaf. Other insects have an egg-laying organ, an ovipositor, with which they can insert their eggs into a crevice, the soil, a plant tissue, or, in the case of parasitic insects, into the body of an insect that will be the host for their offspring. There are two types of ovipositors, an appendicular type that is composed of abdominal appendages, which are essentially modified legs, and a nonappendicular type that is composed of the modified terminal segments of the abdomen. Some beetles, flies, and moths and butterflies have nonappendicular ovipositors. Other insects, among them silverfish, dragonflies, grasshoppers, cicadas, true bugs, and thrips, have appendicular ovipositors.

What is the **ovipositor of a house fly** like?

The ovipositor of a female house fly, much like the nonappendicular ovipositors of other insects, is made up of the four terminal segments of the abdomen, which are thin, lengthened, and telescope into the base of the abdomen when they are not being used. The house fly is deliberate when she is laying her eggs. She walks over the pile of manure or garbage that will be the food for her offspring as she looks for cracks or crevices in which to place her eggs. She uses her extensible ovipositor to place her eggs deep within the cracks and crevices.

How does the **ovipositor of a fruit fly** differ from that of a house fly?

Fruit flies such as the apple maggot and the Mediterranean fruit fly have a nonappendicular ovipositor as do other flies, but their ovipositors come to a sharp and rigid point that is used to pierce a growing fruit and to place an egg within it. These fruit flies, sometimes known as the large fruit flies, are not the same as the pomace flies, or small fruit flies, such as the *Drosophila,* that come to overripe fruit in our homes. The ovipositor of the pomace flies is not adapted for piercing.

What is the origin of appendicular ovipositors?

Appendicular ovipositors consist of paired appendages of two of the segments near the end of the abdomen, the 8th and 9th segments. Sometimes referred to as valves or blades, they are extreme modifications of leg-like appendages of the ancestor of the insects.

What is the **ovipositor of a female grasshopper** like?

The short, stout, and strong blades of her ovipositor are adapted for digging in the soil. As the ovipositor digs its way down into the soil, the segments of the abdomen untelescope, allowing penetration to a depth of as much as two inches below the surface of the soil. There the female deposits from 20 to more than 100 eggs that are inaccessible to most predators cemented together in an ovoid mass.

How do **sawflies** lay their eggs?

Sawflies, which are really primitive relatives of bees and wasps, are well-named because the ovipositor is saw-like. The larvae of almost all sawflies are plant feeders, and the females use the ovipositor to cut a slit, into which they deposit their eggs, into a leaf, stem, or some other part of a plant.

What does the **ovipositor of a parasitic wasp** look like?

It is generally long and slender and is used to inject an egg into the body of the insect that will be the host for its larval offspring. Some parasitic wasps, notably a species that parasitizes sawfly larvae that burrow in wood, have long, thread-like ovipositors that are longer than the rest of the body. Although the ovipositor of one of these wasps is as thin as a horse hair, it can drill through solid wood to enter the tunnel of a sawfly larva and place an egg within its body.

What is the evolutionary origin of the **sting** of a wasp, ant, or bee?

The sting is a modified ovipositor—thus only females can sting—that can pierce by slicing its way into the skin. It is served by venom glands and a sac for the storage of venom. A wasp can sting repeatedly, but a worker honey bee can sting only once in her life. Her sting is barbed and remains firmly fixed in the flesh of the victim. When a bee that has just stung moves away, the whole stinging apparatus is ripped from her body and she soon dies. The discarded stinging apparatus, which is still embedded in the victim's flesh, continues to pump venom into the wound for some time.

What are the first and second things you should do after being **stung by a honey bee**?

If you are near a hive or a nest, the first thing to do is move away quickly. A stinging bee releases an alarm pheromone that incites other bees to come out and defend the colony. The second thing to do is to apply first aid. Remove the sting from the skin without compressing the venom sac and thus forcing more venom into the wound. This can be accomplished by scraping the sting away with a fingernail, a knife blade, or the edge of a credit card. You can then apply ice to ease the pain. If the venom causes a large swelling or a rash, it is best to consult a physician.

INSECT BODIES: THE INSIDE

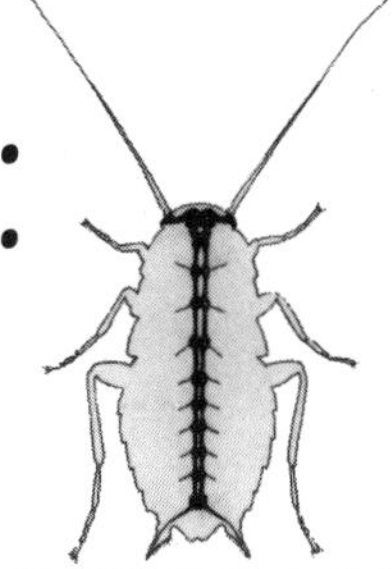

How complex are the **inner workings** of a tiny insect?

They are as complex as our own. Insects have a circulatory system that circulates blood throughout the body, a respiratory system that delivers oxygen to all of its cells, a digestive system that digests and absorbs food, an excretory system that eliminates metabolic wastes from the body, a reproductive system that produces either eggs or sperm, a muscular system that converts energy to movement, an endocrine system that produces the chemical messengers known as hormones, and a nervous system that coordinates the functions of the other systems.

BLOOD AND CIRCULATION

What is the **circulatory system** of an insect like?

While humans and other vertebrates have a closed circulatory system in which the blood flows within a plumbing system of arteries, capillaries, and veins, insects have an open circulatory system. That is, their blood flows freely throughout the body cavity, in other words, the space between the body wall and the inner organs. The insect's body cavity and its attendant blood flow extend out into the appendages, legs, wings, and antennae.

Do insects have a **heart**?

Strictly speaking, no. But they do have a pumping organ that is roughly analogous to the heart of a vertebrate. This organ, known as the dorsal vessel, lies along the center

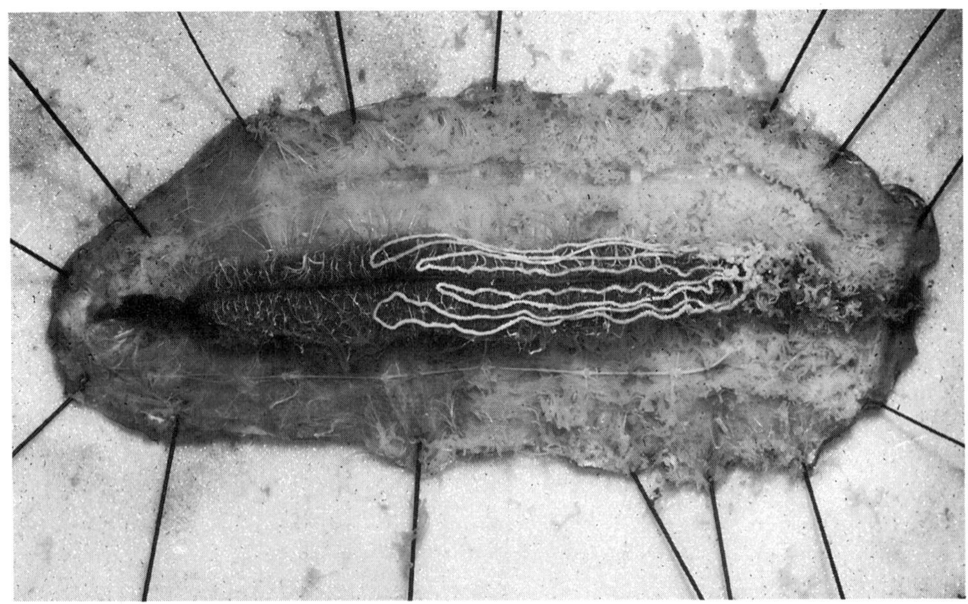

Dissection of a hornworm. (Photo by Edward S. Ross.)

of the body cavity on its upper, dorsal, side. It consists of two parts: the "heart," which lies mainly in the abdomen, and the "aorta," which runs forward through the thorax to the head. The heart, which is composed of several chambers with valves, sucks in blood from the abdominal cavity and pumps it forward through the aorta, which is generally no more than a straight tube. Aided by membranous diaphragms in the body cavity, the dorsal vessel continuously pumps blood toward the head, and the blood then flows back to the abdomen to be pumped forward again. Diaphragms and little pulsatile organs, essentially accessory hearts, aid in the flow of blood into the appendages.

What are some of the **functions of an insect's blood**?

An insect's blood does many, but not all, of the same things that the blood of a vertebrate does. As it circulates throughout the body, an insect's blood carries hormones from the glands that secrete them to their target sites; it transports nutrients from the digestive system to all of the cells of the body; and it carries waste products from the cells to the insect's equivalent of the kidneys. It does not usually distribute oxygen, however, as does the blood of a vertebrate. The insect's blood, or hemolymph, also acts as a hydraulic system that can apply pressure to expand the wings of a newly-molted insect, cause the protrusion of an eversible structure such as a membranous bladder, or extend the coiled siphoning mouthparts of a butterfly.

Why isn't insect blood red?

The blood of an insect may be almost colorless, green, or yellow—but, with only a handful of exceptions, never red. The blood of all vertebrates, from fish to mammals, is red because it contains red blood cells. These cells are red because they contain hemoglobin, a red, iron-containing protein that binds the oxygen molecules that the blood carries from the gills or lungs to the cells of the body. With some exceptions, the blood of insects is not appreciably involved in transporting oxygen. Therefore, it is usually not red because there is no need for hemoglobin. There is, however, free hemoglobin, not contained in cells, in the blood of a few larval midges that live in oxygen-poor mud at the bottom of pools of water or ponds. In these few insects, the blood does transport oxygen. When oxygen becomes plentiful in their environment, enough of it is absorbed through the midge's membranous body wall to meet its needs. The oxygen is dissolved in the fluid of the blood and is thus carried throughout the body. The hemoglobin may be useful only when there is so little oxygen in the environment that the needs of the midge larva cannot be met by the small amount that is dissolved in the blood. Under such conditions, hemoglobin may come to the rescue by carrying oxygen to the cells of the body.

Does an insect's blood have **defensive functions**?

Yes, the first two that are mentioned below are common to all insects and the third occurs in only a few insects. First, among the several different kinds of cells in the blood are phagocytes—a word whose literal meaning, as translated from its Greek roots, is eater of cells. The phagocytes serve the same end as do the white blood cells of humans or other vertebrates. They destroy bacteria and other microorganisms that invade the body. Second, certain blood cells can encapsulate foreign bodies such as parasites and thus render them harmless. The egg or young larva of a parasitic insect that invades the body cavity can be so completely covered by a multitude of flattened blood cells that it dies because its access to oxygen is blocked. Third, some insects have toxic substances in their blood that deter predators. For example, a ladybird beetle or a blister beetle oozes toxin-containing blood from its leg joints if it is attacked.

Can parasites of insects prevent their hosts from **encapsulating** them?

Parasites of insects have evolved several ways, mainly biochemical mechanisms, to prevent their hosts from encapsulating them. It was also recently discovered that certain parasitic wasps that live in the body cavity of an insect as larvae have enlisted an outside agent, a virus, to do this job for them. This virus, specifically known as a polydnavirus, suppresses the host's immune system (the system that triggers encapsulation) in a way that has yet to be discovered. The egg that the mother of the parasite injects into the host insect is coated with a fluid that contains the polydnaviruses that will make the survival of her offspring possible. The egg is bathed in this fluid as it passes through its mother's reproductive tract.

Does insect **blood clot**?

Yes, it does. If an insect is wounded, as when a nip from a predator pierces its body wall, blood cells move to the site of the wound. Phagocytes remove damaged cells, and other blood cells produce a clot that seals the wound until the body wall is regenerated at the next molt.

BREATHING

How do insects **breathe**?

Oxygen gets to the cells of the insect's body through a complex pattern of air-filled tubes known as the tracheal system—named by analogy with the trachea, or windpipe, of a vertebrate. Openings through the body wall called the spiracles connect the tracheal system to the outside atmosphere. The tracheae branch and rebranch, becoming ever thinner as they penetrate farther and farther into the tissues of the body. The last and smallest branches of the tracheal system, the tracheoles, carry oxygen to all of the cells of the insect's body.

Oxygen moves through the tracheae to the cells by simple diffusion. As physics tells us, gases diffuse from where they are in high concentration to where they are in low concentration. Since the insects are using up oxygen, its concentration is lower within the body than in the atmosphere, and it diffuses inward. In the same way, carbon dioxide (the gaseous waste product produced by the metabolism of the cells) diffuses outward from the body, where it is in high concentration, to the atmosphere, where it is in lower concentration. The thin walls of the tracheoles are very permeable to gases, and it is through them that oxygen moves to the cells and that carbon dioxide enters the tracheal system.

The spiracles are not just simple holes in the body wall. They are equipped with valves that open and close according to the insect's need for oxygen. By closing partly or fully when the insect has little or no need for oxygen, the valves minimize the rate at which moisture is lost from the body. Insects have two pairs of spiracles on the thorax and may have as many as eight pairs on the thorax.

Do insects ever **inhale and exhale**?

Many insects do. Generally speaking, small, inactive insects get as much oxygen as they require by diffusion, but diffusion alone cannot satisfy the far greater oxygen requirements of an insect that is flying or otherwise highly active. But the amount of oxygen that enters the insect's body can be considerably increased by respiratory movements, inhalation and exhalation, that pump fresh air into the tracheae. Inhalation and exhalation are made possible by flexible air sacs that are a part of the tracheal system and can expand and contract as do our lungs. (Air sacs are only expandable bladders, and, unlike our lungs, have nothing to do with gas exchange.) A grasshopper, for example, inhales by expanding its abdomen while its abdominal spiracles are open and its thoracic spiracles are closed. Air rushes in to fill the air sacs. It exhales by contracting its abdomen while the abdominal spiracles are closed and the thoracic spiracles are open. This pushes the air out of the sacs and forces it to flow forward through the tracheal system and out through the thoracic spiracles.

How do **aquatic insects** get oxygen?

Aquatic insects obtain oxygen in three main ways. One way, used by insects such as water scorpions, rat-tailed maggots, and most mosquito larvae, is to poke a hollow tube, a snorkel, into the air through the surface film of the water. A second way, used by many aquatic beetles and true bugs, is to bring a bubble of air with them under the water from the surface. The third way is to absorb dissolved oxygen from the water through gills or directly through the body wall. Only immature insects use this method. Among them are the nymphs of damselflies, dragonflies, and mayflies, and the larvae of caddisflies and black flies.

What are **rat-tailed maggots**?

They are the aquatic larvae of certain flies of the family Syrphidae, commonly known as flower flies or hover flies. The drone fly, a convincing mimic of a honey bee, is an example that is familiar to many people. During its larval stage, this fly lives in oxygen-poor environments such as sewage or the liquid in a rotting carcass. It gets its oxygen through a snorkel (a very long, thin tube known as the rat tail) that extends up into the air. The snorkel is so long and thin that it cannot supply enough oxygen by diffusion alone to satisfy even the meager demands of such a lethargic creature as a rat-tailed maggot. The maggot solves this problem by making respiratory movements that suck air down through the snorkel.

How do the **predaceous diving beetles** get oxygen?

These beetles get oxygen from a bubble of air that they get at the surface and keep with them under the water. From time to time, the beetle must go to the surface to renew its bubble. How often it must do this varies with the size of the bubble and the beetle's need for oxygen. In some species, a large bubble is carried under the elytra, the hardened front wings that cover the membranous hind wings. If an experimenter cuts the hind wings off to make more room under the elytra, the bubble is larger, and the beetle goes to the surface for air less often.

Can an **air bubble** function like a gill?

Yes, it can. An air bubble that functions in this way is known as a "physical gill." As an insect uses up oxygen from its bubble, the concentration of oxygen in the bubble decreases, and the relative concentration of nitrogen, the other major component of air, increases. Consequently, the bubble functions like a gill as oxygen diffuses from the water, where it is in high concentration, into the bubble, where it is in low concentration. Enough nitrogen remains in the bubble to maintain a fairly large volume into which oxygen can diffuse for quite a while, because oxygen diffuses into the bubble three times as rapidly as the nitrogen diffuses out. This extends the useful life of a bubble: most insects must still return to the surface periodically to renew it, but less often than would be necessary otherwise. In a few insects, including a small, slow-moving aquatic beetle, the physical gill can function more or less indefinitely. The beetle's body is covered with water-repellent hairs that are bent at an angle. These hairs maintain a thin bubble that covers virtually the whole body of the beetle and has such a large surface area that the diffusion of oxygen into it can meet the needs of the beetle for months. An aquatic true bug is covered by a similar bubble that is maintained by hair on the body so dense that there are 2 million hairs per square millimeter. There are 645 square millimeters in a square inch—hence 1,290,000,000 hairs per square inch.

What is a **tracheal gill**?

Tracheal gills, which absorb dissolved oxygen from water, are thin-walled evaginations of the body wall—often filamentous or plate-like in form— that contain tracheae and many tracheoles. Oxygen dissolved in the water diffuses through the wall of the gill and into the tracheoles. It then diffuses through these tracheoles into the main tracheae and ultimately into the tracheoles at the other end of the system that deliver the oxygen to the cells.

Can aquatic insects survive after their **tracheal gills have been removed**?

Under certain circumstances, some small and relatively inactive insects can survive even after their tracheal gills have been excised. Oxygen dissolved in the water diffuses into their blood through the body wall and is carried to the cells of the body by the circulating blood. During the winter, in highly oxygenated water, or when the insect is at rest, this is enough to keep the insect going, but it may not survive without its gills in summer, when it is active, or in water that does not have enough oxygen dissolved in it.

Does any insect take in oxygen **through its anus**?

Immature dragonflies, which are aquatic, do just exactly that. The immature dragonfly's rectum is enlarged, very muscular, and lined with rows of little, overlapping, plate-like tracheal gills. It "breathes" by sucking in water through its anus. The gills absorb dissolved oxygen from this fresh supply of water. The muscular rectum expels the "stale" water through the anus and then sucks up a fresh supply.

DIGESTING FOOD

What is the **digestive system** of an insect like?

In its broadest aspects, it is roughly similar in both form and function to the digestive system of a vertebrate such as a human. In overall form, the insect's digestive tract, also known as the gut, is a tube that extends through the body from the mouth opening to the anus. Food is moved through it by peristaltic contractions of its walls. As in vertebrates, the insect's digestive system secretes enzymes that digest food, break it down into its component nutrients, and then absorb these nutrients by passing them through the wall of the gut into the blood.

Insects eat an astonishing variety of foods: almost any organic substance, including leaves, plant sap, blood, other insects, carrion, and even dry wood, hair, or feathers. They have, of course, become adapted to dealing with their own particular foods. Consequently, the more detailed aspects of the digestive system vary, often greatly, from insect group to insect group or even from species to species.

What is the **structure of an insect's digestive tract**?

The digestive tract, also known as the gut, begins at the mouth with the esophagus, which transports food to the foregut. The foregut includes a crop where food can be stored and, in some insects that eat solids, a gizzard, or proventriculus, which grinds the food with sturdy cuticular teeth. Embryologically, the foregut is an invagination of the body wall and is thus lined with cuticle. It empties into the midgut, which is not an invagination of the body wall and is, therefore, not lined with cuticle. The two major functions of the midgut are the secretion of digestive enzymes and the absorp-

Digestive System

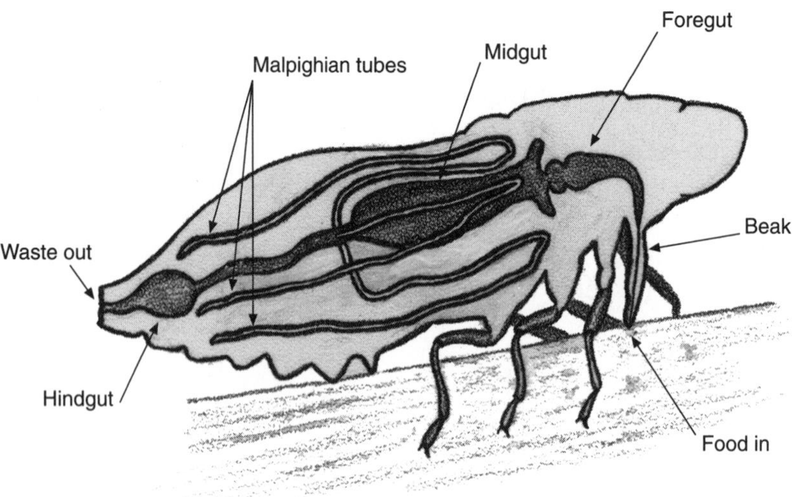

(Illustration by James B. Nardi. Courtesy of Iowa State University Press.)

tion of nutrients. The waste matter that cannot be digested that is left in the midgut after digestion and absorption is passed into the hindgut, which absorbs water, minerals, and other useful substances from the waste before it is formed into feces in the rectum and eliminated through the anus. The hindgut, like the foregut, is an invagination of the body wall and is, therefore, lined with cuticle. When an insect molts, the cuticular linings of the fore- and hindguts are molted along with the cuticle of the exoskeleton.

What is an **enzyme**?

An enzyme is a compound—usually a protein—that acts as a catalyst, a substance that makes a chemical reaction proceed without itself undergoing any permanent chemical change. There are many enzymes with many different functions in the bodies of insects and other animals. Many of them play essential roles in the digestion of food.

What is a **filter chamber**?

The filter chamber is an adaptation of the gut that helps aphids, leafhoppers, and their relatives, all of which suck plant sap, to cope with the huge quantities of water that they must ingest to get the low concentration of nutrients that are dissolved in the watery sap. In the filter chamber, a section of the rear end of the midgut loops back to

Do clothes moths digest wool and hair?

Most animals cannot digest hair. We all know that cats cannot, because we have seen them regurgitate ("cough up") balls of intact hairs. The difficulty is that hair is composed of keratin, a protein that is resistant to almost all digestive enzymes. Feathers, which are eaten by bird lice, are also made of keratin. Clothes moths—and presumably also the hair-eating hide beetles (dermestids) and the bird lice—are among the only animals that secrete the unusual enzymes that digest keratin.

make contact with the front end of the midgut. The filter chamber absorbs water from the ingested sap at the front end of the midgut and passes it to the hindgut, thus conducting the water around most of the midgut. This arrangement benefits the insect because the midgut — the site of digestion and absorption— need not deal with the huge amount of water that would otherwise dilute the food.

Do insects **salivate**?

Insects have a pair of salivary glands that are located in the thorax. A long tube conducts the saliva from the glands to the base of the labium. Saliva lubricates the mouthparts and carries enzymes that begin the process of digestion. In some bloodsucking insects, the saliva contains an anticoagulant that prevents blood from clotting in the mouthparts. The salivary glands of larval caddisflies and larval moths and butterflies secrete the silk that these insects use in weaving cocoons or other shelters. The unusually large salivary gland of male scorpionflies produce large quantities of nutritious saliva that serves as a nuptial gift that the female eats as she copulates with the male.

How do termites **digest wood**?

Wood consists chiefly of cellulose, which most insects and other animals cannot digest. Cellulose is a chain-like molecule that consists essentially of a string of simple sugar molecules that are bound together by tenacious bonds that can be broken only by the enzyme cellulase. Breaking these bonds splits up the cellulose molecule and releases the digestible simple sugars of which it is composed. The termites that eat the wood in our buildings do not make the enzyme cellulase, but their hind intestines are occupied by hordes of protozoa that do make cellulase and digest enough cellulose to meet their own needs as well as those of their host termite. When a termite undergoes a molt, it molts the cuticular lining of the hindgut and thus loses the bacteria and protozoa that are essential to it.

How do termites replace the **symbiotic protozoa** that they lose when they molt?

They do so by means of anal trophollaxis, the eating of feces from the anus of another individual. As disgusting as this may sound to you, it is a blessing to a termite that has just molted. The fecal material from the donor termite restores protozoa to the hindgut. Without its usual complement of these symbionts, the newly molted termite could not digest cellulose and would soon starve to death, even while ingesting copious quantities of wood.

EXCRETION

Do insects have an equivalent of the **kidneys**?

As the kidneys remove metabolic wastes from the blood of a vertebrate, the Malpighian tubes remove metabolic wastes from the blood of an insect. The Malpighian tubes are outgrowths of the digestive tract that empty into the hindgut just at the point where the midgut and hindgut join. They are generally long tubes that are closed at their free end and that writhe about in the blood in the body cavity as they filter dissolved waste products from the blood. Aphids and springtails are the only insects that have no Malpighian tubes. Other insects have anywhere from two to over 200 (as in some large grasshoppers).

How were the **Malpighian tubes** named?

They were named for their discoverer, Marcello Malpighi, a 17th-century Italian microscopist who discovered them while investigating the anatomy of the silkworm. He is even better known for his work on vertebrates. For example, he began the study of embryology and discovered that the arteries of a vertebrate are joined to the veins by the tiny capillaries.

Do insects **urinate**?

Not in the same way that we do. They do, of course, produce urine, the waste product of metabolism, but they do not eliminate the urine from the body as a liquid separate from the feces as we and other mammals do. The insect's organs of excretion, the Malpighian tubes, empty metabolic wastes into the hindgut, where they are mixed with the fecal material. Thus, the feces of an insect contain the urine as well as the indigestible part of the food.

Why is it necessary to remove **metabolic wastes** from the body?

The nitrogenous (nitrogen-containing) wastes, such as ammonia, urea, and uric acid, that result from the metabolism of proteins are toxic to insects and other animals. They must be constantly eliminated from the body so that they do not build up to concentrations that can poison the organism.

In what **chemical form** do most terrestrial insects excrete their metabolic waste?

They excrete it in the form of uric acid, which is less toxic than are the other choices, ammonia and urea, and also considerably less soluble in water, thus requiring less water to flush it from the body. The relative insoluability of uric acid is particularly advantageous to the many terrestrial insects that do not have ready access to free water and must conserve the water that they have in their bodies. Reptiles and birds also need to conserve water and therefore secrete uric acid. Birds, like insects, excrete urine and fecal material together as one package, but the uric acid is readily visible in the dropping of a bird. It is the white part at one end of the dropping.

THE FAT BODY

What is an insect's **fat body**?

The fat body is usually a rather loose aggregation of yellow or white cells that lies in the body cavity and is bathed by the blood. Its structure is ill-defined, seemingly haphazard, and variable from species to species. Nevertheless, its structure and location are relatively constant within a species. In caterpillars, for example, a part of the fat body is just inside the body wall, and another part surrounds the digestive tract.

Does the fat body do **more than store fat**?

The fat body is mainly a storage organ for fat, protein, and glycogen, a complex sugar, but it also has other important functions. It synthesizes proteins, including one involved in the formation of the egg yolk, and it synthesizes the blood sugar, which is the sugar trehalose rather than the glucose of humans. It has cells that store uric acid, a function that is important to insects, such as springtails, that have no Malpighian tubes. In some insects it also has cells that house friendly bacteria that provide the insect with vitamins and other nutrients. The nutrients stored in the fat body are often reserved for later use. Insects that do not feed as adults, such as the cecropia moth and other giant silkworms, depend upon these stored nutrients to provide them with energy and to serve as the building blocks that will constitute their eggs.

MUSCLES

What are the **muscles** of an insect like?

On a fundamental level, insect muscles are comparable in structure and function to the striated skeletal muscles of humans and other vertebrates. Insects do not have the smooth, unstriated muscles of the digestive tract, bladder, and other viscera of vertebrates. Even the muscles of the gut, heart, Malpighian tubes, and other visceral organs of an insect are of the striated type. Some of an insect's visceral muscles can function without being connected to the central nervous system, but its skeletal muscles, such as those that move its appendages, are associated with nerves from the central nervous system that signal the muscle when to contract. Most of the skeletal muscles, including the wing muscles of insects that beat their wings slowly, contract once in response to each nerve impulse. But some skeletal muscles, such as the wing muscles of insects that beat their wings rapidly, can make several contractions in quick succession in response to only one nerve impulse. This explains why some insects can beat their wings at extremely rapid rates: honey bees about 200 times per second; mosquitoes over 500 times per second; and a tiny biting midge over 1,000 times per second.

What do **visceral muscles** do?

They produce movement in such internal organs as the digestive tract, the heart, the Malpighian tubes, and the genital ducts. The waves of peristaltic contractions produced by visceral muscles propel food through the digestive tract, helps the heart circulate the blood, writhes the Malpighian tubes in the body cavity, and creates contractions that move an egg through the genital duct.

How many muscles do insects have?

Since insects are small, you might expect them to have fewer muscles than a much larger animal. But such is not the case. A large insect may have two to three times as many muscles as a person. A human has 529 muscles, but Pierre Lyonnet, an 18th-century French anatomist, counted 1,647 separate muscles in the large, wood-boring caterpillar of a carpenter moth, sometimes known as a goat moth.

How are **so many muscles** packed into such a small body?

An insect's muscles are, of course, miniaturized. Their small size is due in part to a decrease in the size of each muscle cell, or fiber, but has been accomplished mainly through a reduction in the number of fibers per muscle. Some insect muscles are composed of only one or two fibers.

THE NERVOUS SYSTEM

What does an insect's **nervous system** do?

Like the nervous system of a vertebrate, an insect's nervous system coordinates its bodily functions and directs its behavior. It can be divided into three parts that are functionally more or less distinct: the *central nervous system,* which controls voluntary activity and is the integrative and decision-making center; the *peripheral nervous system,* which brings in information from the sense organs and also sends directions to the muscles and other organs; and the *visceral nervous system,* which is the insect's version of the vertebrate sympathetic nervous system. It controls the digestive system, the opening and closing of the spiracles, and is associated with certain endocrine glands.

What is the **structure** of an insect's central nervous system?

Typically, it is a chain of ganglia (aggregations of nerve cells) that extends from the head to the end of the abdomen, one ganglion per segment. The ganglia are joined by paired, longitudinal connectives that consist mainly of nerve fibers. The three most complex ganglia constitute the brain, located in the head above the esophagus. The subesophageal ganglion, actually a complex of three ganglia, is in the head below the esophagus. In primitive insects, such as the bristletails, there is a ganglion in each of the three thoracic segments and each of the first eight abdominal segments. There is, however, a tendency toward the reduction of the number of ganglia in the more advanced insects. For example, some adult flies have only a single abdominal ganglion, which is partially fused with a single, large thoracic ganglion.

What do the **ganglia** of an insect's thorax and abdomen do?

These ganglia are primarily associated with the body segment in which they are located, and they control the muscles of that segment. But it is not always that simple. Muscles in a given segment may also be innervated by muscles from some other segment. For example, the flight muscles of the thorax are controlled not only by nerves from the ganglia of the wing-bearing segments but also by nerves from the ganglia of the first three abdominal segments. The last ganglion in the abdomen is actually a fusion of four ganglia that were separate in the ancestor of the insects. This compound ganglion innervates the genitalia, and is thus intimately involved in the control of egg laying, copulation, and the release of sex attractant pheromones.

Does the brain of a male mantis **control his mating activities**?

The brain —or perhaps some other ganglion in the head—exerts an indispensable inhibitory control on copulation and many other behaviors. This is demonstrated by

Is the brain of an insect comparable to our brain?

Only in a very broad sense. Like our brain, it integrates much of the information that comes in from the sense organs, especially the eyes and the antennae. The interpretation of olfactory information from the antennae is particularly important because it controls the selection of food, the placement of eggs, and the response to pheromones that facilitate locating and identifying mates. Also like our brain, the insect's brain is the location of the "higher centers" of the nervous system that control the most complex aspects of its behavior. In insects that must function in complex societies, such as ants and some bees and wasps, the brain is larger than in nonsocial insects that have less sophisticated behaviors. But the control of behavior is not as completely centralized in the insect's brain as it is in ours. A male praying mantis, for example, can initiate copulation and inseminate a female even after she has devoured his head and the brain along with it.

the fact that the copulatory movements of a male mantis, which are controlled by the last abdominal ganglion, will continue indefinitely and uninhibited if his head is eaten by his mate or removed by an experimenter. This inhibition from the brain prevents the wasteful and no longer appropriate behavior from continuing.

How does a message get from a **sense organ to the central nervous system**?

The message moves as an electrical impulse along nerve fibers that connect the sense organ with the central nervous system. If, for example, an antenna or some other part of the body brushes against an object, one or more sense hairs will be slightly deflected. The movement of the hair in its membranous socket will distort an adjacent nerve ending, which generates an electrical impulse that will travel along the nerve fiber toward the central nervous system. As it speeds toward the brain or one of the ganglia of the nerve cord, the electrical impulse will have to pass from a fiber of one nerve cell to the fiber of another. The two fibers are not physically joined, but branches of one almost touch branches of the other to form a *synapse*. The synaptic gap between the two nerve fibers is crossed by a chemical neurotransmitter that is produced by the nerve from which the signal is coming and that stimulates the generation in the receiving fiber of an electrical impulse that will continue on its way to the central nervous system.

What does the **peripheral nervous system** do?

Broadly speaking, it has two main functions. First, it brings information from the sense organs to the central nervous system. The sense organs are the insect's window on the world, keeping it in touch with what is happening in the outside environment. Second, after the central nervous system has integrated the information and "decided" what action to take, the peripheral nervous system conveys the appropriate orders to the muscles, glands, or other organs that will act on the central nervous system's decision.

Are insects studied as **"model systems"** in neurobiological studies?

Insects such as *Drosophila,* tobacco hornworms, cockroaches, and grasshoppers are being more widely recognized as the best "model systems" for answering fundamental questions about how the nervous systems work. This may seem far-fetched at first glance, but when we consider that insects and vertebrates —even humans—are descended from a distant common ancestor, it becomes apparent that many fundamental characteristics of the nervous system must be shared by insects, vertebrates, and some other animals. Using insects as model systems becomes even more attractive as legislation limits and makes more cumbersome the use of vertebrates such as mice, rats, and dogs as laboratory animals. A significant point that many biologists, especially crusaders against "anthropomorphism," seem to miss is that humans must necessarily serve as a model system for insects to the same extent that insects serve as a model system for humans.

HORMONES

What is the **glandular system** of an insect like?

Insects have two types of glands: *Exocrine* glands have ducts and discharge their products into the outside world or into some internal system such as the digestive system or the reproductive system. Products discharged into the environment are known as *pheromones* and have some behavioral or physiological affect on another member of the same species. *Endocrine* glands typically have no ducts and produce *hormones*, chemical messengers that are usually released directly into the blood. Hormones have many functions in the body of an insect. For example, they are important in regulating certain behaviors, reproduction, molting, metamorphosis, and many other aspects of the insects physiology.

How was it first demonstrated that insects make **hormones**?

Early in the twentieth century, some biologists assumed that insects did not make hormones. It was not until Vincent Wigglesworth, an English insect physiologist,

Insect physiologist Vincent Wigglesworth. (Photo courtesy of Photo Researchers, Inc.)

later to be knighted by Queen Elizabeth, performed a very clever experiment that gave clear proof that insects do make hormones. He did this experiment with a blood-sucking true bug, *Rhodnius,* that molts only after engorging itself with blood — and then only more than a week later. He decapitated two of these bugs and connected them neck to neck with a tube through which blood flowed freely between the bugs. One of the bugs had fed a week earlier and was due to molt, and the other had fed only the previous day. Although the recently fed bug should not have molted for another week, it did molt shortly after it had been attached to the other bug. Since the nervous systems of the two bugs were not connected, the signal that induced the recently fed bug to molt must have been a chemical factor that was brought in from the body of the other bug by the circulating blood—by definition a hormone.

REPRODUCTION

How do insects **reproduce**?

Most insects reproduce sexually, as do most animals. That is, some individuals have male sex organs and others have female sex organs. Throughout the animal kingdom, males are, by definition, the sex that produces the smaller sex cells, the sperm. Females are, by definition, the sex that produces the larger sex cells, the eggs. In the great majority of insects, an egg does not produce an embryo unless it is fertilized by a sperm. Thus, half of an individual's genes come from its mother and half from its father. This is the great advantage of sexual reproduction —the pooling in the offspring of genetic information from the two parents. This creates offspring with new anatomical, physiological, or behavioral characteristics that might better adapt them to current environmental conditions or to new conditions that might arise as the environment changes.

Who was **Francesco Redi**?

Redi's experiments demonstrated the universal importance of reproduction. He was one of the first to show that there is no spontaneous generation of life, that all living things originate from preexisting living things. For centuries, people thought that worms and tadpoles were generated from mud, flies from the carcasses of dead animals, and human body lice from filthy clothing reeking of stale sweat. Redi, a 17th-century Italian scientist, did an experiment that proved conclusively that maggots and flies are not generated by the rotting meat of dead animals. No flies or maggots appeared in containers of meat that were covered with screens that prevented flies from entering them. However, maggots did appear in uncovered containers that were entered by flies. Redi saw flies lay eggs on the meat, and realized that maggots—and ultimately flies—come from these eggs.

What organs comprise the **reproductive system** of a typical female insect?

There is a great deal of variation from family to family and even from species to species, but the reproductive systems of most females are variations of the same groundplan. This consists of a pair of ovaries that lie in the abdomen and produce the eggs; tubes that conduct the eggs to the vagina; a storage organ for sperm, the spermatheca, which empties into the vagina; and a pair of glands, the accessory glands, that also empty into the vagina.

What are the **functions of the vagina**?

The vagina, also known as the genital chamber, opens to the outside. It receives the penis of the male and accepts his semen. The eggs pass through the vagina on their way to the ovipositor, and it is in the vagina that the eggs will be bathed by the secretions of the accessory glands. In a few insects that do not lay eggs, the larva is retained within a "uterus" in the mother's body until it finishes growing. The "uterus" is an enlargement of the vagina.

Is there an advantage to having a **storage organ for sperm** in the body of the female?

The storage organ, or spermatheca, can store living sperm for days, months, or even years. A small gland that empties into the spermatheca produces a secretion that provides the sperm with nourishment and a suitable liquid environment. A queen honey bee, for example, can store sperm for a period of years. She mates several times when she begins her life but will never mate again. Nevertheless, she is capable of laying hundreds of thousands of fertilized eggs during her tenure as queen of the colony, which may continue for several years. A female's ability to store sperm for long peri-

How are the eggs laid?

Waves of peristaltic contractions move the eggs through the tubes that extend from the ovaries to the vagina. The eggs are fertilized by sperm that the female releases as the eggs pass the opening of the duct that runs from the vagina to the spermatheca, the organ that stores sperm. The females of some species can choose whether or not to fertilize an egg. Queen honey bees, for example, determine the sex of their offspring by fertilizing or not fertilizing an egg. Unfertilized eggs produce males, and fertilized eggs produce females. As she moves over the comb, she invariably places fertilized eggs in cells built to accommodate workers and unfertilized eggs in the somewhat larger cells that are built to accommodate drones, leaving no doubt that she can control the release of sperm from her spermatheca.

ods can be highly advantageous because it makes it possible to separate mating and egg laying in time. Males and females can come together in a season propitious for mating, and the female can lay her eggs in a season that offers the most food and other resources to her young. For example, many plant-feeding insects mate in late summer or autumn, when they are most numerous and it is easy to find a mate, but the females do not lay their eggs until the following spring, when tender foliage is available for their offspring to eat.

What do the female's **accessory glands** do?

The functions of the accessory glands are many and may be different in each species. In many insects, the secretions of the accessory glands are responsible for holding the eggs together in a mass or gluing them to a leaf or some other surface. Praying mantises, for example, cover their egg mass with a frothy secretion that hardens to form a protective capsule— in some species as large as a walnut—that remains attached to a plant stem throughout the winter. The accessory glands of female tsetse flies have been converted to milk glands that feed their larva which develop within a genital structure that is analogous to the uterus of a mammal. In bees and wasps, the accessory glands have been modified as poison glands that make the venom that is injected by the stinger.

How does an insect **sperm get into an egg**?

While the egg of a human female can be penetrated by a sperm at any point on its surface, a sperm can enter an insect egg through only one tiny opening in the egg's shell.

The egg of a human, or any other mammal, never leaves the warm and moist shelter of the female's reproductive tract. It can, therefore, afford to be thin-walled, soft, and easily penetrated by sperm. On the other hand, the eggs of most insects are expelled from the mother's body and must survive in the hostile outer environment, often for many months. Consequently, they are covered with an outer shell, usually hard and impenetrable, that keeps them from drying out and protects them against at least some of the parasites and predators that might have designs on them. A sperm can enter an egg only through the micropyle, the tiny opening in its shell. This micropyle is usually very small, presumably to cut down on the loss of moisture from the egg.

What organs comprise the **reproductive system** of a male insect?

The reproductive systems of males, like those of females, are variable and may differ from species to species. But in a typical system there is a pair of testes that lie in the abdomen and produce the sperm. Each testis is connected by a thin tube to one of two seminal vesicles in which the sperm are stored until they are passed into the body of a female. The seminal vesicles empty into an ejaculatory duct that ends in the penis and is lined with muscles that forcefully eject the semen into the female's vagina. A pair of large accessory glands empty into the male's ducts just below the seminal vesicles.

What do a male's **accessory glands** do?

The accessory glands produce many different substances that have various functions. Among them are seminal fluid and sperm packets. In some insects, the sperm are carried in a free-flowing liquid known as seminal fluid. This fluid protects and nourishes the sperm and transports them into the genital tract of the female. In other insects, the sperm are contained in membranous or gelatinous packets known as spermatophores. These packets not only house and protect the sperm, but in some species also provide nourishment to the female when they are absorbed or eaten by her. Accessory gland secretions that are passed into the body of a female may also contain pheromones that will influence her in various ways. They may elicit contractions of her genital duct that aid the movement of sperm; they may stimulate her to lay eggs; or they may affect her sexual behavior so as to prevent her from mating again, thus ensuring that her first mate will be the father of her offspring. A study of the mating behavior of house flies nicely demonstrated the effect of seminal fluid on the female's sexual behavior. House flies copulate for an hour, although almost all of the sperm are transferred to the female during the first ten minutes. During the remaining fifty minutes the male pumps sperm-free seminal fluid into his mate. Females that do not receive this seminal fluid remain receptive and will copulate with another male. Females that do receive this fluid are sexually "turned off" and reject other males for most of the rest of their lives.

Do **male honey bees** pump their ejaculate into the body of their mate?

They do not. In fact, their ejaculatory duct does not have the necessary muscles. Male honey bees, or drones, have evolved a suicidal way of putting their sperm into their mate. After the drone has inserted his penis into the female, a part of his genital apparatus, the part that holds the sperm, everts into the female's genitalia with an almost explosive force that is accompanied by an audible popping sound. The male's genitalia then tear loose from his body, and he falls to the ground and dies.

Do male insects get **erections**?

Some do. Males that do not form a sperm packet may facilitate the transfer of their seminal fluid by erecting the penis so that it can more easily enter the vagina of the female. Erection may be accomplished in two ways: by means of muscles or, as in humans, by the pumping of blood under pressure into the penis.

INSECT DIVERSITY

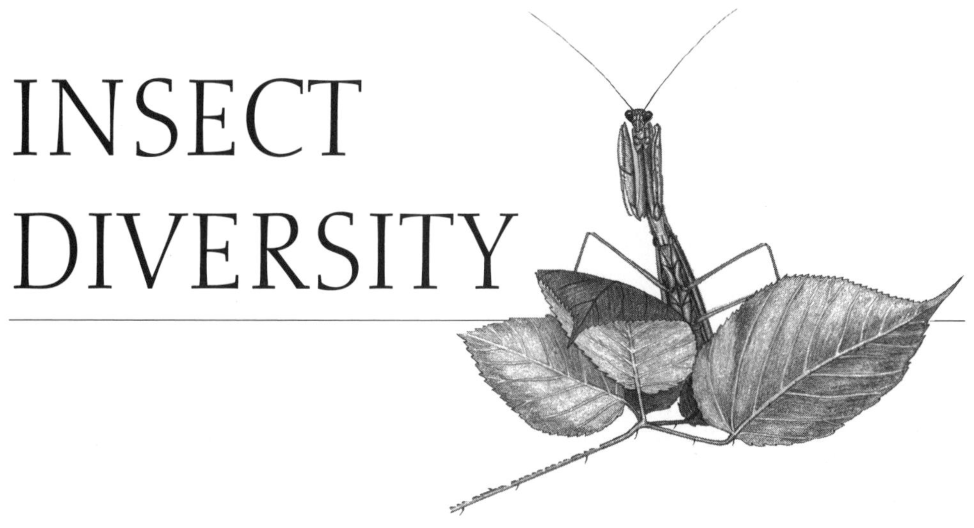

How many **different kinds** of insects are there?

This should really be a two-part question: How many insects are known to science? and How many insects have yet to be discovered? According to reasonable estimates, about 900,000 species of insects have thus far been discovered, named, and described. The estimates of how many remain to be discovered range from a conservative 9 million to a high of about 30 million.

How many species of insects live in the **United States and Canada**?

According to a recent estimate, somewhat more than 88,000 known species, only about 10 percent of the world's known insects. Mt. Desert Island in Maine has over 6,000 species, North Carolina over 12,000, and New York State over 15,000. There are surely quite a few North American species that have yet to be discovered, and the totals keep increasing. The insects of North America belong to 659 families. To give you some perspective, slightly more than 800 species of birds have been recorded from North America, including strays from Europe, Asia, the Caribbean, and Latin America that do not nest in North America.

Why are there **so many different kinds** of insects?

Because insects are so small that they can fit, so to speak, into the "cracks and crevices" of the environment. They can live in places that are too small for larger animals, and they can survive on resources that are too meager for larger animals. Consequently, they occupy hundreds of thousands of ecological "niches" that are not available to larger animals. During millions of years, more and more insects have evolved to split up the earth's resources ever more finely, until now there is a huge number of insect species. A fruit fly larva can grow to maturity in a small cherry. Various species of maggots and beetles can share one cow pat. A rice weevil finds everything that it needs in a single kernel of grain. The larva of a wasp lives in the tiny egg of a moth.

Carolus Linnaeus (Carl von Linne). (Photo by Edward S. Ross.)

What are **taxonomists** and what do they do?

A taxonomist is a scientist who names, describes, and classifies organisms. Insect taxonomists usually specialize on some limited group. There are just too many insects for any one person to deal with them all.

How do taxonomists keep track of **so many different species of insects**?

They pigeon-hole or classify them by arranging them in nested categories of decreasing inclusiveness. Consider, for example, the classification of the German cockroach:

Kingdom Animalia
Phylum Arthropoda
Class Hexapoda
Order Orthoptera
Family Blattelidae
Genus Blattella
Species *Blattella germanica*

Who was **Linnaeus**?

Carolus Linnaeus (the Latin form of Carl von Linne), a Swedish botanist who lived from 1707 to 1778, was the founder of modern taxonomy. He devised systems of classification for plants and animals, and introduced the use of binomial (two part) scientific names that replaced long and cumbersome names that sometimes included dozens of descriptive words. The tenth edition of his *Systema Naturae,* published in 1758, is internationally recognized as the starting point of animal nomenclature.

What **characteristics** of insects are used in classifying them?

Many characteristics. Any characteristic that will separate two species or reveal relationships between species is useful. For example, the piercing-sucking mouthparts of the true bugs are different in structure from the piercing-sucking mouthparts of all other insects. This tells us that the bugs are a group of related species, and that this group is separate from all of the other insects with piercing-sucking mouthparts. Differences and similarities in the wings of insects are particularly important in defining the subclasses that are the major subdivisions of the class Insecta, and the orders, which are the major subdivisions of the subclasses. The scientific names of the orders reflect the importance of the wings in defining the orders. The Greek root *pter* means wing. The orders Orthoptera, Thysanoptera, Hemiptera, Coleoptera, Lepidoptera, Diptera, and 15 others have names that end with *ptera*.

What is the **classification** of insects to the level of orders?

Class Hexapoda
- Subclass Apterygota—wingless insects
  - Order Collembola—springtails
    - Thysanura—bristletails
- Subclass Pterygota—winged and secondarily wingless insects
  - Division Exopterygota—insects with gradual metamorphosis
    - Order Ephemeroptera—mayflies
      - Odonata—dragonflies, damselflies
      - Orthoptera—grasshopper and relatives
      - Isoptera—termites
      - Psocoptera—booklice, barklice
      - Mallophaga—chewing lice
      - Anoplura—piercing-sucking lice
      - Hemiptera—true bugs
      - Homoptera—cicadas, hoppers, aphids, scales
      - Thysanoptera—thrips
  - Division Endopterygota—insects with complete metamorphosis
    - Order Neuroptera—lacewings and relatives
      - Coleoptera—beetles and weevils
      - Mecoptera—scorpionflies, hangingflies
      - Siphonaptera—fleas
      - Diptera—midges, mosquitoes, flies
      - Trichoptera—caddisflies
      - Lepidoptera—moths, butterflies
      - Hymenoptera—wasps, ants, bees

A few seldom-seen orders are omitted, but this classification includes at least 98 percent of the insects that you are likely to see. As with any other classification, there is some disagreement among taxonomists with respect to the organization of the classification of insects.

What is the **meaning of the names** of the class, subclasses, and divisions of the insect classification?

Hexapoda means six-legged and is derived from two Greek roots: *hex,* meaning six, and *pod,* meaning foot. *Apterygota,* which means wingless, is derived from the Greek root *a,* without, and *pter,* a wing. These insects are primitively wingless, that is, they are descended from ancestors that never evolved wings. *Pterygota* means winged, and is derived from the Greek root *pter.*

Some of these insects are secondarily wingless, that is, they lost their wings to accommodate a particular life-style such as living as a parasite amongst the hairs of a mammal. *Exoptergota* is derived from *pter* and the Greek root *ex,* outside. It refers to the externally visible developing wings of the insects with gradual metamorphosis. *Endopterygota* combines *pter* and *endo,* a Greek root that means within. It refers to the internal development of the wings of insects with complete metamorphosis.

Can the **Pterygota** be subdivided by criteria other than the external or internal development of the wings?

Some taxonomists divide the Pterygota into two subgroups: the Paleoptera, which includes only the orders Ephemeroptera and Odonata, and the Neoptera, which includes all of the other orders of the Pterygota. This division recognizes an evolutionary landmark, a structural modification of the wings that made it possible for the Neoptera to evolve an enormous number of new species that spread into ecological niches that are closed to the Paleoptera. The Neoptera (from the Greek roots *neo,* new, and *pter,* wing) can fold their wings down close to the body when they are not in use, allowing them to enter tight places such as cracks and crevices, and to burrow in the soil, decaying wood, the various structures of living plants, and many other places where they find food, shelter, and other resources. On the other hand, the Paleoptera (from the Greek roots *paleo,* ancient, and *pter,* wing), cannot fold their wings and can only hold them awkwardly out to the side or straight up over the body. They cannot exploit the multitude of ecological niches that are open to insects that can enter tight places.

Where do springtails live and what do they do?

Springtails are common and often very abundant, but we seldom notice them because they are so small and usually live in places where they are hidden from view. Many species live in the soil, often as large populations of as many as 4,000 individuals per cubic foot of surface soil. Others live in decaying wood or other rotting vegetation, in crevices in bark, or in fungi. One species, *Podura aquatica*—which has no common name—sometimes occurs on the surface of freshwater ponds by the millions, closely packed and forming big gray mats. Another species, the seashore springtail, sometimes occurs in very large numbers along the shore between the low and high tide lines. A collembolan known as the snow flea may be found in large numbers on the surface of the snow in winter. A few species are guests in the nests of termites or ants. Springtails are mainly scavengers that eat decaying vegetation, pollen grains, and the feces of arthropods. A few eat the tissues of living plants, notably the lucerne flea, which may seriously damage alfalfa crops.

SPRINGTAILS

What is a **springtail**?

Springtails, the members of the order Collembola, are tiny, wingless insects that are usually much less than a quarter of an inch long. They are easily recognized by a fork-like jumping organ, the furcula, that is folded forward on the underside of the abdomen, and whose two prongs hook onto a clasp-like structure. When the furca is tensed and suddenly released by the clasp, it strikes the ground with enough force to propel the springtail as much as four inches into the air. Many entomologists think that the springtails are so different from the other insects that they should be placed in a group of their own outside of the Class Hexapoda. Worldwide, there are about 6,000 species.

BRISTLETAILS

What is a **bristletail**?

The common name bristletail is almost a literal translation of the scientific name of the order to which these insects belong, *Thysanura,* which comes from the Greek roots *thysan,* a fringe, and *ur,* a tail. This is a small order with fewer than 400 species worldwide. They are of moderate size and wingless; those that people are likely to see are about one-half inch long. Bristletails are distinguished by their carrot-shaped bodies, which are often covered with scales, by their long antennae, and by the three long, slender, and bristly (fringed) tails at the end of the abdomen. These insects live in soil, decaying wood, leaf litter, or even in the nests of termites, ants, or mammals. We do not know what most of them eat, but some species are known to eat starchy substances.

What are **silverfish and firebrats**?

They are bristletails that live in our homes or other buildings. They are generally harmless, but may chew holes into cloth or paper coated with starch such as wall paper and book bindings. For unknown reasons, they may eat rayon fabric, although it is indigestible and cannot sustain life. Silverfish and firebrats prefer different habitats. Cool and damp places such as basements and bathrooms suit silverfish. Firebrats prefer hot places and will not lay eggs at ordinary room temperature, but breed rapidly at temperatures between 90°F and 102°F. They occur in bakeries and near furnaces.

MAYFLIES

What are **mayflies**?

Mayflies (the order Ephemeroptera), sometimes called fishflies, are winged insects that are aquatic in the nymphal stage. Over 3,000 species are known. They are unique among the insects in that they go through one additional molt after they have become winged adults. Their scientific name refers to the fact that the adults, which cannot feed, are ephemeral, living only for a few hours or a few days, just long enough to copulate and lay eggs. The males form flying swarms that are visited by mate-seeking females. Many species just spew their eggs into the water as they fly above the surface. Some species do not actually lay their eggs; their egg-laden abdomens simply break off and fall into the water. Various aquatic habitats are occupied by nymphs of different species. In lakes and slow-moving rivers, they often burrow in the bottom muck. Some cling to aquatic plants, and in fast-flowing streams they are likely to hide under rocks or cling to their upper surface. Except for a few carnivorous species, mayfly nymphs feed on algae or plant detritus.

What **characteristics** identify mayflies?

The nymphs, which are often flattened but may have various other shapes, can be recognized by the three long tails at the end of the abdomen and the plate-like or feather-like gills along the sides of the abdomen. Adults have two pairs of wings that are held together straight up over the back. The hind wings are smaller than the front wings and in some species may even be absent. The adults, like the nymphs, have three long tails at the end of the abdomen.

Mayfly. (Photo by Edward S. Ross.)

What is unusual about the way **mayflies copulate**?

The male has two penises, each one separately associated with one of the two testes. The female complements the male in having two vaginas, each one separately associated with one of the two ovaries. During copulation, a penis is inserted into each of the vaginas.

Do mayflies **serve any purpose**?

They certainly do. Viewed ecologically, the nymphs are important and often essential components of many aquatic ecosystems. For example, they are often so abundant that they are the major food for trout and other fish. The importance of both nymphal and adult mayflies in the diet of trout is reflected by the artificial "flies," usually made of feathers and fur or hair, that are used as bait in fishing for trout. Many "wet flies," which are fished under water, resemble mayfly nymphs. Some "dry flies," which are fished on the surface, resemble adult mayflies.

Are **mayflies ever pests**?

Swarms of mayflies that are large and dense enough to constitute a nuisance appear along the shores of the Great Lakes, along the Mississippi River, or along rivers that flow into the Mississippi. They are attracted to lights at night, and in cities and towns along these waters dead mayflies can accumulate in huge drifts that must be cleared away with front-end loaders and dump trucks. To people who are allergic to them, these swarming mayflies may be much more than a nuisance. Such huge swarms once occurred commonly along the shores of Lake Erie but all but disappeared because of pollution. Mayflies are very sensitive to pollutants and are generally good bioindicators of water pollution. In recent decades, the pollution of Lake Erie has been much reduced and the mayflies are making a comeback.

DRAGONFLIES AND DAMSELFLIES

What insects are included in the order **Odonata**?

This order of about 5,000 species includes the dragonflies and the damselflies, both large and often gorgeously colored insects. The adults are easily recognized by their huge compound eyes, their very long and slender abdomen, and four elongated, membranous, and many-veined wings that resting damselflies hold together up over the back and that resting dragonflies hold out to the side like the wings of an airplane. All adult damselflies and dragonflies are predators, and most of them catch their prey on the wing. The nymphs, which are all aquatic, breathe by means of gills: three large, leaf-like ones at the end of a damselfly nymph's abdomen and many small, plate-like ones lining the rectum of a dragonfly nymph. The nymphs are also predators that eat aquatic insects and even small fish or tadpoles. They lie in wait for their prey, some species sitting on an aquatic plant and others more or less buried in the bottom muck, sometimes with only their eyes showing. When a prey animal comes close, they snatch it with their long, raptorial labium, which is folded under the head when not in use.

How do dragonflies and damselflies **copulate**?

In a peculiar and unique way. The male's genital opening is at the end of his abdomen, but he has a "secondary" penis and other copulatory structures at the base of his abdomen. When he is ready to copulate, he loops his abdomen down and forward to charge his secondary copulatory organs with sperm from his genital opening. When he finds a willing female, he grasps her by the back of her neck with the genital claspers at the tip of his abdomen. She then loops her long abdomen up to bring her vagina in contact with his secondary penis. The two then form a complete loop. In many species, the male retains his hold on the female's neck even after their genitalia have separated. The pair then flies in tandem as the female deposits her eggs in the water. The male guards her to prevent other males from inseminating her, thus ensuring that the eggs she lays that day will be fertilized by his sperm.

How do the **Japanese** feel about dragonflies and damselflies?

The Japanese love and respect them both. In its ancient mythology, Japan was called *Akitsushima,* land of dragonflies. While North Americans have almost no common names for their dragonflies and damselflies, the Japanese have well-established folk names for most of the 200 species that occur on their islands—testimony to a long-time and widespread interest in these lovely insects. Today the "Dragonfly Kingdom" in Nakamura City has a dragonfly museum of over 7,000 square feet and a dragonfly sanctuary. Both are operated by the nationwide *Tombo to Shizen Wo Kangaerukai,* Corporation for Consideration of Dragonflies and Nature, founded by Nitsutoshi Sugimura, an enthusiastic amateur student of dragonflies and damselflies.

GRASSHOPPERS AND THEIR ALLIES

ORTHOPTERA

What insects belong to the order **Orthoptera**?

This order, which is split up into several smaller orders by many entomologists, is made up of a varied assemblage of about 28,000 species including mantises, walkingsticks, cockroaches, and rock crawlers, as well as the jumping Orthoptera, crickets, katydids, and grasshoppers. These insects are so varied in structure that it is difficult to characterize the Orthoptera as a whole.

What do the **jumping Orthoptera** have in common?

The crickets, katydids, and grasshoppers are so similar to each other in so many ways that it is obvious to the eye that they are closely related. But two commonalties are outstandingly obvious: all of them have the hind legs conspicuously modified for leaping, and the males attract females by stridulating—making sounds by rubbing one body part against another. Crickets and katydids rub their front wings together, and grasshoppers rub a hind leg against a front wing. The majority of the jumping Orthoptera are plant feeders except for some katydids that eat other insects and some crickets that are omnivores.

Locust swarm in Ethiopia. (Photo by Gianni Tortoli. Courtesy of Photo Researchers, Inc.)

What is a **locust**?

This name is applied to grasshoppers that migrate in huge swarms and do tremendous damage to vegetation. The locusts of Europe, Africa, and Asia often occur in vast swarms that can travel hundreds of miles in a day and may extend over hundreds of square miles. These swarms may include 300 million individuals—about 500 tons of them per square mile. When such swarms land, they eat every leaf and every blade of grass, leaving the land bare. The Bible, Exodus 10:15, tells us that the eighth plague that Jehovah visited upon the Egyptians was a great swarm of locusts that "covered the face of the whole earth, so that the land was darkened; and they did eat every herb of the land, and all the fruit of the trees . . . and there remained not any green thing . . . through all of the land of Egypt."

Do **locusts** occur in North America?

At one time they did, but they are now either extinct or no longer form swarms. In the 1870s, huge swarms of locusts, called Rocky Mountain grasshoppers, swept across the Great Plains. A surveyor in Nebraska reported a swarm that was 100 miles wide, 300 miles long, and a half-mile high. He calculated that it included 124 billion grasshoppers. They ate everything green in their path: trees were stripped of their leaves and green bark; there were holes in the ground where grass or herbaceous plants had stood; and they even ate the dry straw of brooms. The land was left as barren as if it had been burned.

What are **Mormon crickets**?

Cricket is a misnomer in this case. These creatures are really wingless katydids that can be quite destructive in the western United States. They come down from the hills, crawling overland in hordes that may cover a square mile. When a vanguard of Mormon settlers arrived in the Salt Lake Valley in 1847, they planted grain, but their crop was destroyed by Mormon crickets. When the main band of setllers arrived in 1848, they again planted grain and a horde of Mormon crickets appeared and began to eat the crop. But, as if by a miracle, flocks of California gulls came from nearby marshes and ate the "crickets." In 1913, the Mormons memorialized their rescue from starvation with a golden statue of this gull that they erected in Temple Square in Salt Lake City.

What are **praying mantises**?

Praying mantises are large, solitary, slow moving, and predaceous insects that catch their prey with their front legs. They do not have jumping hind legs. Of the 20 species of mantises that occur in North America, the introduced Chinese mantis, at a length of as much as four inches, is the largest. Mantises are ambushers that sit on a plant, often near a blossom, as they wait for prey to come close. They feed mainly on insects, but on rare occasions the larger species capture hummingbirds. In late summer or early autumn, the female encases her eggs—sometimes more than 200—in a frothy substance that hardens to form the sturdy egg case. These egg cases are conspicuous on twigs or plant stems in winter. The rounded, beige cases of the Chinese mantis may be more than an inch in diameter and are often found attached to the dead stems of goldenrod or other herbaceous plants.

What are **walkingsticks**?

They are large, sluggish herbivores that generally feed on the leaves of shrubs and trees. Most of the North American species are two or three inches long, but one, the longest insect in the United States, attains a length of seven inches. Some tropical species may be as much as twelve inches long. With only one exception, the American species are wingless and camouflaged by their slender bodies resembling long, skinny twigs. Their long spindly legs are almost threadlike and modified neither for jumping nor grasping. Many tropical species are winged and resemble leaves. Walkingsticks, unlike most insects, simply let their eggs fall to the ground one at a time, where they lie until they hatch the following spring. In some species, many of the eggs do not hatch until the second spring after they are laid. Since walkingsticks have only one generation per year, these species tend to be most abundant in alternate years.

What are **cockroaches**?

They are medium to large insects, with the body somewhat flattened, the antennae long and thread-like, and with a shield-like part of the thorax concealing the head from above. They are swift runners with long legs. Generally speaking, they are omnivores that feed mostly on decaying plant and animal matter. Cockroaches live in ground litter, under loose bark, on low plants, in caves, and even in the soil. Most of them are tropical, but there are about fifty species in temperate North America, a few of which are household pests. The eggs of most cockroaches are enclosed in a hard case that may be dropped or carried about on the mother's abdomen, but some species are live-bearers.

What are **rock crawlers**?

This is a strange and primitive group of the Orthoptera, whose members share characteristics of cockroaches and crickets. The 20 known species live in perpetual winter conditions at the edges of snow fields and glaciers in the mountains of Siberia, Japan, and the northwestern United States. They eat things such as dead insects blown up from lower elevations, and thrive at cold temperatures that would kill other insects. They are active below freezing and cannot survive temperatures much above a chilly 53°F.

Are **cockroaches** and **termites** related?

There is little doubt that the termites evolved from cockroach-like ancestors. Wingless cockroaches of the genus *Cryptocercus,* which are similar to cockroaches in several ways, are the "missing link" between the termites and the cockroaches. One species of this genus occurs in the mountains of both the eastern and the western United States in subsocial colonies in decaying logs. Their primitive society may well be the forerunner of the much more organized and complex societies of the termites. These cockroaches eat wood as do many termites and, like termites, cannot digest it without the aid of microorganisms, flagellated protozoa, that live in their hind guts. Also like termites, they ingest the fecal material of another individual to replace the microorganisms that they lose when they molt the lining of their hind gut.

TERMITES

What are **termites**?

The termites, also known as white ants, constitute the Isoptera, an order with about 2,000 members. Although termites and ants are both social and form colonies that

What kinds of cockroaches live in our homes?

Quite a few, but, except in the southern states, four species commonly infest North American homes and other buildings. All four are originally creatures of warm climates and in the North survive only in heated buildings. All of them hide in the daytime and become active only in the dark. Although most of them have wings, they rarely fly. The small German cockroach, about a half-inch long as an adult, is light tan and is distinguished by two dark stripes on the shield that covers the head. It prefers moist areas and is most often seen in kitchens and bathrooms. The brown-banded cockroach is slightly smaller than the German cockroach, mostly tan in color, and has two light yellow bands that cross the base of the wings. It prefers relatively dry areas and is commonly found in living rooms. The American cockroach, about one and a half inches long as an adult, is chestnut-brown in color and can be distinguished from similar species by the yellow posterior border of the shield that covers the head. It occurs in the basements of homes and in grocery stores, bakeries, restaurants, and other food-handling businesses. The Oriental cockroach is uniformly black and about an inch long. Unlike the other cockroaches just mentioned, it cannot fly. Adult females are nearly wingless, and the wings of the male are much shorter than his body. They are more moisture-loving than the other pest cockroaches, and generally occur in damp basements and in sewers.

may include thousands of individuals, the name white ant is a misnomer. Termites and ants belong to separate orders and are related only in that both are insects. While termites are soft-bodied and usually light in color, ants have hard bodies and are usually dark in color. Both termites and ant workers are wingless, but the wings of their reproductive castes are very different. The front and hind wings of termites are similar in size, shape, and venation, and are folded down over the back at rest. The hind wings of ants are considerably smaller than the front wings and when at rest are held together above the body. Ants have a "wasp waist": the abdomen is constricted at its base. Termites do not have a wasp waist; their abdomens are broadly joined to the thorax.

What is the structure of a **termite society**?

The members of a termite society, a colony, belong to one of four castes of specialized individuals that have different forms and that perform different functions. Each termite caste consists of both sexes, but in wasp, ant, and bee societies, the soldier worker castes consist only of females. Members of the *primary reproductive caste* are dark

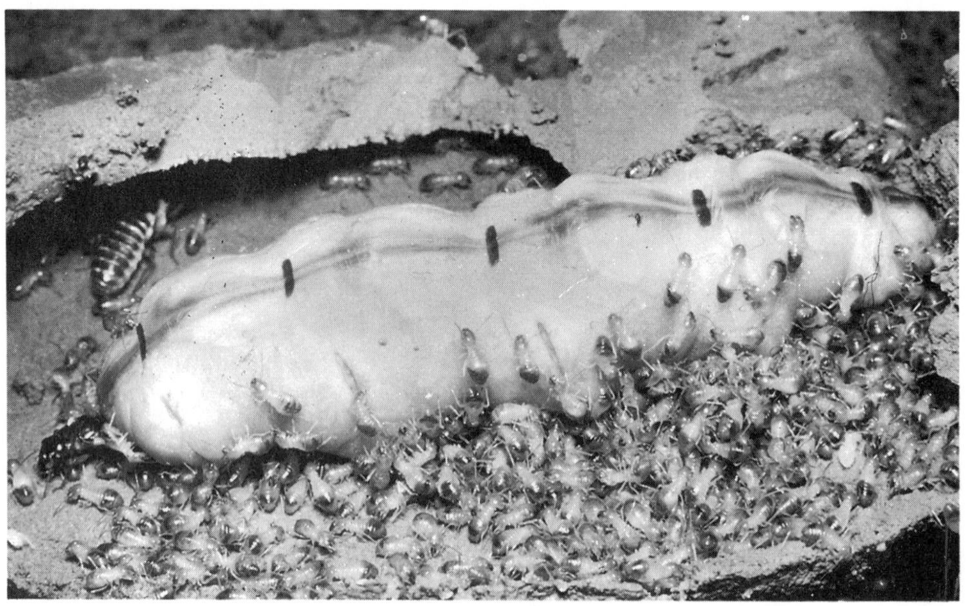

Pregnant queen termite surrounded by workers. (Photo by Edward S. Ross.)

in color, have a somewhat hardened cuticle, and are the only members of a colony that have fully developed wings. Their functions are to found new colonies and to carry on reproduction within the colony. *Secondary reproductives* are paler than primary reproductives and never have fully developed wings. If the primary reproductives die, the secondary reproductives assume the duties of reproduction. *Workers* are small, pale, soft-bodied, and sterile, and make up most of the population of a colony. As their name indicates, they do most of the work: building and repairing the nest, foraging, and feeding and grooming the members of the other castes. Members of the *soldier caste* have greatly enlarged heads and large, strong mandibles, formidable weapons used to defend the colony against invaders such as ants.

How are **termite colonies founded**?

New colonies are founded by a pair of primary reproductives, a king and a queen. In spring or summer, termite colonies produce large numbers of primary reproductives that leave the colony as a swarm. After flying for some distance, they alight on the ground, shed their wings, and form pairs. The pair then search for a suitable place to found a colony, often in moist soil where wood is in contact with the ground. The pairs will remain together and mate repeatedly throughout their lives. Once impregnated, the queen's abdomen swells to accommodate her large ovaries; she becomes an egg laying machine. In some tropical species, her abdomen may expand to be two inches long, while her relatively tiny head and thorax may be only about a quarter of an inch long.

How do **termite soldiers** defend their colony?

The soldiers of most species use their powerful mandibles to wound, dismember, or even behead attackers, which are most often predatory ants. Some termites use a chemical defense instead. The mandibles of the soldiers of these species are not enlarged, but the head is elongated to form a forward-pointing nozzle from which a sticky substance is emitted that will disable an enemy.

What are **dry-wood termites**?

The common termite of most of the eastern United States, the subterranean termite, cannot survive unless its nest is near moist soil. Dry-wood termites, which occur in the tropics, in the southern United States, and along the Pacific Coast, can invade and survive in dry wood, such as a piece of wooden furniture. A table or a chair that shows no outward sign of termite damage may be so riddled internally with galleries that it will collapse when someone puts weight on it. Since dry wood contains very little moisture, dry-wood termites depend mainly upon the metabolic water that is formed, along with carbon dioxide, when they metabolize carbohydrates to release energy.

Do all termites **eat wood**?

Most termites eat wood, and wood feeding seems to be their ancestral habit. Since they cannot digest cellulose, the major component of wood, termites use microorganisms that inhabit their hind guts (flagellate protozoa in some species and bacteria in others) to help them digest the ingredient. Some termites leave the nest to harvest seeds, leaves, grass, or other vegetable matter; some eat humus; and certain species feed on a fungus that they grow on a bed of decaying vegetation in their nest.

PSOCIDS

What are **booklice**?

A few members of Psocoptera, a small order of 2,400 species worldwide, are known as booklice. The Psocoptera, or psocids, are small, seldom as much as four-tenths of an inch long; relatively soft-bodied; and either winged or wingless. The booklice are wingless and found indoors feeding on various organic substances, sometimes on the mold that grows on old books. The name barklouse is broadly applied to psocids that live under bark or in leaf litter, under rocks, or on vegetation—often dead leaves clinging to trees. Although they are loosely referred to as lice, none of the psocids are parasitic. They feed on algae, lichens, fungi, pollen, decaying plant matter, and occasionally dead insects or other dead animal matter.

BIRD LICE

What are **chewing lice**?

The chewing lice, sometimes known as the bird lice, constitute a small order, about 2,700 species worldwide, known as the Mallophaga, which translates from the Greek as "eaters of wool." Chewing lice are small, some only about four one-hundredths of an inch long; all secondarily wingless; usually greatly flattened from top to bottom; and with mouthparts that are basically of the chewing type. All are ectoparasites that live on the outside of the host's body—usually amongst the feathers of a bird and sometimes in the fur of a mammal. The great majority eat feathers, hair, or fragments of skin, but a very few ingest blood that they obtain by lacerating the skin of the host with their mandibles. Some entomologist combine the Mallophaga and the Anoplura, the piercing-sucking lice, to form one order with the difficult-to-spell name Phthiraptera.

Do chewing lice ever **leave their host**?

When two hosts are in close bodily contact, as during copulation or brooding, these lice will move from one host to the other. Otherwise, they remain on their host until the host dies. Lice mate on their host, fasten their eggs to its feathers or hair, and often go through several generations on the same host animal.

PIERCING-SUCKING LICE

What are **piercing-sucking lice**?

They are the members of a small order —only about 500 species— known as the Anoplura. Some entomologists combine the Anoplura with the Mallophaga to form the order Phthiraptera. These lice are all small; a human body louse, for example, is

How specific are chewing lice in their choice of hosts?

Some chewing lice can live on several unrelated species of birds, but others are very choosy and will live on only a few closely related birds or mammals. The lice of cuckoos are among the most selective species. Some of the cuckoos of Eurasia are nest parasites; these birds lay their eggs in the nests of other birds of various species and abandon them to be raised by their hoodwinked foster parents. But the many species of lice that infest the foster parents never infest the parasitic nestling cuckoos. A cuckoo can deceive the foster parents but it cannot deceive their lice.

only about one-sixth of an inch long. They are all secondarily wingless, flattened from top to bottom, and have mouthparts modified for piercing and sucking. All are ectoparasites that live in the fur or hair of a mammal, and their only food is the blood of the host. Like the chewing lice, the piercing-sucking lice spend their entire lives—from egg to adult—on the host, usually for several succeeding generations. They transfer from one host to another only when two hosts are in close contact, as when they copulate or nurse their young. Piercing-sucking lice are even more choosy about their hosts than are the chewing lice, generally infesting only one species of mammal or a few closely related species.

THRIPS

What is a **thrips**?

Thrips is a peculiar word that ends with an "s" both in its singular and the plural forms. Thrips belong to the order Thysanoptera, which includes about 4,000 species. They are slender and small, seldom more than one-eighth of an inch long, and have several peculiar characteristics. Some are wingless, but the wings of the others are reduced to a narrow blade with a flying surface consisting of a fringe of long, stiff hairs. The head is prolonged as a cone-shaped protuberance housing needle-like mouthparts that rasp the surface of a leaf or petal to form a slurry that the thrips sucks up through its cone-shaped snout. Thrips are the only insects that do not have claws. The tarsus, or "foot," the last segment of the leg, is hoof-like in shape and contains an eversible sticky bladder that helps the thrips to climb on slippery surfaces.

What is the masked hunter?

It is a species of assassin bug that is often found in houses, where it feeds on bed bugs and occasionally bites people. The common name of this species derives from the peculiar camouflage of the nymphs. The nymph's body, including legs and antennae, is covered with a sticky substance to which particles of dust and fibers adhere. The nymph is thus "masked." It looks like a clump of lint, and usually escapes notice unless it moves.

Where do thrips **live** and what do they **eat**?

Most species live on green vegetation and many species in flowers, where they can be seen slinking around the pistil and stamens. A few species live on the ground in decaying vegetation. Most thrips feed on plant sap, but a few eat fungi, and a few others prey on tiny insects and other arthropods.

TRUE BUGS

What are **true bugs**?

Narrowly and technically speaking, the only creatures that are properly referred to as bugs are the members of the order Hemiptera. The literal translation of the name of this order is "half wing," referring to the unusual structure of the front wings. The basal portion of the front wing is thickened, leathery, and lacks veins. The apical portion is membranous and usually has veins. The hind wings are entirely membranous. All Hemiptera have piercing-sucking mouthparts that are sheathed by a long beak that arises from the front part of the head and that is held appressed against the lower side of the body when it is at rest. The Hemiptera, which has about 50,000 species worldwide, is the largest of the orders of insects that have gradual metamorphosis.

Where do true bugs live?

True bugs live in almost all terrestrial and freshwater habitats. In terrestrial habitats, most of them live on plants, under bark, in leaf litter, or in the soil. A very few live in the nests of birds and an even smaller number live in the fur of bats. The aquatic species, most of which are associated with fresh water, include semi-aquatic species that live on or in wet soil at the shore line, many species that live in the water, and a few that spend their lives on the surface of the water. There are a few marine bugs that live on the surface of the oceans.

How and what do **true bugs eat**?

They use their piercing-sucking mouthparts to suck juices from a huge variety of plants and animals. Most of the aquatic and semi-aquatic bugs—the water striders, backswimmers, water scorpions, giant water bugs, toad bugs, and others—feed on other arthropods and even small fish and tadpoles. The water boatmen are the exception; many of them eat algae. The terrestrial true bugs are much more varied in their feeding habits. The majority—among them seed bugs, plant bugs, lace bugs, leaf-footed bugs, and most of the stink bugs—suck sap from plants. Included among the bugs that eat other insects are the ambush bugs, assassin bugs, damsel bugs, and some of the stink bugs. A few species suck blood from vertebrates, like the assassin bugs and the bed bugs, most of which feed on birds or bats except for one species that attacks people. The most specialized of the true bugs are probably the blind and wingless bat bugs, which live as blood-sucking ectoparasites on the bodies of bats.

What are the **giant water bugs**?

These predaceous bugs are well named. Some of them are indeed giants. A South American species that can attain a length of four inches is the largest true bug in the world. None of the North American species are that big, but some of them are as long as two inches, big enough to capture such prey as tadpoles and small fish with their raptorial front legs.

What are **lace bugs**?

They are plant-feeding bugs that have a lacy appearance because their wide wings and the large, broad flanges of their thorax are reticulated and gauze-like. One of the most common species is the sycamore lace bug, whose feeding sometimes causes the leaves of sycamores to turn brown. These pretty little bugs, about three-sixteenths of an inch long, spend the winter under loose flakes of bark on the trunks of sycamores. You will probably find some of them if you turn over a few bark flakes this winter.

APHIDS AND THEIR ALLIES

What kinds of insects belong to the order **Homoptera**?

There is no one common name that includes all of the Homoptera. Among the 32,000 species of this order are the cicadas, leafhoppers, planthoppers, treehoppers, spittlebugs, whiteflies, aphids, scale insects, and mealybugs. The Homoptera and the true bugs are so similar that many entomologists lump the Homoptera together with the Hemiptera.

What characteristics distinguish the **Homoptera**?

Except for the cicadas, which may be two inches long, the Homoptera are small insects that are generally no more than a quarter of an inch long. Like the true bugs, they have piercing-sucking mouthparts, but, unlike the true bugs, the beak arises at the back of the head, sometimes looking almost as if it comes from between the front legs. Quite a few Homoptera are wingless, but, with the exception of male scale insects, the winged species have two pairs of wings. The front wings are not divided into two parts as are the front wings of the true bugs; they are of the same appearance and texture throughout, either entirely transparent and membranous or entirely leathery and opaque.

Where do homopterans **live and what do they eat**?

Except for a few aquatic aphids, the Homoptera are terrestrial. Homopterans spend most of their lives on plants. A few, such as the destructive grape phylloxera, live on roots in the soil, but the great majority live above ground level. Some live within galls that they cause the plant to form, but most are exposed to view on the leaves or other structures of a plant. They eat only the sap of plants: cell sap, phloem sap, or xylem sap, depending upon the species of homopteran.

What are **periodical cicadas**?

Periodical cicadas are among the longest lived of all the insects. The nymphs live underground sucking sap from the roots of trees for either 13 or 17 years. In the spring of their 13th or 17th year, they emerge from the soil to molt to the adult stage as they cling to the trunk of a tree or some other support. The males form singing choruses that may include hundreds or thousands of individuals. The loud, shrill song of the male attracts other males and females. Males stay with the chorus, but females only visit briefly, just long enough to mate and obtain the sperm that will fertilize their eggs. The females use their saw-like ovipositors to lay their eggs in punctures that they make in the twigs of trees, as many as thirty eggs per puncture. The eggs hatch from six to ten weeks later, and the tiny nymphs drop to the ground and burrow into the soil, where they will feed and grow for the next 13 or 17 years. There are 15 "broods" of periodical cicadas in the United States. Most of those in the South are 13-year broods, and most of those in the North are 17-year broods. A brood emerges somewhere in the United States every year.

Aphids feeding on plant sap. (Photo by Edward S. Ross.)

How many periodical cicadas are present during an emergence?

The number varies, but some emergences are immense. When brood XIII (13) emerged in the Chicago area in 1956, entomologists estimated that there were about 133,000 cicadas per acre in an upland forest and about 1,500,000 per acre in a lowland forest. In the lowland forest, the biomass (total weight) of cicadas averaged about one to two tons per acre. Thus, there were almost a billion cicadas and a biomass of about 533 tons per square mile of lowland forest. Since the cicadas occupied an area of many square miles, the entire emergence consisted of many billions of individuals.

What are **spittlebugs**?

Spittlebugs, also known as froghoppers, are small jumping insects that live on trees, shrubs, herbaceous plants, and grasses. The adults wander about on the plants, but the nymphs live in masses of little bubbles that are on a plant, often on the stem, and that look like globs of spittle. Some people incorrectly call these spittle nests "frog spit" or "snake spit." The spittle actually consists of a mixture of fluid that comes out through the spittlebug's anus and a mucilaginous secretion from glands at the end of the abdomen.

What are **whiteflies**?

They are minute homopterans that often infest plants in greenhouses and sometimes infest house plants. If one disturbs an infested plant, a flurry of tiny, white adults with a wing span of less than a tenth of an inch bursts into the air. Their wings are broad and covered with a white, waxy powder. The first instar nymphs are active, but older nymphs are sessile and covered with an oval, white, waxy, scale-like case.

Can **scale insects** be compared to parasites of animals?

Yes, they can. Their relationship to their host plant, especially in the case of armored scales, parallels the relationship of a parasite of an animal to its host. Take the San Jose scale, a destructive pest of orchard and shade trees, as an example. Excepting only first instar nymphs and adult males, these scales lack appendages and eyes; they are essentially sacks with an anus at one end and mouthparts, which are permanently embedded in the bark of a twig or small branch, at the other end. They are completely covered by a waxy scale that they secrete and enlarge as they grow. First instars, known as crawlers, have legs and antennae and crawl about for a few hours before they insert their mouthparts and undergo a molt in which they lose their appendages and after which they secrete a scale. The adult males, which have one pair of wings and all of the other usual appendages, fly to the pheromone-releasing females and inseminate them. The sack-like female gives live birth to crawlers. These two active stages are very important in the life cycles of scale insects. Only the crawlers can move to new places—sometimes carried on the body of a bird or a large insect—and found new populations. Sexual reproduction is possible only because the adult males are able to travel to the sessile females.

LACEWINGS AND THEIR ALLIES

What kinds of insects belong to the order **Neuroptera**?

The Neuroptera is a relatively small order of about 5,100 species. All of them are predators that mainly eat other insects, except for a few species that feed on freshwater sponges. Otherwise, they are difficult to characterize as a group, because they belong to several dissimilar families that include the dobsonflies and alderflies (which are aquatic as larvae), and the snakeflies, mantispids, lacewings, and antlions (which are terrestrial in all life stages).

What are **lacewings**?

The lacewings, also known as the aphid lions, are probably the most familiar of the Neuroptera —especially the green lacewings that are commonly found on herbage and the foliage of shrubs and trees. The larvae live in aphid colonies and use their long, sickle-shaped mouthparts to suck the juices from the aphids. The adults, which also eat aphids, have long antennae, eyes of a metallic gold color, and broad, lacelike green wings.

What are **mantispids**?

Adult mantispids parallel praying mantises in anatomy and hunting behavior. Like mantises, mantispids are ambushers that wait quietly on plants for their prey to come close enough to grab. The similarity in the structure of the thorax and the front legs of these two unrelated insects is an amazing example of parallel evolution. In both mantises and mantispids, the first segment of the thorax is greatly elongated and moveably hinged to the preceding segment of the thorax, and the front legs are lengthened and modified for grasping—adaptations that give these insects a long and flexible reach. Nymphal praying mantises, which have gradual metamorphosis, eat and live as the adults do. But larval mantispids, which have complete metamorphosis, live in the egg sacs of spiders, feeding on the eggs.

What are **antlions**?

Adult antlions are graceful insects that resemble damselflies. The larvae, which are sometimes called doodlebugs, are the "lions" that prey on ants and other small insects that crawl on the ground. They dig steep-sided pitfall traps in sandy soil, usually in a place that is protected from the rain, as under an overhanging rock or beneath a building. They lie hidden in the sand at the bottom of their conical pit, waiting for a crawling insect to fall into it and slide down its steep side into their sickle-shaped jaws. If the prey insect starts to crawl back out of the pitfall, the antlion uses its flat, shovel-like head to bombard it with tiny scoops of sand in an attempt to start it sliding back into the pit.

BEETLES AND WEEVILS

What are **beetles**?

The beetles, all 370,000 of them, belong to the Coleoptera, which is by far the largest order of insects. Just in America north of Mexico, there are 115 families of beetles that include over 23,000 species. Despite there being so many species, adult beetles are a relatively homogeneous group and are, with few exceptions, easily recognized. The lar-

Acorn weevil. (Photo by Edward S. Ross.)

vae, which are commonly known as grubs, all have chewing mouthparts but otherwise vary greatly in form. Adults also have chewing mouthparts and are easily recognized as beetles by their greatly modified front wings, which are called elytra. The elytra have no veins, are opaque, and are sometimes leathery but usually hard and rigid. They have become a part of the body armor that covers the membranous hind wings and the vulnerable abdomen. In most beetles, the elytra cover the entire abdomen, but in a few, such as the rove beetles, they are short and leave much of the abdomen uncovered.

What are **weevils**?

Adult weevils look like most other beetles except for their long proboscis-like snouts, which are actually prolongations of the front of the head capsule and bear chewing mouthparts at their tips. Weevils are all plant feeders. Some feed on leaves, but the larvae of many feed within fruits or seeds.

What are **whirligig beetles**?

They are aquatic beetles that swim at the surface and eat small insects that fall onto the water. John Henry Comstock described their behavior in his *Introduction to Entomology:*

What is a "Spanish fly"?

The "Spanish fly" is a European species of blister beetle that was once used to prepare medicinal blister plasters that were incorrectly thought to alleviate fevers and a host of other ills. Dead, dried, and pulverized beetles were made into a paste that produced blisters when applied to the skin. The blisters are caused by cantharadin, an oily and irritating fluid that oozes from the bodies of the Spanish flies—and all other blister beetles, as well—when they are threatened by predators. Spanish fly was thought to be an aphrodisiac when taken internally, but it is a dangerous poison and there is little evidence that it actually acts as an aphrodisiac.

> As familiar to the country rover as the gurgling of the brook or the flecks of foam on its "golden-braided centre," or the trailing ferns and the rustling rushes on its banks, are these whirligigs on its pools. Around and around each other they dart, tracing graceful curves on the water, which vanish almost as soon as made. They are social fellows, and are almost always found in large numbers, either swimming or resting motionless near together. They rarely dive, except when pursued; but are so agile that it is extremely difficult to catch them without a net.

Do **burying beetles** really bury things?

Yes, they do. They bury small dead animals as food for their offspring. When a pair of these large beetles locate a small corpse, often a rat or a mouse, they dig under it until it settles down beneath the surface of the ground. They then complete the burial by covering the corpse with soil. If the corpse is lying in an unfavorable spot, the beetles will move it to a place where the soil is suitable for a burial. Eggs are laid on the wall of a shaft in the soil that connects with the corpse. As she waits for her eggs to hatch, the female prepares a cavity in the corpse, regurgitating digestive juices into it and thus preparing the partially digested food that the larvae will eat. When the newly-hatched larvae arrive at the cavity, presumably led there by the odor, their mother feeds them by regurgitating partially digested flesh from the corpse. In a few days, the larvae begin to feed on their own, at first in the feeding cavity, but then on the rest of the corpse. When they are full grown, they pupate nearby in the soil.

How do **blister beetles** live?

Adults and larvae have very different habits. Adults eat the foliage of plants, while the larvae live in and feed on the egg pods of grasshoppers or, in other species, the stores

Do fleas have big appetites for food?

Adult fleas certainly do. They have been known to suck blood continuously for four hours, ingesting far more than their stomachs can hold. Most of the blood that they ingest passes through the gut undigested, is squirted out through the anus drop by drop, and ends up in the host's bedding. This seemingly profligate feeding benefits any larval fleas that are feeding in the host's nest, since dry blood is a required part of their diet.

in the nests of solitary bees. The eggs of species that eat grasshopper eggs are laid in the soil. The first instar larva, agile and very active, runs over the soil until it comes to a place where the egg pod of a grasshopper lies beneath the surface. The larva then burrows into the egg pod and feeds on the eggs until it is full grown. Some species associated with bees' nests lay their eggs directly on a blossom, but others lay their eggs in the soil. Larvae from the soil may climb up a plant to a blossom. In either case, they wait until a bee arrives at the blossom, then clamber onto her hairy body and hold on tightly as the unsuspecting bee returns to her nest. They eat the eggs, larvae, and stored pollen in bees' nests. Since it is very difficult for a tiny first-instar larva to locate an egg pod or a bee's nest, blister beetles must lay many eggs in order to be survived by even a few progeny.

What are **white grubs**?

White grubs are the large, white, c-shaped larvae of June beetles that have large, somewhat swollen abdomens. They live just beneath the surface of the soil, where they feed on the roots of grasses and many other kinds of plants. They often injure or even kill turf grass in lawns. The large, brown adults spend the daylight hours in the soil, but come out at night to feed on the leaves of trees. They are attracted to light and at night may be seen bumbling about on the ground under lights. At the first crack of dawn, they retreat into the soil, where the females lay their pearly white eggs. The grubs feed and grow slowly during two summers and the beginning of a third summer. They then molt to the pupal stage, but do not emerge from the soil until the next spring, the fourth spring of their lives.

How did the **Colorado potato beetle** get its name?

This beetle is currently one of the most important pests of the white potato in North America and much of Eurasia. Until about 1859, however, it was an obscure inhabitant of the eastern foothills of the Rocky Mountains, where both the larvae and adults fed on the leaves of an herbaceous plant known as the buffalo bur or sand bur. When the early settlers arrived in Colorado in the mid-1800s, they planted the white potato, a native of the Andes in South America and a close relative of the buffalo bur. The beetles, later to be known as Colorado potato beetles, soon began to feed on potatoes and began to move eastward from potato patch to potato patch. They arrived at the Atlantic coast in 1874, only fifteen years later, and are now spreading across Eurasia. The humpbacked, reddish larvae and the rather rotund black-and-yellow-striped adults are now familiar to anyone who has grown potatoes.

SCORPIONFLIES

What are **scorpionflies**?

The scorpionflies are named for their large and bulbous male genitalia, which look something like the sting at the end of a scorpion's abdomen. Scorpionfiles, hangingflies, and a few obscure groups make up the order Mecoptera, a small order that includes a worldwide total of less than 500 species. Hangingfly males do not have bulbous genitalia. The scorpionflies and the hangingflies are noteworthy because the males provide their mates with food. Male scorpionflies that are ready to mate gather dead insects—their usual food—and stand guard over them as they release a sex attractant pheromone. Visiting females eat this food as they copulate with the male. Hangingflies do it differently. The male captures a living insect and holds its body with his hind legs as he hangs from a plant by his front legs and releases his sex attractant pheromone. His mate feeds on the dead insect and will copulate with him as long as the meal lasts.

FLEAS

What are **fleas**?

The fleas, about 2,300 species, constitute the order known as the Siphonaptera, an especially informative scientific name that is a terse but apt description of an adult flea. The Greek root *siphon,* (a tube or a pipe) refers to the flea's piercing-sucking mouthparts, and *aptera* means wingless. Adult fleas are quite small, flattened from side to side, and have jumping legs. The larvae look a bit like tiny, legless caterpillars. They have chewing mouthparts and a few long hairs on the body.

How do **fleas live**?

The adults are blood-sucking parasites of mammals or birds and use their jumping legs to get on and off their hosts. Their flattened body and the secondary loss of their wings are adaptations that enhance the ability of adult fleas to maneuver in the hair of a mammal or the feathers of a bird. They lay their eggs in the nest or lair of the host. The larvae live in the sleeping place of the host, where they feed on organic debris, including dried particles of undigested blood that are passed from the anus of adult fleas. Full-grown larvae molt to the pupal stage in a silken cocoon that they spin in the host's bedding.

Why are **humans the only primates** that have fleas?

Because they are the only primates (monkeys, apes, humans, and others) that have a permanent dwelling place. Gorillas build nests but abandon them every morning and build a fresh one later. Fleas cannot survive on a host that wanders and does not regularly return to an accustomed sleeping place. The larvae, which always live some place other than on the host's body—normally in its nest or den—must return to the host for an essential meal of blood after they become adults, an impossibility if the host does not occasionally return to the place where the larvae live.

What can be done to alleviate a **dog's flea problem**?

The population of dog fleas in a home can be greatly reduced without the use of insecticides. The first step is to give the dog its own special sleeping place and to discourage it from sleeping elsewhere. If this can be accomplished, the fleas will lay most of their eggs in the dog's bedding. The next step is to launder the dog's bedding about once a week and thus destroy the flea eggs and larvae before they can become blood-sucking, egg-laying adults.

How do **fleas survive** if their host is gone?

Even after it is fully developed, an adult flea can lie dormant within its cocoon for months or even more than a year without feeding, until some outside stimulus triggers its emergence. The stimulus is likely to be vibrations caused by movements of the returning host. By the time a long-missing host returns, all of the eggs and other immature fleas in its nest will have become adults but will still be within their cocoons. When they are stimulated by the return of the host, they pop out of their cocoons almost instantly and simultaneously. Even after an adult flea has emerged from its cocoon, it can survive for quite a long time without taking a blood meal, as long as 17 months in the case of a captive rat flea. The ability to survive without feeding is obviously advantageous. The longer a flea can hold out, the more likely it is to be rescued from starvation by the return of the host or the arrival of a new host.

FLIES

What insects belong to the order **Diptera**?

All of the insects that are properly called flies, such as the crane flies, horse flies, deer flies, fruit flies, blow flies, and flesh flies, belong to the order Diptera. In all of these names, "fly" remains a separate word. The word fly is a part of the name of many insects that are not Diptera: mayfly, dragonfly, damselfly, sawfly, and butterfly among them. These names are written as compound words in which "fly" does not stand as a separate word. Although "fly" is not a part of their common names, the midges, mosquitoes, and gnats are true members of the order Diptera.

What is the **literal meaning** of the word Diptera?

It means two-winged, from the Greek roots *di,* meaning two, and *pter,* meaning wing. The name tells us the most apparent and significant characteristic of these insects. The front wings are almost always present, but the hind wings are always absent, represented by tiny knobbed, thread-like organs called halteres, which are also known as balancers. With only a few exceptions, those being male scale insects and some mayflies, Diptera are the only insects that have front wings but lack hind wings. Only a few of the 120,000 species of Diptera do not have front wings, and they live on windswept islands or are external parasites of birds or mammals as adults.

What are **immature flies** like?

Generally speaking, the larvae are of two quite different types. Larvae of the more primitive Diptera, such as crane flies, midges, and mosquitoes, are legless—as are the larvae of all Diptera—but, unlike the higher Diptera, such as the house fly, blow flies, and flesh flies, primitive Diptera have a distinct head with some variation or another of chewing mouthparts. The larvae of the higher Diptera, usually known as maggots, are unique among the insects in that the head has virtually disappeared. What little is left of the head is withdrawn into the body of the maggot. The pupae of the more primitive Diptera are generally naked, but those of the others are completely enclosed in a puparium, which is the modified skin of the last larval instar. It is formed when the larva assumes an ovoid shape and darkens and hardens its cuticle. The puparium separates from the body of the pupa but is not shed. The insect remains within the puparium, protected as if by a cocoon, until the newly molted adult escapes by pushing off the head end of the puparium.

What do **adult flies eat**?

The feeding habits of the adults are varied, but not as varied as those of the larvae. A few adult flies, some bot flies, for example, lack mouthparts and do not feed, but all of the others have mouthparts fitted for sucking—sometimes also for piercing—and take liquid food of one sort or another. Some adult flies are predators that suck the juices from insects; some suck blood from vertebrates; and many drink nectar, flowing sap, and/or liquids from feces or rotting flesh. A few, such as the bush fly of Australia, annoy people by sipping pus from sores or discharges from the eyes, nose, or mouth.

What do **larval flies eat**?

The larvae of Diptera occur in many different habitats and eat many different foods. Some are parasites that live in the nasal sinuses of sheep, the stomachs of horses, or the muscles of many animals, including cattle and humans. A great many live as parasites in the bodies of many different kinds of insects. Among the plant feeders are some that bore in roots, stems, or fruits; some that live and feed in galls that they cause to form on plants; and even some that spend their lives mining in the thin layer of tissues between the upper and lower surfaces of leaves. Many are scavengers that eat animal wastes or dead and decaying animal and vegetable matter. Some of the aquatic species are filter feeders that strain tiny single-celled algae and other organic particles from the water.

What are **lovebugs**?

The lovebug is a species of march fly. They were named in recognition of the fact that they are often, if not usually, seen as copulating pairs. Lovebugs, which occur in the Gulf States, sometimes form enormous swarms in May and September. They are so abundant that automobiles that drive through a swarm are soon covered with them; they obscure the driver's vision by covering the windshield and clog the radiator so that the automobile overheats.

What are **moth flies**?

They are minute flies that are rarely more than one-sixth of an inch long. The moth flies are so named because their broad, hairy wings make them look like tiny moths. They are often very numerous around sewage disposal plants, but those most familiar to people live in bathroom and basement drains. Relatives of the moth flies, known as sand flies, are blood suckers that transmit several diseases of humans.

What is a **bee louse**?

It is a tiny wingless fly, only about one-sixteenth of an inch long, that spends its entire life in a honey bee nest. As a larva, it feeds on honey as it burrows beneath the capping of honey cells. As an adult, it lives as an external parasite on the body of a queen or, less often, a worker bee. It usually stays on the bee's head and eats honey and pollen that it takes directly from the bee's mouth. Although the bee louse occurs in many parts of the world, it is the only species in its family.

What are robber flies?

They are all predators that suck the juices from their insect prey, which are usually snatched from the air. Most robber flies have elongate abdomens, and most are large—some more than an inch long. Some of the larger species are densely covered with yellow and black hair and resemble bumblebees, a resemblance that gives them some protection against insect-eating birds. If handled, robber flies are likely to deliver a painful bite by stabbing with their beaks.

What are **goldenrod gall flies**?

They are rather large and attractive fruit flies with banded wings. They cause the formation of one of the most familiar and easy to find of the plant galls, a spherical growth about an inch in diameter on the stem of a goldenrod. In winter these galls are readily visible and often abundant on the dead stems of these plants. The larva, which lived by eating the tissue at the center of the gall, spends the winter in its feeding cavity. In fall, it excavates a tunnel to the gall's surface in preparation for its emergence as an adult fly in the spring. Goldenrod gall fly larvae are used as bait by people who fish through the ice in winter and are a favorite winter food of downy woodpeckers, which peck a hole through the side of the gall.

What are **blow flies**?

Many blow flies, among them the well-known bluebottle, are metallic blue or green. They are fairly large, slightly larger than a house fly. Some larvae live in wounds on the bodies of animals; some feed only on dead, decaying tissue and others do real damage as they eat healthy tissue. Most blow fly maggots are valuable members of their ecosystems, rendering service as scavengers that eat animal wastes or carrion.

CADDISFLIES

What are **caddisflies**?

The caddisflies, about 12,500 species worldwide, belong to the order Trichoptera. The adults are small to medium-sized and somewhat resemble moths in appearance They have thread-like antennae that are sometimes longer than their body, and two pairs of membranous wings that are clothed with long, silky hair. The wings are held rooflike over the abdomen when at rest. Adult caddisflies are attracted at night to lights near the aquatic habitats of the larvae, which range from quiet ponds to swift-flowing streams.

How do **caddisfly larvae** live?

The slow moving and rather caterpillar-like larvae all live in fresh water and can be found on the bottom or on aquatic plants. Broadly speaking, they can be divided into three groups according to their habits: free-living species, net makers, and case builders. The free-living species live under rocks, construct neither cases nor nets, and are primarily predators that eat small aquatic creatures. The net-making species live in streams. Their silken nets are often fixed to the downstream side of a rock over which the water flows. Their open end faces upstream and, depending upon the species, they may be shaped like a tiny cup, a trumpet, or the finger of a glove. The larva tends its net from a nearby shelter and eats organic matter that is caught in it. The case makers are plant feeders and live in the shelter of the tubular, conical, or even snail-shaped cases that they build of sand grains, pebbles, or tiny sticks of plant material. Some species cement these materials together while others attach them to a lining of silk. The larva's abdomen is inside the case, but its head and thorax protrude from an opening at one of its ends as it crawls about.

MOTHS AND BUTTERFLIES

How can **moths** be distinguished from **butterflies**?

Both belong to the order Lepidoptera and are very similar, but they can be told apart by the shape of their antennae and, with some exceptions, by their behavior. All butterflies have long, thread-like antennae that end in a small knob. The antennae of moths may be comb-like, feather-like, or thread-like, but they never end in a knob. Butterflies are active during daylight and, with few exceptions, only when the sun is shining. A few moths are active during the day, but most of them are nocturnal. Moths and butterflies also differ in how they hold their wings at rest. Moths hold them out to the side like an airplane, folded down flat over the body, or wrapped around the body. Butterflies rest with their wings held together up over the body and only occasionally, out to the side like an airplane, ususally when they are basking in the sun.

By what characteristics can an **adult Lepidopteran** be recognized?

There are many Lepidoptera, about 170,000 species, but they are similar enough so that almost all of them are instantly recognizable on sight. The wings, which are broad and membranous, are covered with rows of tiny, pigmented scales—the colored "powder" that rubs off on your fingers—that overlap like the shingles on a roof. The Lepidoptera are named for the latter characteristic; *lepi* is Greek for a scale and *ptera* is Greek for a wing. Another striking characteristic of adult moths and butterflies is the form of the mouthparts. A few moths have vestigial mouthparts and the members of one very small and very primitive family have chewing mouthparts, but all of the other Lepidoptera have siphoning mouthparts, unique to this order, that consist of a long, thin tube that is coiled under the head like a watchspring when it is not extended to probe for nectar in a blossom.

Butterfly (Lepidoptera) feeding. (Photo by Edward S. Ross.)

How can **larval moths and butterflies** be recognized?

Larval moths and butterflies, known as caterpillars, are distinctive and, with very few exceptions, easily distinguished from other insects. They are long and soft-bodied, and to some people they look rather worm-like. Their mouthparts are of the chewing type, and, except for a mere handful of predaceous species, they feed on leaves and other plant matter. Caterpillars have three pairs of short legs on the thorax, and two to five pairs of fleshy prolegs on the abdomen . At the end of each proleg— the "sole of the foot", so to speak — there are many tiny hooks called crochets, which enable the caterpillar to hold tightly to a leaf or to whatever surface it may be on. If you let a caterpillar sit on your finger, the tiny crochets will dig into the superficial layer of your skin. They don't hurt, and you can't feel them, but if you pull the caterpillar off your finger, you can feel a very slight tug as each pair of prolegs pulls loose.

Do all moths and butterflies **spin cocoons**?

The caterpillars of many moths spin a silken cocoon that will house them during their pupal stage, but butterfly caterpillars and some moth caterpillars do not. Cocoons may be sturdy and tough, giving protection against most parasites and predators, or they may be so thin and skimpy that they seem to offer no protection at all. Moth caterpillars that do not spin cocoons pupate in protected places, often in a burrow in the soil or on a plant stem. Some butterfly pupae, such as those of monarchs, hang upside down from a leaf, a stem, or some other surface. They dangle from spines at the end of their abdomen that are embedded in a pad of silk that the caterpillar lays down on the supporting surface before it molts to the pupal stage. Others, such as swallowtails, attach themselves to a vertical surface. Spines at the end of the abdomen are held fast in a pad of silk, and the pupa is held more or less upright by a girdle of silk around the middle of its body, much like a window washer who leans back in his or her safety belt.

Are there moths that **suck blood**?

As fantastic as it may seem, there is in Southeast Asia a moth that pierces the skin and sucks blood from mammals such as pigs, cattle, and even elephants. The tip of this moth's siphoning proboscis is hard, sharp, and armed with little teeth that can tear through skin and flesh. This blood-thirsty creature is apparently descended from moths that took the first steps toward the blood feeding habit, such as species that board animals to sip sweat, skin oils, and other secretions — even blood oozing from wounds such as those made by biting insects.

What are those **big, green caterpillars on tomato plants**?

These huge caterpillars, which may be three to four inches long when full grown, are either tobacco or tomato hornworms. These caterpillars are the growing stages of two species of the narrow-winged sphinx moths that we sometimes see in the evening hovering in front of flowers like hummingbirds. The upward-projecting "horn" at the end of the abdomen gives these green caterpillars (which also sport white bars along their sides) their name. The tobacco hornworm, like its close relative the tomato hornworm, is a greedy consumer of tomato leaves and is the more common of the two in the northern United States and southern Canada. Both species are "host specific." That is, they will feed only on plants of the nightshade family: tobacco, tomato, potato, eggplant, and related wild species.

What are **carpenterworms**?

They are large—up to two inches long—heavy-bodied caterpillars that tunnel in the wood of various kinds of trees such as maple, elm, oak, willow, locust, ash, and others. The adult moths lay eggs in crevices of the bark. Upon hatching, the tiny caterpillars quickly tunnel into the wood, ultimately making very large tunnels that are sometimes over an inch in diameter. They grow slowly on their diet of wood, which is low in nutritive value. After three years, they molt to the pupa in a large cell that they excavate in the wood. Just before transforming to the adult, the pupa wriggles its way to the opening of its burrow.

Tent caterpillars. (Photo by Edward S. Ross.)

Where do those **big silken nests** on wild cherry or apple trees come from?

Built in the crotch of a branch and attaining a length of about 18 inches, these tent-like nests are the daytime shelters of the communal eastern tent caterpillar. When the caterpillars hatch in spring from an egg mass that girdles a twig and that may contain several hundred eggs, they join forces to spin a small tent that they continuously enlarge as they grow. The caterpillars spend the daylight hours resting in the tent or basking in the sun on its surface. At night they leave the tent to feed on the leaves of the tree, and will ultimately nearly strip it. After feeding for a month or more, they are full grown in early June, at a length of about two inches. They then scatter to spin cocoons on the trunk of the tree or some nearby object. After about three weeks the adults emerge and lay eggs that will not hatch until the next spring, more than nine months later.

What are those **cocoon-like bags** that dangle from the branches of junipers?

They are the silken cases in which evergreen bagworms, the caterpillar stage of a moth, spend their lives. The bags, festooned with bits of leaves and twigs, are continuously enlarged as the caterpillars grow, and are about one and a half inches long in late summer when the caterpillars have finished growing. The females, which become wingless adults in September, remain in their bags until they have mated and laid their eggs. Then they drop to the ground and die. The little, black, winged males are attracted to the females by a sex pheromone and do not live for much more than a day, because they cannot feed. In winter, a bag that had been occupied by a male is empty but may still have a pupal skin protruding from the valve-like opening at its tip. A bag that was occupied by a female contains her pupal skin, which will house hundreds or as many as two thousand soft-shelled, white eggs that will not hatch until the following June.

WASPS, ANTS, AND BEES

What do **wasps, ants, and bees** have in common?

They belong to the 130,000-member order Hymenoptera, and are all characterized as adults by a "wasp waist," a narrow constriction between the thorax and the abdomen; chewing mouthparts; and usually a stinger at the end of the female's abdomen. A large group of gall-forming and parasitic wasps have a piercing ovipositor rather than a stinger at the end of the abdomen. The most primitive of the Hymenoptera, the sawflies, do not have a "wasp waist"— the abdomen is broadly joined to the thorax—and have a caterpillar-like larva rather than the white, grub-like larva of the other Hymenoptera.

How do **sawfly larvae** and caterpillars differ?

Like the great majority of caterpillars, almost all sawfly larvae are plant feeders, and most of them feed externally on foliage. Sawfly larvae also look much like caterpillars, but they differ in the number of eyes and prolegs that they have. Caterpillars have six small, simple (not faceted) eyes on each side of the head, but sawfly larvae have one rather large simple eye on each side of the head. Caterpillars have a maximum of five pairs of prolegs on the abdomen, while sawfly larvae have a minimum of six pairs.

Are the **Hymenoptera important to people**?

Very much so! While a few of them, such as some sawflies, ants, and stinging wasps, may sometimes be pestiferous, the great majority of them are highly beneficial. Many, such as bees, serve as pollinators and a great many as parasites of other insects. There is no doubt that, from the human point of view, the Hymenoptera are the most beneficial of the insects.

Why are bees such **important pollinators**?

They are certainly the most important of all the creatures that pollinate plants. First, there are a great many species, about 3,500 in North America alone, and all but the honey bee and the bumble bees are solitary rather than social. Second, all of them visit

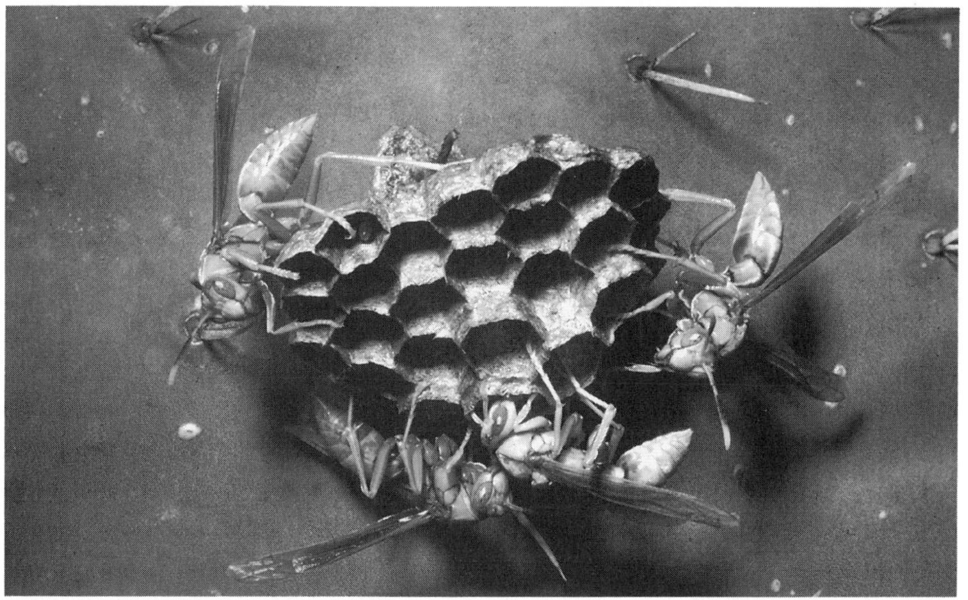

Wasps making nest. (Photo by Edward S. Ross.)

flowers frequently, because their only food is pollen and nectar. The adults subsist mainly on nectar and feed their larval offspring a mixture of pollen and honey, the latter consisting of nectar that has been concentrated by evaporation. Third, they are specially adapted for collecting and transporting pollen. The body hairs of bees, unlike those of wasps, are branched or feather-like, well adapted for retaining pollen grains that the bee brushes against as it moves about on a flower. Much of this pollen is transferred by the bee from its body hairs to the pollen baskets on the outer surfaces of the hind tibiae. The pollen in these baskets is carried back to the nest, but some remains clinging to the body hairs and may fertilize the next flower that the bee visits. The bee's pollen baskets are on the outer surfaces of the hind tibiae, and consist of the smooth and somewhat convex face of the tibia surrounded by the stiff hairs that form the "walls" of the basket.

How important are the **parasitic wasps**?

They are the most important of the many parasites of insects. About 115,000 species of insects are parasites of other insects; an astonishing 100,000 of them, about 87 percent, are wasps. Adult wasps are not parasitic but use their piercing ovipositors to place their eggs within the bodies of the insects that are the hosts of their parasitic larvae. The larvae grow to maturity within the host's body and will ultimately kill it. Some remain within the host's body during their pupal stage, but some emerge from the host to pupate in a silken cocoon that they spin on or near its body.

How do wasps make paper?

They make paper by mixing their saliva with fibers of weathered wood. It is said that the Chinese, the first people to make paper, learned the art by watching wasps. Examining a hornet's nest will show that the wasps used several sources of fiber. The paper in the nest is composed of little layers of different colors. Some are made from fibers that the wasps took from a weathered branch or fence post and appear silvery-gray. Others, made of fibers collected from a decaying log, are reddish-brown.

Are **all wasps parasitic**?

No. Non-parasitic wasps are predators that feed their young insects or other arthropods that they have paralyzed with venom from their stings. Most of them are solitary species that nest in burrows in the soil or plant stems, or build mud nests of various shapes, some of which are commonly seen under the eaves of houses or on the ceilings of open porches. The nests are stocked with the arthropods that the larvae will eat. Many of the solitary wasps are very fussy about what they feed to their larvae. Some of the potter wasps stock their nests only with caterpillars, and others only with the larvae of leaf beetles. The large black and yellow cicada killers stock their underground nests only with adult dog-day cicadas. The spider wasps stock their nests, which may be in rock crevices or burrows in the soil or rotten wood, with nothing but spiders.

What do the **social wasps** feed their young?

The social wasps include the familiar black and white hornets and the black and yellow yellowjackets, which build paper combs enclosed in a multilayered paper envelope. The football-shaped nests of hornets, sometimes over a foot in diameter, hang from the branch of a tree or shrub. The nests of yellowjackets are similar but built in a hole in the ground. The equally familiar polistes wasps, or paper wasps, hang their uncovered combs from the underside of a branch, the eaves of a house, or some other overhang that gives protection from the rain. All of these wasps feed their larvae insects, often caterpillars, that they prepare by chewing them up.

Are all **ants social**?

Without exception, all of the known ants are social. A colony usually consists of three basic castes that are made up of only females: workers, soldiers, and a queen. All but the queen are sterile. She monopolizes reproduction in the colony. The wingless workers make up most of the population of a colony and are responsible for doing its

Soldier army ant. (Photo by Edward S. Ross.)

work. Some species do not have soldiers, but in others they are a large and important part of the colony. They use their large and powerful mandibles to kill intruders and otherwise defend the colony. Successful colonies produce swarms of winged females (future queens) and winged males that fly off, mingle with winged individuals from other colonies, and form pairs. As soon as the queen is inseminated, she seeks a nest site and begins to lay eggs. At first she does all of the work, but she is soon relieved by her worker offspring. Colonies vary in size, from a few dozen individuals in some species to hundreds of thousands in others.

How **abundant** are ants?

According to Bert Hölldobler and Edward O. Wilson's, *The Ants,* there are 8,804 known species of ants, but far more are still unknown. Although other groups exceed the ants in numbers of known species, ants may be the most numerous of all the insects. In the Amazon rain forest, for example, there are over 3,500,000 ants per acre. William Morton Wheeler, the outstanding authority on ants of the early 20th century, wrote as follows: "Ants are to be found everywhere, from the Arctic regions to the tropics, from timberline on the loftiest mountains to the shifting sand of dunes and seashores, and from the most damp forests to the driest deserts. Not only do they outnumber in individuals all other terrestrial animals, but their colonies even in very circumscribed localities often defy enumeration."

What do **ants eat**?

The first ants were predators of other arthropods, as are the great hordes of army ants that scour the tropical forests of the New World for their prey. But ants have diversified to exploit a great variety of foods. Harvester ants feed mainly on seeds that they collect, sometimes at some distance from the nest, and store in underground granaries. Some ants, notably the pharaoh ant, which is often a household pest, are virtually omnivorous, feeding on sugar, greasy particles of food, dead insects, and other organic substances. Among the most interesting of the ants are species that have become farmers and keepers of domestic animals. The leaf-cutter ants of South America eat a fungus that they grow on a mulch, which they prepare from pieces of fresh leaves that workers bring to the nest. Many ants collect the "honeydew," or sugary excrement, secreted by aphids. Some simply collect it from aphids that they chance upon, while others tend and protect aphids much as people keep cows or other domestic animals.

GROWTH AND METAMORPHOSIS

GROWTH

How can an insect covered by a **lifeless and largely rigid cuticle** grow?

Just as a growing child must every so often be outfitted with new and larger clothes, a growing insect must from time to time replace its existing cuticle with a new and larger one that will allow for growth. Insects—and all other arthropods—undergo periodic molts in which they shed the outgrown cuticle to replace it with a roomier one. The new cuticle has slack, largely in the form of folded membranes, that will be taken up as the insect continues to grow.

What happens when an insect **molts**?

The first sign of a molt is the separation of the cuticle from the underlying epidermal layer. Next, molting fluid is secreted into the space between the epidermis and the now detached cuticle. After the epidermal cells have secreted a new cuticle beneath the old one, enzymes in the molting fluid digest the chitin and protein of the inner layer of the old cuticle. They will be salvaged and ultimately reused by the insect. In the next step, the old cuticle, which now consists of little more than its hard outer layer and the epicuticle, splits open along the midline of the back, and the insect withdraws from it, head and thorax first, much as a person withdraws a hand from a glove. Looking like a pale ghost of its former self, the insect is now clothed only in its new cuticle, which is as yet neither darkened nor hardened and is so soft and fragile that it can be ruptured by the touch of a finger. Before the new cuticle hardens, the insect swallows enough air—water in the case of an aquatic insect—to swell up its body and thus expand the new cuticle. Now the insect has room to grow. When it has grown enough to fill the new cuticle, taking up the slack provided by its folded membranes, it will molt again.

Cockroach next to molted cuticle. (Photo by Edward S. Ross.)

How **many times** do insects molt?

The number of molts varies from species to species and sometimes from individual to individual, but usually ranges somewhere between three and twenty. If nutrition and other environmental factors are adequate, many insects undergo a constant and genetically fixed number of molts. Tobacco and tomato hornworms, for example, molt a total of seven times. Mosquitoes and flies generally undergo a total of five molts. But environmental factors can slow growth and thus increase the number of molts. For example, the hornworms already mentioned undergo an extra molt if they are fed a poor diet. On a good diet, clothes moths molt six times, but on an inadequate diet they may molt as many as forty times. Khapra beetles, which feed on stored grain, molt six times at 90°F, but ten times at 70°F. With a few exceptions, insects do not molt after they have become adults. The exceptions are springtails and bristletails, which molt many times as adults, and mayflies, which undergo one additional molt after attaining adulthood. A bristletail may molt as many as 60 times during its life.

What is an **instar**?

Molts divide an insect's life into stages that are known as stadia. Between hatching from its egg and its first molt, an insect is in the first stadium and is known as the first instar. Between the first and second molts, the second stadium, it is known as the second instar, and so on until it attains the status of adult instar, after which all but the most primitive insects do not molt.

What is Dyar's law?

Harrison Gray Dyar (1866–1929), an American entomologist, found that the width of the head capsule of caterpillars increases as a regular geometrical progression from instar to instar. In other words, in each succeeding instar the width of the head capsule will be a constant multiple of the width of the head capsule of the preceding instar. Thus, in a series of caterpillars whose head capsules, beginning with the first instar, have widths of 0.8, 1.3, and 2.1mm, the constant multiplier is 1.62, 1.3/0.8 = 1.62, 2.1/1.3 = 1.62. Using this multiplier we can predict what the head capsule width of the following instar will be, 3.4mm (1.62 x 2.1). Thus, if we have a series of caterpillars representing several instars, we can tell if an instar is missing by determining if the head capsules form a regular geometric progression. There are exceptions to Dyar's law, but it is more often than not a useful aid in unraveling the life history of an insect.

How much do insects **increase in size** as they grow?

Some grow relatively modestly from birth to maximum size. An aphid increases its weight by a factor of only 16 times, a diving beetle by 52 times, and a locust by 126 times. But the increase in size of caterpillars is enormous, especially compared to humans, who increase in weight from birth to maturity by a factor of from about 20 to 25 times. When a silkworm caterpillar reaches its maximum size, it will have increased its weight by a factor of over 8,000 times. The champion seems to be a slow-growing, wood-boring caterpillar that increases its weight by a factor of about 72,000 times!

Do insects grow **throughout their lives**?

They do not. An insect grows only during the life stage that immediately follows its birth or hatching from the egg: the nymphal stage in insects with gradual metamorphosis, and the larval stage in those with complete metamorphosis.

METAMORPHOSIS

What is the difference between a **nymph and a larva**?

A nymph is the immature, growing stage of an insect with gradual metamorphosis. The developing wings, or wingpads, of nymphs are external, borne in plain view on the

What is the most conspicuous change that comes about during metamorphosis?

In winged insects it is certainly the acquisition of wings. Unlike birds and bats, no insect that has wings as an adult has visible wings when it is hatched or born. Thus, entomologists agree that all winged insects metamorphose during their development. Wingless insects, such as lice and fleas, which descended from winged ancestors, undergo a similar metamorphosis except for the acquisition of wings.

outside of the body. A larva is the immature growing stage of an insect with complete metamorphosis. Its wings develop internally, concealed beneath the body wall.

What is **metamorphosis**?

Metamorphosis is defined as a change in form. It is the course of development that transforms a first instar nymph or larva to the adult. Particularly remarkable examples of metamorphosis are the transformation of a tadpole to a frog or a toad, and the transformation of a caterpillar to a moth or a butterfly.

Do **all insects** undergo metamorphosis?

The changes in form of springtails and bristletails are so slight—not much more than what occurs in a person from infancy to adulthood— that some entomologists say that these insects do not undergo a metamorphosis. In a bristletail the only notable changes are the acquisition of a covering of scales on the body and the addition of a few segments to the already long and many-segmented antennae.

What are the life stages of insects with **gradual metamorphosis**?

There are three: the egg stage, the nymphal stage, and the adult stage. Embryonic development occurs in the egg. The nymph is the growing stage, and except for the absence of fully developed wings, closely resembles the adult. Almost anyone would, for example, recognize a grasshopper nymph as a "baby" grasshopper. Nymphs usually behave much like adults, live in the same habitat, and eat the same food. Mayflies, dragonflies, and damselflies are exceptions. These nymphs are aquatic and have gills, while the adults are terrestrial and do not have gills. Nymphs have several instars, the last of which molts to the adult stage. The adult is the reproductive stage. Only in this stage do insects with gradual metamorphosis copulate and bear young.

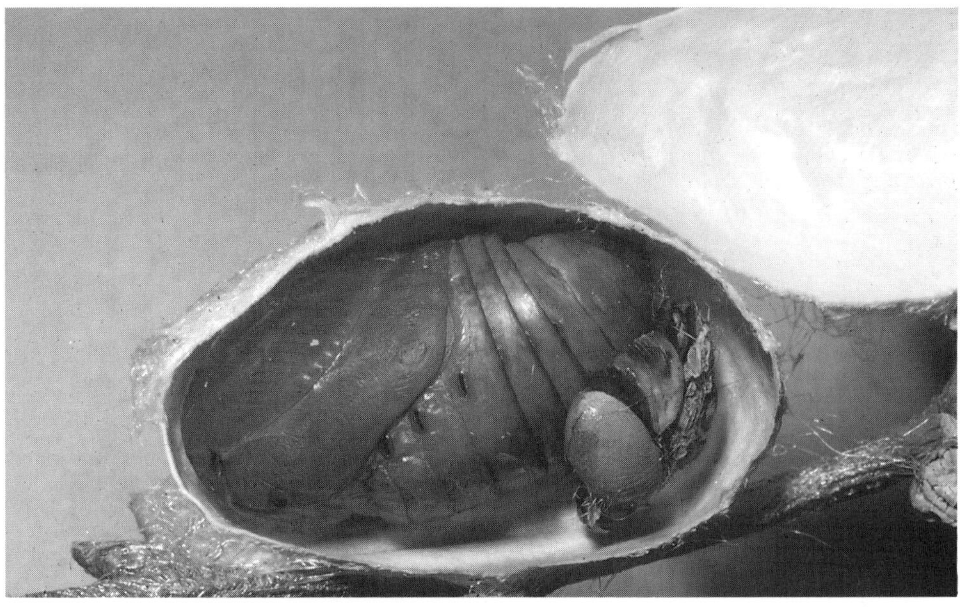

Moth pupa in its cocoon. (Photo by Edward S. Ross.)

What **kinds of insects** have gradual metamorphosis?

The insects with gradual metamorphosis, also known as the exopterygota (Greek for external wings), include mayflies, dragonflies, damselflies, grasshoppers, crickets, katydids, stick insects, mantises, cockroaches, earwigs, termites, stoneflies, booklice, barklice, chewing lice, blood-sucking lice, thrips, true bugs, aphids, leafhoppers, and others.

What are the life stages of insects with **complete metamorphosis**?

There are four: the egg, the larva, the pupa, and the adult. The egg stage, in which embryonic development occurs, is absent in live bearers such as tsetse flies and certain flesh flies. The larva is the growing stage and bears little or no resemblance to the adult. For example, a maggot, the larva of a fly, looks nothing at all like an adult fly, and a caterpillar, the larva of a butterfly, looks nothing like an adult butterfly. Furthermore, larvae and adults often differ in behavior, habitat, and food choice as well. A maggot that lives in and feeds on carrion or fecal matter will, as an adult, use its sponging mouthparts to take nectar from flowers. Caterpillars ingest huge amounts of leaf tissue, but as adults they use their siphoning mouthparts to sip nectar from flowers. Larvae have several instars, the last of which molts to the pupal stage, the stage in which the transformation to adulthood takes place. It is sometimes referred to as the resting stage. While the great majority of pupae do not move about—most of them are barely capable of wriggling—they are certainly not at rest. During this stage, most of the organs and tissues of the larva are broken down to a viscous and largely amorphous mass that is reorganized to form the tissues and organs of the adult. After the transformation is complete, the pupa molts to the final stage, the adult. Only in this stage does copulation occur, allowing insects with complete metamorphosis to reproduce.

What are **pupae** like?

With very few exceptions, pupae are virtually inactive and can do little more than make wriggling movements of their abdomens. Their appendages—antennae, legs, and wings— are generally nonfunctional. The appendages of the pupae of moths and butterflies are so closely fused to the body that the pupa looks like a stylized bas-relief of an adult carved on a small, brown nut. In other insects, the appendages of the pupa are not fused to the body but are folded against the body and are rigidly immobile.

Are there **active pupae**?

Although the great majority of pupae are virtually inactive, the pupae of a few insects can move about with great agility. For example, mosquito pupae, known as tumblers, are as active as the larvae and do just about everything that the larvae do except eat. Their legs and wings are nonfunctional, but they can swim very rapidly by lashing the abdomen up and down. They spend a lot of time just below the water surface, breathing through two trumpet-like tubes on the thorax that protrude through the surface film. If a shadow passes over them, they swim rapidly down to the safety of the bottom.

How are pupae **protected** against predators?

Since pupae are generally immobile, the larvae must take steps to safeguard themselves after they have molted to the helpless pupal stage. Some pupae are naked and exposed, as are those of butterflies; they are likely to be camouflaged and difficult to see, or sometimes brightly colored as a warning that they are not good to eat. In preparation for pupation, some insects—among them certain moths, beetles, lacewings, ants, wasps, and fleas—spin silken cocoons that will house them after they become pupae. The larvae of other insects retreat to some protected place where they will be hidden after they molt to the pupal stage. Codling moth caterpillars, the infamous worm in the apple, leave the fruit and crawl under a loose scale of bark. Tobacco and tomato hornworm caterpillars descend from the plant on which they have been feeding and pupate several inches under the soil surface. Like hornworms, Colorado potato beetle larvae leave the plant to tunnel into the soil before pupating.

What is pedogenesis?

Pedogenesis, the production of offspring by an immature stage, is exceedingly rare and occurs in only a few species, including some gall midges and a rare beetle, *Micromalthus,* that lives in decaying wood. The larvae of *Miastor,* a gall midge, occasionally lay eggs but more often give birth to larvae. These young larvae, which are in the body cavity of the parent larva, eat the tissues of its body, and eventually escape by making their way through its body wall. In other gall midges, pupae may produce larvae. Adult *Micromalthus* have reproducing larvae of three types: some that produce only females, some that produce only males, and others that produce both males and females. A male-producing larva lays a single egg that sticks to its body. When the larva hatches from this egg, it eats its parent.

Do flies spin **cocoons**?

No, but the pupae of house flies, flesh flies, blow flies, and the other "higher" flies are stored within a tough protective case that serves the same function as a cocoon but is not a cocoon. This case, the puparium, is the hardened skin of the third instar maggot. When the time to pupate is near, the maggot crawls to a protected place, changes its shape from the carrot-like form of the maggot to the ovoid form of the puparium, and darkens and hardens its cuticle. The molt to the pupal stage occurs within the puparium, but the puparium is not shed, and the fly does not emerge from it until after it has molted to the adult stage.

What kinds of insects have complete metamorphosis?

The insects with complete metamorphosis, also known as the endopterygota (Greek for internal wings), include lacewings, antlions, dobsonflies, beetles, weevils, scorpionflies, hangingflies, caddisflies, moths, butterflies, mosquitoes, midges, flies, fleas, wasps, ants, bees, and others.

Is complete metamorphosis **advantageous**?

Yes, it is, because larvae and adults can advance on two different evolutionary tracks and become separately specialized to perform their different roles. The larva, whose functions are to survive, eat, and grow, has become specialized as an efficient and often ravenous consumer of food. Caterpillars, for example, have been described as digestive systems on a caterpillar tread. Their chewing mouthparts are nicely adapted for eating leaves or other solid foods, and their stubby legs give them a firm grip on their host plant. The adult moths or butterflies have been called flying machines devoted to sex. Their *raison d'être* is to survive and reproduce. Their wings give them the ability to cover long distances as they search for mates or suitable places to lay their eggs. Their long, slender legs are the landing gear, and their siphoning mouthparts sip up the sugar-rich nectar that fuels the muscles that beat their wings. Insects with gradual metamorphosis, on the other hand, have not been able to specialize in the same ways since there is no transformation stage. Nymphs and adults are similar in anatomy and behavior, eat the same sort of food, and generally live in the same habitat. The adults have functional wings and genitalia, but are not otherwise specialized for growth or reproduction. The anatomy and life-style shared by nymphs and adults must suffice for both functions.

Is there any evidence that complete metamorphosis is **more advantageous than gradual metamorphosis**?

The difference in the number of species in each category leaves little doubt that complete metamorphosis is an evolutionarily more successful strategy for survival than is gradual metamorphosis. Of the approximately 900,000 known species of insects in the world, only about 135,000 (15 percent) undergo gradual metamorphosis, while about 765,000 (85 percent) undergo complete metamorphosis.

DIAPAUSE

How do insects **survive the winter**?

They survive in an inactive state of arrested development known as diapause. Until diapause is terminated, eggs do not hatch; nymphs, larvae, and pupae do not go on to the next life stage; and females neither lay eggs nor give birth. Most, but not all, diapausing insects are inactive. Most protect themselves against freezing temperatures by producing an antifreeze, an alcohol such as glycerol, sorbital, or mannitol. Their low metabolic rate, usually one-tenth or less of that of a nondiapausing insect, allows them to feed off of their store of body fat so that they can survive through the long winter.

In what **life stage** do insects diapause?

Considering insects as a whole, diapause can occur in any life stage or instar: egg, nymph, larva, pupa, or adult. But any given species of insect generally diapauses in only one of its life stages. Bagworms and tent caterpillars diapause as eggs, fritillary

Yellowjacket in diapause, wings and antennae tucked under its body. (Photo by Edward S. Ross.)

butterflies as first instar larvae, European corn borers as full-grown larvae, cecropia moths and swallowtail butterflies as pupae, and bean leaf beetles and mourning cloak butterflies as adults.

How do insects know when to go into the state of diapause?

Most insects initiate diapause in response to the short days of late summer and autumn, the only reliable clue to the approach of winter. Cold temperature is not a reliable clue. In a warm year, cold weather may be delayed until development has proceeded past the point of no return. Thus, an insect that diapauses as an egg will not go into diapause if cold weather is delayed and will hatch so late in the season that it will freeze to death before it can become an adult.

How does an insect know when to **terminate diapause**?

Diapause must be terminated in a timely manner in spring or early summer if the insect is to get off to a good start and produce as many generations of descendants as possible before winter. Many insects terminate diapause in response to warm temperature—but only after they have experienced a sufficiently long period of cold weather. This requirement for a long initial exposure to cold prevents a suicidal termination of diapause in response to a period of warm weather in fall or to a brief spell of warm weather in winter.

When does the **cecropia moth** terminate diapause?

The cecropia moth terminates diapause in response to warmth only after it has been sufficiently chilled. You can prove this to yourself with a simple experiment. In autumn or early winter collect a dozen or more cecropia cocoons. Put half of them in a cage at room temperature and the other half in a refrigerator. After ten weeks take the cocoons out of the refrigerator and put them in a separate cage next to the moths that have been at room temperature all along. The pupae in the chilled cocoons will almost immediately begin to develop and will emerge from their cocoons as a fairly well synchronized group in about three weeks. The pupae that were not chilled will produce adults at long intervals over a period of many months, and some of them will probably die without developing.

How do the **diapause of insects and the hibernation of mammals differ**?

They are similar in that both are dormant or resting states. But they differ in that insect diapause usually ends only after a period of chilling, while hibernation ends in response to warmth with no need for a previous period of chilling.

FINDING A MATE AND MATING

How do insects **find mates**?

This is not a problem for the few insects that reproduce parthenogenetically, without the need for a male. Neither is it a problem for some gregarious species in which males and females live cheek by jowl, although even gregarious species need to have a way of *recognizing* an individual as a member of the opposite sex. But finding a mate is a problem for solitary species. A solitary insect was most likely abandoned as an egg by its mother. It has probably never seen an adult of its own species and may be far removed from the closest potential mate. It thus has two problems. It must find a mate, and it must recognize it as a member of its own species. Many insects locate mates through signals that can be perceived from a distance, such as sounds, odors, or visual characteristics. Others meet their mates at trysting places where the two sexes congregate. As a general rule, mates are recognized at close range by a species-specific pheromone that they emit.

Why have **aphids** been called a race of Amazons?

Like the Amazons, that legendary race of women warriors, aphids have but little use for males. Throughout most of the year, no male aphids are to be seen. Take the rosy apple aphid, an occasional pest of apple trees, as an example. They, like most aphids, survive the winter as eggs fixed to a plant on which they feed—in this case, tucked away in a crevice in the bark of an apple twig. When these eggs hatch in the spring, they produce only wingless females. These first aphids of the spring mature in about two weeks and then, reproducing parthenogenetically, they give live birth to a generation of daughters, which in turn give live birth to a second generation of daughters. This goes on for several generations during spring and summer. Finally, in the fall, the next to last generation gives live birth to both males and females. These females

Do any insect species consist of only females?

Yes, but probably no more than a handful, although there are a few other species in which males only rarely occur. No male of the white-fringed beetle has ever been found. Nevertheless, this insect, an introduction to the United States from South America and a serious pest of several crops, seems to be doing well. This is at least partly due to its potential for very rapid population increase. After all, there are no non-reproductive males. The whole population consists of parthenogenetically reproducing females that may each lay many hundreds of eggs, up to a maximum of well over 3,000.

mate with males and rather than giving live birth, lay the eggs that will be the sole representatives of the rosy apple aphid during the winter.

FINDING A MATE WITH PHEROMONES

What is the composition of a **sex attractant pheromone**?

Sex attractant pheromones are, generally speaking, odorous substances that diffuse through the air and are carried by the breeze. When pheromones were first discovered, it was thought that a sex attractant consisted of a single chemical compound that was unique to one species. We now know that a sex attractant is usually a mixture of several compounds, some of which may occur in other species. But each sex attractant is unique because it contains these compounds in characteristic proportions. Sex attractants, innately recognized by the opposite sex, are usually emitted by the female, but in a few species—boll weevils and hangingflies, for example—they are emitted by the male.

How does a male cecropia moth **find a female** of his species?

By flying to the source of a sex attractant pheromone that is released by the female. Not until after she has mated does the newly emerged adult female move more than a few inches away from the cocoon in which she spent the winter as a pupa. About an hour before the first dawn of her life—about 18 or 19 hours after she came out of the cocoon—she everts a little yellow gland from the end of her abdomen and begins to release her sex attractant pheromone. The pheromone is blown downwind by the breeze, forming—like smoke from a chimney—an invisible, expanding plume that ultimately becomes too diffuse for a male cecropia to sense. At the same time of day, the males begin to fly. If a male happens to fly into a perceptible plume of pheromone, he turns upwind and continues to fly upwind as long as he smells the pheromone. If he blunders out of the plume, he makes a searching flight that, with luck, will bring him back into the plume. If he finds the female, he lands beside her and immediately makes genital contact.

How **powerful** is the cecropia sex attractant?

This question puts the cart before the horse. It is much more informative to ask about the sensitivity of the male's "nose." We do not know how sensitive male cecropias are to the pheromone released by their females, but we do know something about the sensitivity of the male silk moth of commerce to the attractant pheromone produced by females of his species. The male cecropia's sensitivity is probably more or less the same. The male silk worm can respond to as little as a few hundred molecules of pheromone in a volume of about 0.06 cubic inches of air. Thus, he can perceive a few hundred molecules of pheromone mixed in with about 25 quintillion (25 followed by 18 zeroes) air molecules.

From how far away can a male cecropia find a female?

From much farther away than you might guess. This is not the same as asking from how far away a male can perceive a female's attractant pheromone. From an ecological and evolutionary perspective, the former question is more interesting than the latter because it bears on the question of how low—and consequently how dispersed—a cecropia population can be and yet reproduce itself and survive. A part of the male's journey to a female consists of upwind flight directed by his perception of the pheromone, but the other, sometimes much longer, part is random movement that may, by luck, bring him closer to the female. By using traps baited with pheromone-releasing female cecropia moths, it was found that a few males will locate a female from three or four miles away. The distance record for cecropia is held by a male that had been released eight miles away from the trap in which he was caught. The distance record for moths is held by a promethea male, a close relative of cecropia, that had been released 23 miles away from the trap that caught him. It took him three days to make it—but make it he did.

What is **bombykol**?

Bombykol is the sex attractant pheromone that is emitted by the female silk moths of commerce, the mothers of the caterpillars that secrete the silk from which our blouses and neckties are made. This was the first insect pheromone to be chemically isolat-

How do male bumble bees use a pheromone to locate mates?

The males mark a series of perches on plant stems with a pheromone from their mandibular glands that is attractive to females. Females that are ready to mate are attracted to these marked perches and will land on them to await the arrival of a male. Males patrol their "trap line" of marked perches, checking and rechecking each one. They copulate with any females that they find waiting for them.

ed and characterized—in 1959 by the German chemist A. Butenandt and his colleagues. At that time chemists had worked with large quantities of moths because the microanalytical techniques of today were not yet available. Thus, they had to extract the terminal ends of the abdomens of about a half-million virgin silkworm females to obtain about 4/10,000 of an ounce of the pure sex attractant. Minute quantities of this attractant were as attractive to male silk moths as were the females themselves.

Do insects make sex **pheromones other than attractants**?

They also secrete aphrodisiac pheromones and, in a few species, even antiaphrodisiacs. According to the *Oxford English Dictionary*, an aphrodisiac is something that arouses sexual desire. Students of insect behavior take a somewhat broader view, including among the aphrodisiacs substances that facilitate courtship or put mates in the mood for copulation. These substances are usually, but not always, made by males; act only at short range; and come into play only after the pair have come together. Aphrodisiacs have been discovered in several different groups of insects, including flies, butterflies, and caddisflies. A cockroach produces an aphrodisiac that is eaten by the female. This substance, waggishly named seducin, is secreted on the male's back. A female who comes to a male's sex attractant pheromone will not let the male copulate with her until she has ingested some seducin.

FINDING A MATE BY EAR

Do many insects **make sounds to attract mates**?

According to one authority, insects of tens of thousands of different species have the ability to produce sound. In the great majority of these species, the sounds are sexual signals intended for the ears of the opposite sex, often loud signals that can attract mates from a distance. Generally speaking, the signal senders are males and the receivers are females, but in some species the signal is received and acted upon by members of both sexes. Among the many insects that make sounds to signal the opposite sex are various species of grasshoppers, crickets, katydids, cicadas, true bugs, and beetles.

How do insects make sounds?

The ability to produce sounds has evolved independently among the insects several times, and insects now produce sounds in several different ways. Many species, among them grasshoppers, crickets, and katydids, stridulate—that is, they make a sound by rubbing one part of the body against another. Grasshoppers draw a file-like row of pegs on a hind femur against an edge of a forewing. Crickets and katydids rub one forewing against the other, drawing a rasping organ, or file, on one wing across a scraper on the other wing. The shrilly, high-pitched drone of a dog-day cicada, which is heard high in trees during the hot days of July and August, is produced in an entirely different way by a pair of organs at the base of the abdomen. Sound is produced when a convex timbal, a structure like a tiny drum head, is rapidly vibrated by a muscle. It is repeatedly drawn inward and released, similar to pressing down and then releasing the lid of a tin can. Pulling the timbal down makes a click, and another click is produced when it is released and springs back up. A cicada's timbal makes about 390 clicks per second. The death watch beetle, which often burrows in the wood of old houses, makes its spooky ticking sound by banging its head against the wall of its burrow. The Madagascar hissing cockroach produces a loud hiss when membranes are set to vibrating by a rush of air through the spiracles.

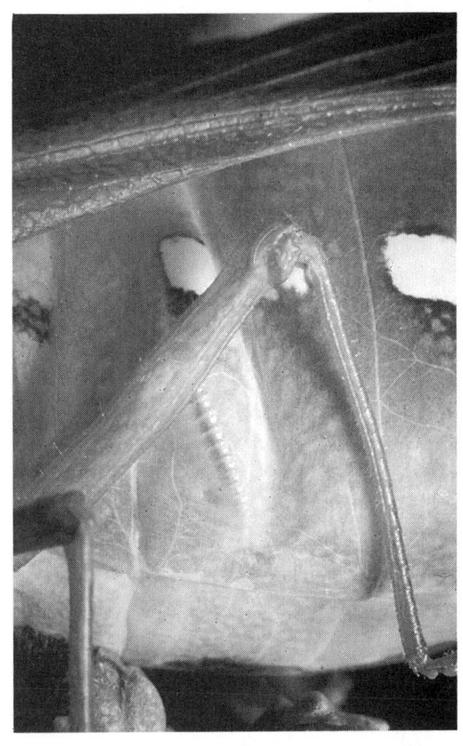

Grasshoppper hind leg and "file." (Photo by Edward S. Ross.)

Do crickets use **megaphones**?

While some crickets have no way of intensifying their songs, others can considerably intensify them by singing from tunnels in the earth that they dig in the shape of bandshells or megaphones. A male mole cricket, for example, sings from behind the entrance to his burrow, which is shaped like a double megaphone. This considerably intensifies his song, which can be heard by a person from almost 2,000 feet away.

How does the **temperature affect the rate** at which crickets call?

Crickets are "cold-blooded," meaning they have no internal mechanism for controlling their body temperature. Thus the rate at which they sing varies with the air temperature: the warmer the night, the faster they chirp. The relationship between air temperature and calling rate may be so predictable that you can determine the temperature by counting calls. For example, the air temperature in degrees Fahrenheit can be calculated by adding 40 to the number of calls that a snowy tree cricket, also known as the thermometer cricket, makes in 13 seconds.

What is the **meaning of a cricket's song**?

Some crickets sing three different songs with three different meanings. A loud and belligerent song announces that the singer is on his territory and that he will defend it against usurping males. Another song, loud but different from the territorial proclamation, is directed at females and will attract them from a distance. When a female arrives at his burrow, the male stops singing the loud calling song and switches to the third song, the softer and quieter courtship song. Since this song cannot be heard from far away, distant males do not hear it, thus averting unwelcome intrusions upon the courting couple.

Do male crickets **fight**?

Yes. If an intruding male enters another male's territory, the two will at first try to out-sing each other. This "battle of the tenors" often settles the conflict, and usually in favor of the original occupant of the territory. If this does not work, the males get physical. They whip each other with their antennae, spar with their forelegs, or even use their jaws to tear off each others appendages. The Chinese take advantage of this behavior to stage fights between crickets. Two males, each valued for its combativeness, are put together in a small, bare cage. If this confrontation does not soon progress beyond a chirping match, the crickets' handlers incite them to physical combat by stroking the tips of their antennae with a fine straw. Wagers are made, and money is won or lost on the outcome of these Lilliputian battles.

Do female crickets **respond to telephone calls** from males?

They do. Just before the beginning of World War I, a German scientist showed that female crickets are attracted to a telephone if a male of their species is singing at the other end of the line. This showed that females will respond to the calling song alone without an assist from chemical or visual signals.

Are male crickets **cuckolded** by other males?

A singing male may be cuckolded by a silent male that lurks nearby. Although these males, known as satellite males, have the organs for chirping, they do not sing. They let the holder of the territory do the singing, and when a willing female approaches, they sneak out to intercept her and sometimes manage to seduce her and inseminate her before she reaches her vociferous suitor. Although a silent satellite male may obtain fewer matings than a more forceful singing male, he may profit by "keeping his mouth shut," and thereby avoiding the attention of the egg-laying, parasitic flies that are attracted to singing crickets. The eggs that the fly lays on the cricket hatch to produce maggots that burrow into its body and ultimately kill it. In a year when these parasites are abundant, silent satellite males are likely to father more offspring than are the noisy calling males.

How do **periodical cicadas** attract mates?

While dog-day cicadas sing alone, male periodical cicadas—which appear en masse every 13 or 17 years—attract females by banding together in singing choruses that may include hundreds or even thousands of males. An emergence of these insects, which may include billions of individuals spread over a large area, consists of three different species. All seems to be chaos. Cicadas are flying everywhere, and the singing males make a deafening racket. Nevertheless, the three species manage to sort themselves out and form separate choruses. Confusion and matings between different species are averted, because each species has its own distinctive song and because the three species sing at different times of the day. One species calls mainly in the morning, another during the middle of the day, and the third mainly in the afternoon.

What happens in a **chorus of male periodical cicadas**?

The male's song attracts both males and females. As more and more males arrive at the chorus tree, the chorus becomes louder and thus more attractive to females. During a period of about two weeks, a chorus may grow to include a great many males that are so perfectly synchronized with each other that they sound like a single voice. The larger and louder a chorus is, the more females it will attract. Most matings occur within a chorus, and males that join a chorus are likely to mate more often than lone males. Females mate soon after they arrive at a chorus but do not stay for long. Once she has been inseminated, she leaves to get on with the all-important and time-consuming business of laying her eggs. The male remains behind with the chorus in hope of mating with another female.

FINDING A MATE BY SIGHT

Do insects use **visual signals** to attract mates?

Although most insects rely upon chemical or auditory signals to attract mates, there are quite a few that use visual signals. Visual communication by insects and other animals has been a popular subject for research because we easily perceive visual signals and because they have a dominant role in our own behavior. Visual communication has significant advantages over the other possible modalities of communication, particularly the chemical modalities. The potential complexity of visual signals makes possible limitless variations that can convey many different meanings. Consider the many possible permutations of just some aspects of a visual signal: color, shape, posture, movement, and tempo. Furthermore, if a predator appears, a visual signal can be quickly turned off, which, unlike a chemical signal, does not leave a lingering clue to the presence of a signal sender.

Why do **fireflies flash**?

As a female firefly, actually a kind of beetle, rests in the grass or other vegetation, she flashes signals that attract the notice of flying males who will flash in response. Her signal announces her location and her willingness to welcome a suitor. Her signal is in code. The number of flashes that she makes, their duration, and the length of the intervals between them are characteristic of her sex and her species. The male's signal may be different from the female's, but it is also in code, is characteristic of his species and sex, and tells the female that he has noticed her signal and is on his way. The male zeroes in on the female as the two flash back and forth at each other.

How do fireflies **produce light**?

The light-making organ is at the hind end of the abdomen. Light is produced by a complex chemical reaction that converts chemical energy to light energy. This reaction is amazingly efficient. About 98 percent of the energy involved is released as light. Almost no heat, a useless byproduct, is produced. Contrast this with a far less efficient incandescent light bulb that produces enough unwanted heat to burn your hand.

What are firefly ***femmes fatales***?

This appropriately descriptive term was used by James E. Lloyd to designate female fireflies that eat males of other firefly species that they lure with false flash signals. They respond to males of their own species with their own species-specific signal, mate with them, and usually do not eat them, but they respond differently to the flash signals of males of other species. These carnivorous females have broken the code that other species of fireflies use. They falsify the flash signals of other females and thereby attract males of these other species and then devour them.

Do groups of fireflies **flash synchronously**?

In southeast Asia and the western Pacific from Burma east to New Guinea, some species of fireflies gather in huge groups of thousands of individuals in "firefly trees" and produce spectacular displays as they flash synchronously. Engelbert Kaempfer, a Dutch physician who traveled along the Chao Phraya River from Bangkok to the sea in 1680, is quoted by John and Elizabeth Buck:

> The glowworms . . . represent another shew, which settle on some Trees, like a fiery cloud, with this surprising circumstance, that a whole swarm of these insects, having taken possession of one Tree, and spread themselves over its branches, sometimes hide their Light all at once, and a moment after make it appear again with the utmost regularity and exactness . . .

Although both sexes are present in these trees, only the males flash. They do so in unison at intervals of from less than a second to as much as three seconds, depending upon the species. A lone firefly flashing in the dense tangles of vegetation in the swamps along the river would be difficult to find, but a firefly tree is a beacon that mate-seeking fireflies can see from far away.

How do fireflies **synchronize** their flashes?

Many explanations have been proposed, ranging from telepathy to the unhelpful suggestion that these insects have an innate sense of rhythm. It was even suggested that the rhythmic flashing of these fireflies is an illusion caused by the twitching of the observer's eyelids. The most reasonable explanation is that an internal pacemaker or clock keeps the fireflies in synchrony once they have been triggered to flash. This clock, a timer of sorts, keeps each individual in step with the others by triggering each flash a set time after the preceding flash.

FLIES

How do flies **use visual signals** to locate mates?

Some male flies, among them certain parasitic flies, hover flies, and flesh flies, find mates by a behavior known as "station taking." The male watches for potential mates from a perch, perhaps a leaf or a branch, that gives him a clear view of the air space around him. When an insect of about the right size flies into view, he flits out and

Mating robber flies. (Photo by Edward S. Ross.)

grapples with it. If it turns out to be a female of his own species, he and his newly found mate will retreat into the nearby vegetation to copulate. The two probably recognize each other at close range by means of pheromones, quite likely a distinctive flavor that they perceive through taste organs that they are known to have on their feet. If the "station taking" male contacts a male of his own species or a member of some other species, he quickly breaks contact and returns to his perch. You can trick a "station taking" male by flipping a small, dark object in front of him. He will probably dart out to contact it, proving that he responds to visual cues, but cannot recognize a female by vision alone.

Grayling Butterflies

How do male **grayling butterflies** locate mates?

Like certain flies, they may "take a station" and dart out to pursue likely candidates for mating. If the candidate passes muster on contact, presumably because she tastes or smells like a member of the opposite sex of his own species, he induces her to alight and convinces her to mate by an elaborate courtship that ends with his bowing before her as he catches her antennae between his front wings, each of which bears a patch of specialized scales that rub against her antennae and release a pheromone that is presumably an aphrodisiac.

What is a supernormal stimulus?

It is an exaggerated stimulus, usually artificial, that is more attractive than the real thing. For example, a gull can be tricked into abandoning its own eggs by offering it a larger-than-life artificial egg. Male silver-washed fritillaries ignored realistic dummies to pursue supernormal dummies that were more orange and four times as large, and flapped more rapidly than a real female.

What **experiments** showed how male grayling butterflies perceive females?

Experiments with dummies, a technique often used by ethologists, scientists who view behavior from a biological perspective. Paper dummies, or models, attached to a fishing line and a rod were waved in front of sitting males. They often responded by pursuing the dummy. Dummies of various colors, shapes, and sizes all evoked responses. Some of them looked like butterflies and others were only circles or rectangles of paper. The most responses were elicited by dummies—not necessarily shaped like a butterfly—that were moved in a fluttery manner, that were as dark as possible, and that were brought as close as possible to the male being tested. Although males pursued some paper dummies just as they pursued females of their own species, they invariably rejected them as soon as they made contact with them.

Fritillary Butterflies

What clues do male fritillary butterflies use to **recognize females** of their species?

When a male of the European silver-washed fritillary is not in a mood for sex, he orients to green objects, the color of the foliage on which he rests, or to blue or yellow ones, the colors of the flowers from which he sips nectar. But males that have sex on their minds, recognizable by their zigzag, searching flight, are attracted to orange objects, the color of the female. In experiments, males eagerly pursued orange dummies of a certain size that appeared to fly and to flap their wings rapidly. They paid no attention to the shape of a dummy. Pursuing males never tried to court or copulate with a dummy. They lost interest when they got within four inches. But their interest perked up when a live female in a small cage was hidden under a dummy so that only her scent was perceptible. When presented in this way with a combination of visual stimuli and the female's pheromone, they courted the dummy and tried to copulate with it.

TRYSTING PLACES

Where do male insects **go to find females**?

To the places where females go. Just as people meet potential mates in churches, libraries, and laundromats, male insects that do not sense their mates from a distance by pheromone, sound, or sight look for females in the only two places where they are likely to be, where they eat and where they lay their eggs. In Africa, male tsetse flies watch for females as they follow or sit on wildebeests, antelopes, or other large animals that the females visit in order to take blood meals. Some male hover flies, also known as flower flies, frequent both the flowers at which females feed and the rot cavities in trees where they lay their eggs. In the morning, both sexes can be found at patches of flowers; in the heat of the afternoon, they both retire to shady woodlands where females search for rot cavities.

Why do some insects **gather on mountain tops**?

The mountain top is a trysting place where the sexes meet—the insect equivalent of a singles bar or a Florida beach during the spring break. Many species of beetles, butterflies, flies, wasps, and bees rendezvous on hills, mountain tops, or at other prominent topographic features. Both sexes are genetically programmed to go to such places. Their genes certainly do not inform them of the location of a particular site, but, rather, outline a program of behaviors that will take them to a likely place. A trysting place may offer no resource other than members of the opposite sex. A bare, rocky mountain top, for example, provides little shelter and no water, food, or places to lay eggs. There are usually more males than females at these meeting places. Females usually leave right after they mate to lay their eggs. Males usually stay on in the hope of inseminating another female.

COURTSHIP AND MATING

Do insects go through an **elaborate courtship** before they mate?

Some do and some do not. A male cecropia moth makes genital contact with a female just as soon as he arrives at her side. There is no apparent courtship or foreplay. Other insects do have a courtship—sometimes brief and simple and sometimes as elaborate as the courtship of a peacock or a bower bird. Courtships of insects, birds, or other animals are stereotyped, ritualistic, and uniquely characteristic of their species. For example, a male queen butterfly (which does sound contradictory, doesn't it?) that spots a flying female makes a hurried straight-line flight to catch up with her. When he is a few inches above her, he bobs up and down in the air. At this point he probably picks up her scent and is thus reassured that she really is a female of his own species. Next, he flies forward a bit and dusts her antennae with a glistening aphrodisiac dust that falls from brush-like "hairpencils" at the end of his abdomen. If she is willing to go on with the courtship, she lands on a plant. The male then hovers over her and again dusts her antennae with the aphrodisiac. If she is ready to copulate, she closes her wings over her back. The male lands beside her, closes his wings, and makes genital contact. Shortly thereafter, the male flies off with the passive female dangling from his genital claspers and settles into the vegetation with her. He soon inseminates her, but they will stay coupled for several hours.

How can male insects increase their **evolutionary fitness**?

Only by increasing the number of surviving progeny that they leave behind. This can be accomplished in two ways: by fathering as many progeny as possible, or by fathering fewer and increasing the probability that they will survive. A male can increase the number of progeny that he fathers by mating with as many females as possible or by guarding his mate to prevent other males from injecting her with sperm that will compete with his own sperm. The second and less frequently seen option can be accomplished by giving parental care to his offspring or by improving the odds that his mate will survive to lay the eggs fertilized by his sperm, perhaps by giving her food or some other assistance.

Do all insects use direct **internal fertilization**?

Almost all insects do so by using the penis to inject semen into the female's vagina. A very few insects, the most primitive ones, practice indirect internal fertilization. That is, the male ejaculates outside of the female's body, and it is up to the female to insert the ejaculum, which is in the form of a sperm packet, into her genital opening. Springtails and silverfish mate in this primitive and awkward way.

In what ways are **insect penises** modified?

Modifications are important factors in the competition between males to fertilize a female's eggs. The penis of some insects has recurved spines that prevent it from slipping out of the vagina when a competing male tries to forcefully dislodge a copulating male. The "race to the ovaries" has resulted in the evolution of some extraordinary penile modifications as males compete to fertilize a female's eggs. Some insects have a very long penis, sometimes as long as the body, that can thread its way into the female's genital tract to reach her spermatheca or even her ovaries. A bed bug's penis is enclosed in a sword-like sheath that penetrates his mate's body wall so that he can inject his sperm into the blood in her abdominal cavity. The sperm then swim to her ovaries. There is little doubt that this bizarre sexual practice, known as traumatic insemination, evolved as males tried to beat out other males by finding a shortcut to the ovaries.

HOW NOT TO BE EATEN BY YOUR MATE

Do carnivorous females **eat their mates**?

Sometimes they do. The female has no more use for the male after she has gained possession of his sperm. She already has him in her grasp, and she might as well eat him. After all, food is hard to come by, and she needs nourishment to develop her eggs. Some males more or less willingly sacrifice themselves. If there is but little chance of finding a second female to inseminate, the male can do no more to increase his fitness than nourishing the mother of his offspring with his body and thereby improving the odds that she will survive to lay the eggs that will be fertilized by his sperm. The males of other species do their best to avoid being eaten by their mates, since there is a good chance that they will be able to inseminate more than one female and thereby increase their fitness.

How do male dance flies keep from being **cannibalized by their carnivorous mates**?

They offer them a substitute meal. The males of some species do not feed their mates and are sometimes eaten by them. The courting males of other species offer their mates a nuptial gift of food, a freshly-killed insect that may be as large as the male himself. The female sucks the juices from his nuptial gift as she copulates with him, but she will continue to copulate only until she has sucked her nuptial meal dry.

Are the **nuptial gifts** of all dance flies real food?

In some species, often called balloon flies, the presentation of the nuptial gift has become a ritual in which the courting male offers his mate nothing more than a symbol of a meal: a large, empty, silken balloon that he spins before he approaches her. She neither eats the balloon nor uses it in any other way, but she accepts it and does not eat her mate. Different species of dance flies show different degrees of this ritualization, which may represent evolutionary steps that led to the replacement of a real meal by an empty balloon. The first evolutionary stage begins with species that wrap a few threads around a nuptial gift of the usual size. In the next step, the male attaches

Is there an element of conflict in a courtship?

There very often is. Both individuals are likely to be ambivalent—feeling a desire to flee at the same time that they want to proceed. A male defending a territory is ambivalent as he watches an approaching individual. Is it a willing female, or is it a male who may try to take over his territory? A male approaching a carnivorous female hopes that she will mate with him but may also fear that she will eat him. One of the functions of a courtship ritual is to mitigate such conflicts.

a small balloon to a large, fresh insect that the female will eat. In the next to the last step, the female receives a much larger balloon to which is attached a small and often dry insect that she won't even try to eat. The final step is, as you already know, the presentation of a large, empty balloon that is only the symbol of a real meal. Why the female is willing to accept this useless symbol remains a mystery.

Do nuptial gifts serve some **purpose other than placating a hungry mate**?

A male's edible nuptial gift will nourish his mate and may thus increase his evolutionary fitness by helping her to produce and lay the eggs that will be fertilized by his sperm. Nuptial gifts are of several forms. They may be an item of prey that the male catches and delivers to the female, or they may be a nourishing substance produced by his body.

Do male **hangingflies** feed their mates?

Yes. They can entice a female to mate only if they offer her a nuptial gift of food, a fresh insect that they catch with their raptorial hind tarsi as they hang from a low plant by their front legs. If they catch a small insect, they will most likely eat it themselves. If they catch a large one, they will usually save it and release a sex pheromone that will attract a female. It behooves the male to offer his mate a large insect. She will continue to copulate with him only as long as the meal lasts. If the nuptial gift is a small insect, she will probably eat and run before the male has inserted his sperm into her body. Female hangingflies seldom hunt. They mate often and get most of their meals from their sex partners.

What **nuptial gift** do male scorpionflies offer to females?

A special nutritious secretion from his exceptionally large salivary glands. Males of the genus *Panorpa* obtain the wherewithal to produce this secretion by eating dead insects, the usual food of their species, which they sometimes steal from spider webs. They secrete a large blob of this salivary substance onto a surface and guard it against other males as they release a sex attractant pheromone to attract females. Receptive females eat this nuptial gift and mate with the male. Some males may offer an alternative gift of dead insects. After securing some dead insects, the male scorpion flies guard them against competing males as they release their sex attractant pheromone.

Does **rape** occur among insects?

It appears that it does. Sometimes male scorpionflies dispense with nuptial gifts and go in search of a female that they will force to copulate. The male rushes toward the female and grabs a wing or a leg with the large and powerful genital forceps at the end of his abdomen. After he forces the female into a position that suits him, he tries to make genital contact with her. An occasional male manages to clutch a female's genitalia with his own and inseminate her.

Does a male's genital tract produce **nutrients for females**?

Some males, among them certain beetles, butterflies, crickets, grasshoppers, and katydids, form spermatophores (sperm packets) that contain nutrients that females can eat or absorb through their genital tract. Hungry female crickets survive longer if they receive spermatophores from males. Laboratory studies showed that the very same protein molecules that a male grasshopper provides in his spermatophore are incorporated in the female's developing eggs within 72 hours. The females of some insect species prefer to mate with large males that produce large spermatophores.

ENSURING FIDELITY

How often do cecropia moths mate?

Some female insects will mate many times, but a cecropia female will mate only once in her lifetime. Once she has acquired a load of sperm, she will live for only four or five days and has no time to waste on superfluous sex. Her evolutionary fitness is measured by how many surviving progeny she leaves behind to pass her genes on to future generations. The best thing that she can do to enhance her fitness is to bestow what little care she can on her eggs, to distribute them over a wide area, and to fasten them to the leaves of plants that will be suitable food for the caterpillars that will soon hatch from them. Male animals, on the other hand, can increase their

How does a male prevent other males from inseminating his mate?

There are several ways in which males ensure the fidelity of their mates. Some take her to a concealed place where other males are not likely to find them. Another option is to guard her and chase off intruding males. Some species fit their mates with a "chastity belt" by inserting a mating plug in the vagina or sealing it shut. The same end may be accomplished biochemically, by injecting into her genital tract, along with his semen, a pheromone that turns off her desire to mate. Yet another tactic is to apply to the outside of her body a substance, known as an antiaphrodisiac, that masks or otherwise nullifies the effectiveness of her sex attractant pheromone.

fitness in two ways: by giving their offspring parental care or by maximizing the number of offspring that they father. Cecropia males and many other male animals give no parental care but are sexually promiscuous, trying to inseminate as many females as possible.

How can a female insect's **desire to mate be turned off**?

It is obviously turned off by mating with a male, but exactly how this is accomplished differs among species. In some, the female is turned off by the mere physical presence of a sperm packet in her body. It does not matter if the packet contains sperm; some female cockroaches can be turned off by inserting glass beads into their genital tract in lieu of a sperm packet. In some insects, cecropia, for example, sperm must be present. The sexual behavior of a female cecropia that mates with a castrated male is not turned off since castrated males' sperm packets contain no sperm.

What is **matrone**?

This is the name the late George B. Craig Jr. gave to a pheromone that turns off a female mosquito's desire to mate: that, in other words, keeps her matronly. The male yellow fever mosquito, as well as some other mosquitoes, passes matrone into the female's genitalia along with his semen. Craig's elegant experiments demonstrated the effect of matrone and showed that it is secreted by the male's accessory glands. He dissected accessory glands from males and implanted them in the bodies of living, virgin females. The females survived but refused to mate even though they were virgins. They behaved as if they had already been inseminated. On the other hand, females that he implanted with nonglandular tissue from a male willingly mated.

What is an **antiaphrodisiac**?

It is a scent that some male insects daub on their mates to make them less attractive to other males. The sexual behavior of mealworm beetles provides an interesting example of the use of an antiaphrodisiac. Females secrete a sex attractant pheromone that calls in males from a distance. They continue to release this pheromone even after they have been inseminated. But a male that has inseminated a female applies to her body an antiaphrodisiac pheromone that makes her sex pheromone much less attractive to males.

How do male **stick insects** guard their mates?

Some male stick insects, or walkingsticks, keep their mate from being inseminated by other males by staying coupled with her until long after they have passed their sperm into her genital tract. They are living "chastity belts." The record for prolonged copulation by insects, 79 days, is apparently held by a pair of walkingsticks.

How do male **dragonflies and damselflies** guard their mates?

After inseminating her, the male holds on to his mate for the rest of that day as she flies from place to place distributing her eggs. He may even guide her to a good place to lay them, such as an aquatic plant that protrudes above the surface of the water. He releases her at nightfall, but the eggs that she laid on that day were fertilized by his sperm. The male uses the genital claspers at the tip of his abdomen to hold his mate by the back of her neck, establishing his hold on her even before he starts to copulate with her. But how does he copulate while his genitalia are otherwise occupied? The answer is that he has a secondary penis and some accompanying structures at the base of his long, thin abdomen. His claspers and genital opening are at its tip. When a male prepares to copulate, he loops his flexible abdomen down and forward to charge his copulatory organ with sperm from his genital opening. Copulation is accomplished when the female, all the while being held by her neck, loops her abdomen forward so that her vagina can be entered by the secondary penis at the base of her mate's abdomen. After she has been inseminated, she uncouples her genitalia and the pair fly off in tandem as the male continues to hold her by the neck.

What is a **mating plug**?

Some males plug or somehow seal their mate's vagina so that she cannot receive sperm from other males. In a few species, the plug is a part of his genitalia that he leaves behind in the female's vagina as a suicidal finale to mating. In other species, the female is plugged in a less drastic way. The male deposits a secretion that blocks his mate's vagina internally or applies a secretion that will seal her vagina shut from the outside.

How does a **drone honey bee** plug his mate's vagina?

Male honey bees sacrifice their intromittent organ to plug their mate's vagina. After he has inseminated her, the male's genitalia tear loose and remain behind in her vagina. Although she can eventually remove it, this plug does tend to restrict the number of males that will inseminate her and will thus limit the number of competing sperm that will be present in her spermatheca. The male dies soon after mating. His sacrifice seems great, but his loss is probably outweighed by his gain even though it is small. There would have been only a minuscule chance of his mating with another queen, since drones outnumber queens by a factor of hundreds to one.

Grasshoppers mating. (Photo by Edward S. Ross.)

How does a male **migratory locust** plug a female's vagina?

He inserts into her genital tract a packet of sperm, a spermatophore, that doubles as a mating plug. The spermatophore, which is thin and over three-quarters of an inch long, fills her spermatheca and thus makes it impossible for another male to inseminate her until the spermatophore dissolves on the fourth day. By then the first male's sperm will probably have fertilized all or most of her eggs.

How do **mealworm beetles** use an antiaphrodisiac?

Among the insects that secrete antiaphrodisiacs are male mealworm beetles. Mealworm larvae, sold by pet shops as food for birds and lizards, are familiar to many. The female beetle releases an attractant pheromone to which males orient from a distance. But the first male to mate with a female tries to keep other males away from her by daubing her body with an antiaphrodisiac pheromone. An extract of a female's body, which presumably contains her sex attractant pheromone, is highly attractive to males, but becomes much less attractive after it is mixed with an extract of a male's body, which presumably contains the antiaphrodisiac.

Can males **interfere with the sperm of a previous male**?

Yes, they can. Generally speaking, the last sperm to go into a female's spermatheca are the first that will come out to fertilize eggs, a phenomenon known as sperm precedence. Some male insects use their penis to shove a previous male's sperm to the back of the spermatheca, thereby making more room for their own sperm and making it possible to place them near the opening through which sperm pass on their way to fertilizing an egg. The penis of some insects is specially modified for this function. That of a male dragonfly, for example, ends in two inflatable structures that appear to fit into the paired spermathecae of the female, and that are probably used to push the sperm of a previous male deeper into the spermathecae.

How do **male damselflies** deal with a previous male's sperm?

Some have a specialized penis that can, in addition to ejaculating in the female, remove and discard a previous male's sperm from her spermatheca.

CARING FOR OFFSPRING

Do insects **care for their young**?

There is a spectrum of parental care. At one end are insects that give their offspring no parental care, such as mayflies that simply spew their eggs into the water and walkingsticks that let their eggs fall from a tree to the ground below. At the other end of the spectrum are social insects, such as termites, ants, some wasps, and some bees, that care for their young from hatching to maturity. The insects between these extremes all give some parental care, ranging from many that do no more than deposit their eggs in a favorable place and then abandon them, to some that give their young nearly as much care as do the social insects.

Why give **parental care**?

Giving parental care will probably enhance the parents' evolutionary fitness. In other words, improving the survival rate of their progeny increases the probability that their genes will survive in future generations. Organisms, both plants and animals, can increase the odds that they will leave behind descendants in two ways: by producing a great many offspring, to whom they give no care, in the hope that a few of them will survive, or by producing fewer offspring and helping them to survive by caring for them. Oysters epitomize the former strategy. A single female may release into the sea from 16 to 60 million eggs in one season. Birds and mammals, all of which produce relatively few young but give them elaborate care, epitomize the second strategy. Among the insects, mayflies, blister beetles, and others lay many eggs and give them no care. Wasps of the family Trigonalidae, parasites of caterpillars, scatter and abandon about 10,000 eggs on the leaves of various plants. A parasitic trigonalid larva can survive only if it is inadvertently swallowed by a leaf-eating caterpillar when it is still an egg. A surprising number of insects give their young some form of care. The most

Egg-laying tick. (Photo by Edward S. Ross.)

rudimentary consists of laying the eggs at a place and time suitable for the development and survival of the young. This simple form of care is almost universal among the insects. A few insects, scattered among several orders, give their young care comparable to the care that birds and mammals lavish on their offspring.

What provision do bee flies make **for their larvae**?

The larvae of many of the bee flies are parasites that live in the nests of solitary bees. The mother gives her larval offspring a small but significant head start in life by placing her eggs within small holes in the ground that may be—but are not necessarily—entrances to the subterranean nests of solitary bees. As she hovers in front of such a hole, she hurls her eggs into it by repeated downward and forward flicks of her abdomen.

What provision do **moths and butterflies** make for their young?

Generally speaking, they lay their eggs on plants that their caterpillar larvae are adapted to eat. The great majority of caterpillars feed on plants, most often on the leaves. In common with some true bugs, beetles, and other insects, many moths and butterflies are host specific. That is, they will feed on only a few closely related plants—perhaps some members of a single plant family or, more narrowly, only members of one genus. Host specific insects are so bound to their own particular host plants that they

How do grasshoppers protect their eggs?

They lay them well beneath the surface of the soil, where they lie hidden—in most species throughout the winter—and are at least somewhat protected from parasites, predators, and the elements. The short, stout ovipositor of the female scoops its way down into the soil until her abdomen has stretched to its maximum length—in the migratory locust to a depth of as much as five inches. Then she lays about twenty eggs, covering them with a secretion that will harden and bind them together.

will usually refuse to eat anything else. Tobacco hornworm caterpillars, for example, will starve rather than eat the leaves of a plant other than tobacco, tomato, or some other member of the nightshade family. The adult females behave accordingly. They lay their eggs only on plants of the nightshade family. In captivity, gravid (pregnant) females readily lay eggs on plants of this family, but will die without laying even one egg if they are caged with nothing but a plant from some other family.

How do some moths **use stinging hairs** to protect their eggs?

A few caterpillars are clothed with venomous, needle-sharp hairs that can cause a severe irritation if they break off in a person's skin or in the skin lining of the mouth of a bird or some other predator. Adult female moths do not grow venomous hairs but salvage stinging hairs from the larval skins she's cast off, entangling them in a tuft of nonstinging hairs at the tip of the abdomen. The female covers her egg mass with these stinging hairs.

Do some insect eggs have their own **built-in protection**?

Some do. They may be camouflaged so that they blend in with the habitat and thus escape the notice of predators. But a giant silk moth of Mexico lays conspicuous eggs that are marked with a round black spot that looks like the emergence hole of a parasite. Foraging birds may not even attempt to eat these eggs because they know from experience that eggs with emergence holes have already been emptied by parasites.

How do **fruit flies** protect their eggs?

The fruit fly known as the apple maggot protects her eggs from parasites, predators, and desiccation by thrusting them deep into an apple with her sharp, piercing ovipositor. There the maggots feed until they are full grown and drop to the ground to pupate. She also protects them against competition from other apple maggots for the

Female stink bugs guarding empty eggs. (Photo by Edward S. Ross.)

limited supply of food by smearing a deterrent pheromone onto the surface of the fruit in the area where she places her eggs, thereby preventing other females from laying eggs in that area.

Do **stink bugs** care for their eggs?

Quite a few species do. *Antiteuchus tripterus,* a tropical stink bug of the New World, stands over her compact clutch of eggs—much as a hen broods her chicks—as she guards them against parasites and predators such as marauding ants. When an experimenter removed the guarding females from some egg clutches and left the female on other nearby clutches undisturbed, none of the unguarded eggs survived, although half of those that were guarded by their mothers survived to hatch. The eggs that did not survive had been parasitized by tiny wasps that managed to elude the mother's surveillance. Because she is a slave to instinct, she always faces in the same direction as she guards her eggs. She can ward off egg-laying wasps that approach from her front and sides but is not even aware of those that sneak up behind her.

Do any insects **enlist babysitters** of other species?

Certain female treehoppers, members of the order Homoptera, herd their young together and stand watch over them, chasing off ladybird beetles and other predators.

Ants often guard these insects in order to obtain honeydew, the sugary, liquid excrement of treehoppers and many other Homoptera. Some treehoppers will abandon a brood of young to the care of ants in order to raise another brood.

How do **cicada killers** provide for their offspring?

The female cicada killer wasp digs in the soil a branching burrow with cells in which her offspring will live and grow to maturity. She stocks each cell with one or more paralyzed dog-day cicadas, lays a single egg on one of them, and then closes the cell and leaves her offspring to fate. She finds the cicadas in trees that may be as much as a hundred yards from her nest. It seems that she hunts by vision rather than sound, since most of her prey are mute females rather than noisy, singing males. She stings each victim on the underside of its abdomen, injecting a venom that paralyzes it but does not kill it. Thus, the cicadas will not decompose before the larvae can eat them.

How do hunting wasps **find the way back to their nest**?

They memorize landmarks that mark the way home. Niko Tinbergen, the Nobel Prize–winning Dutch ethologist, did a simple but elegant experiment that proved that the European wasp known as the beewolf recognizes the entrance to its burrow in the soil by means of landmarks. He noticed that departing wasps make circling flights around the entrance before flying off to hunt for bees. Could these be "orientation flights" during which the wasps fix landmarks in their minds? To answer this question, Tinbergen put a circle of pine cones, a conspicuous landmark, around an entrance hole while the wasp was in her burrow. When she came out, her orientation flight lasted longer than usual. Tinbergen let the wasp make several trips back and forth from her nest. When he judged that she had become accustomed to the circle of pine cones, he moved them several feet to one side of the nest entrance while she was off hunting. When she returned she went directly to the center of the circle of pine cones rather than to the nest entrance. The wasp was obviously using the circle of pine cones as a landmark.

What provision do **dung beetles** make for their offspring?

The most widely known of the dung-feeding beetles, relatives of the June beetles, is the sacred scarab of ancient Egypt, which feeds on the dung of cattle and related animals. When she is ready to lay eggs, the female forms a large, spherical ball of dung with her legs and rolls it to a place where the soil is suitable for digging. She then digs a shallow burrow into which she rolls the dung ball. After laying a single egg on the ball, she seals the burrow and leaves. The larva eats the dung, pupates in the burrow, and ultimately emerges from the earth as a full-grown beetle.

Sacred scarab beetle with dung ball. (Photo by Edward S. Ross.)

What makes those big **circular holes** in the **leaves of redbuds and roses**?

They are made by solitary leaf-cutter bees that use them to line their brood chambers. The bees remove large pieces from the edges of leaves, circular ones about the size of a dime and oblong ones that are about as wide but twice as long, and they use them to build thimble-shaped cells in holes that they find or dig in the soil or wood. They form the bottom and sides of the cell from oblong pieces, fill this cell with a paste of pollen and honey, lay a single egg in the cell, and then cap the cell with a circular piece of leaf. Several such cells may be placed end to end in one burrow. The bee pays no further attention to a cell after she has capped it.

How do **giant water bugs** care for their eggs?

They carry them on their backs until they hatch. But in these insects the sex roles are reversed. Immediately after a pair copulates, the female glues her eggs to her mate's back—so many of them that they almost cover his wings. She then swims off to look for another male. About 97 percent of the eggs hatch if they remain attached to their father, but all of them are killed by a fungus if they are removed or left attached to a dead male. The male is obviously essential to the survival of the eggs, but how does he protect them from the fungus? In some species, the male stays near the surface of the water, occasionally exposing the eggs to the air. An experiment showed that exposing the eggs to air has a beneficial effect. Eggs that had been removed from a male but kept in shallow water and sometimes exposed to the air were not as likely to be killed by the fungus as were eggs that had been kept completely submerged. Exposure to air saved about 20 percent of the eggs. The males further increase the survival rate of the eggs—to over 90 percent—by frequently stroking them with their hind legs, a maneuver that presumably cleans them and prevents the growth of the fungus.

INSECT BEHAVIOR

Why is it difficult for people to **comprehend the behavior of insects**?

Because, to oversimplify a little, insects and people view the world through different senses. Compared to insects and many other animals, the chemical senses, taste and smell, are not well developed in humans. We rely mainly on our senses of vision and hearing. Insects, on the other hand, do not have acute vision, and are often deaf. They rely mainly on their chemical senses. For example, while people mark trails with visual signs, perhaps by blazing a tree, ants mark their trails with chemical signs, "blazes" of pheromones that they deposit on the soil or even on your kitchen floor. It is these differences that make it difficult for humans to understand the behavior of insects. We cannot, for example, smell the chemical blazes with which ants mark their trails. We can perceive them only by means of the techniques of analytical chemistry.

Do insects feel **pain or experience pleasure**?

No one knows, and it may never be possible to know. Pain and pleasure are human feelings that can't, strictly speaking, be ascribed to other animals. You can't even be sure that your dog, a fellow mammal and a reasonably close relative of humans, feels pleasure in the human sense when you scratch its belly. Insects are so very different from us that it is difficult for us to conceive of their feeling pain or experiencing pleasure. But consider this: insects will repeatedly return to a source of food, and they can learn to avoid electric shocks and other unpleasant stimuli. When a honey bee sips sweet nectar from a flower, does it not experience a feeling that tells it to come back and do that again? Is that feeling the insect's equivalent of pleasure? When an insect is shocked, does it not experience a feeling that tells it to move away and not come back? Is that feeling the insect's equivalent of pain?

Soldier carpenter ant preening antennae. (Photo by Edward S. Ross.)

What is **ethology**?

Ethology, the biological approach to the study of animal behavior, focuses on observation and experimentation on animals in nature, where they are exposed to the other animals and plants of their natural habitat and where they can exhibit, unimpeded, their entire repertoire of behaviors. This contrasts with the usual, largely laboratory oriented, approach of psychology, the other major discipline that seeks to analyze and understand the behavior of animals. As the late Kenneth D. Roeder, who focused his research on insect behavior, put it, the psychologist puts the animal in an uncomfortable cage and observes it from the comfort of his laboratory, while the ethologist confines himself in an uncomfortable "cage," a blind, and observes the animal as it lives its life in the comfort of its natural habitat.

Is there such a thing as **fossilized insect behavior**?

As Robert and Janice Matthews wrote, "behavior does not fossilize well." Nevertheless, there are a few fossils—all of them the *products* of behaviors—that give us glimpses of what insects did millions of years ago. There are fossils of the serpentine mines that caterpillars excavated as they ate their way between the upper and lower epidermal layers of a leaf. Ancient fossilized dung balls made by scarab beetles have been found, dung balls that are similar to those that modern scarabs still form and bury in the soil with one of their eggs. A fossilized nest of weaver ants found in Africa shows that 60 million years ago these ants had already evolved the behavior of fastening leaves together to form a nest.

What is **habituation**?

Habituation is the simplest form of learning and the one that is most often seen in insects. It consists of learning to ignore or become less responsive to a stimulus that it repeatedly experiences. The workers in an ant colony, for example, will attack a glass rod poked into the nest. If this disturbance is repeated frequently, the ants gradually become less responsive. Many insects, praying mantises among them, become habituated to frequent handling and can thus be "tamed."

Are insects capable of learning?

Learning is defined as the ability of an animal to modify its behavior in response to its experiences. Most insects are capable of some form of learning—most often only the simplest form of learning but sometimes more complicated forms. Nevertheless, learned behavior is only a tiny part of an insect's total behavioral repertoire; most of its behaviors are largely instinctive, determined and guided by its genes.

What is **imprinting** ?

Imprinting is a form of learning that proceeds rapidly, that is usually irreversible, and that occurs only or almost only during a particular "sensitive period" of an animal's life. The newly hatched goslings that imprinted on Konrad Lorenz, the great German ethologist, and accepted him as their parent constitute a well-known example. Insects also learn by imprinting. Ants that have just emerged from the pupa quickly learn to recognize the characteristic odor of their own colony. Newly hatched tobacco hornworm caterpillars will feed on many plants of the nightshade family, among them tobacco, tomato, petunia, and nightshade. But they imprint on the first of these plants that they are offered and will thereafter prefer it to other plants of the nightshade family.

Are insects capable of learning that is more **complex than habituation** ?

Some species certainly are. A honey bee can remember the location of a patch of flowers and return to it time after time to collect pollen and nectar. Wasps that go far afield to hunt for the insects they feed to their larvae memorize landmarks that guide them on the return trip to their nest. A praying mantis can learn not to strike at an object that gives it an electric shock. Captive dragonfly nymphs in an aquarium learn to associate food with the appearance of the person who feeds them.

How long can insects **remember things** ?

Many insects have short-term memories. Hunting wasps can remember the landmarks that lead them back to their nests for hours. *Heliconius* butterflies return to the same sleeping site night after night for several months. Obviously, they can remember the location of the site from one evening to the next. Some social insects, notably honey bees, have longer memories. Honey bees regularly remember the location of a place where they found food, sometimes up to eight days. On one occasion it was apparent that honey bees remembered a feeding site for two months. After two

Do insects sleep?

As best as anyone can tell, they do sleep. At any rate, some insects are totally inactive for long periods of time, a state that some biologists refer to as *akinesis,* which translates from Greek as the absence of movement—in other words, inactivity. Generally speaking, diurnal insects sleep at night, and nocturnal insects sleep during the day. Some insects sleep alone, and some, even species that are loners during the day, form sleeping aggregations at night. Most of the insects that form sleeping aggregations can sting or are otherwise noxious to insect-eating creatures. The stinging, shiny-blue, spider-hunting wasp known as *Chalybion* is solitary during the day but at night forms sleeping aggregations that may include a hundred or more individuals. An individual may benefit by joining an aggregation. If a lone individual is found by a predator, it is almost certain to be attacked and may be injured or even killed as it tries to defend itself. But an individual that is "lost in the crowd" in a sleeping aggregation may not be the one that the predator attacks, and the predator is likely to be dissuaded from making further attacks on the aggregation if it is stung by even one individual or if it is made ill by eating one.

months of winter confinement, these bees used the waggle dance to communicate the location of a food source they had been exploiting just before their confinement began.

How can we tell if a behavior is **genetically programmed** ?

The "deprivation experiment," often used by ethologists, is one way to demonstrate that a behavior is genetically controlled. For example, some hand-raised birds that have been deprived of even a glimpse of a nest are capable of building nests that are much like the nests built by other members of their species. A cecropia caterpillar spins a complex silken cocoon that is typical of its species even though it has never before seen a cocoon. The information necessary for constructing the nest or the cocoon was obviously not learned—in other words, it did not come from the animal's environment. The necessary information must, then, have been contained within the body of the nest builder or cocoon spinner, within its genes. Molecular biologists have now isolated some of the genes—functional segments of the DNA molecule—that control certain behaviors. Among them is the gene that enables fruit flies to maintain their daily rhythm of activity and inactivity. There is no doubt that this gene controls this rhythm; if the gene is changed by a mutation, the nature of the rhythm is changed.

How do insects control their body temperature?

Insects are generally considered to be poikilothermic (cold-blooded), unable to control their body temperature, but this is not strictly true. Homoiothermic (warm-blooded) animals like birds and mammals, have internal physiological mechanisms for controlling body temperature. Insects have behavioral mechanisms for accomplishing the same end. They may warm themselves by basking in the sun and cool themselves by staying in the shade. Some insects, among them the hummingbird-like sphinx moths, warm themselves by increasing muscular activity. Although sphinx moths cannot fly unless their body temperature is between 95 degrees Fahrenheit and 100 degrees Fahrenheit, they can fly when the air temperature is as low as 50 degrees Fahrenheit. A pre-flight warm-up raises their bodies to the requisite temperature as their wing muscles generate heat by vigorously vibrating the wings. This is not unlike the shivering of the body that people experience when they are chilled.

Do insects **use tools** ?

The use of tools is extremely rare among insects. Only three species are known to exhibit this behavior. *Conomyrma,* a desert ant found in Arizona, uses small pebbles as weapons, dropping them down the nest entrances of other species of ants that compete with them for food resources. This assault nearly puts a halt to the foraging activity of the competing ants. A wasp of the genus *Ammophila* uses a pebble held in its mandibles to tamp down the soil around the entrance to its burrow. Weaver ants use living larvae from their own colonies as tools. These ants build nests by using silk to sew together living leaves on a tree. The adult ants cannot secrete silk, but the larvae can. Adults hold silk-extruding larvae in their mandibles as they use them to fasten leaves together.

Do insects perceive **magnetic fields**?

A few insects are known to have the ability to perceive the earth's magnetic field, and it seems likely that this sense is widespread among insects and other animals as well. By sensing the earth's magnetic field an insect can determine directions as does a magnetic compass. A compass is obviously an aid to navigation and to other behaviors that depend upon a sense of direction. Convincing evidence for the existence of a magnetic sense in insects came from a study of how honey bees orient their hanging combs so that they are parallel to each other. In a beekeeper's hive, the orientation of the combs is determined by the parallel placement of the frames in which the bees build their combs. But when a swarm of bees sets up housekeeping in a hollow tree or some other natural site, they have to determine the orientation of the combs for themselves. When an experimenter moved bees from a beekeeper's hive to an empty cylinder with an entrance hole centered in its bottom, the bees built neatly parallel combs whose directional orientation corresponded exactly to the orientation of the combs in the hive that the bees had been taken from. But when a powerful magnet was placed outside of the cylinder, the same bees built combs whose orientation differed by 40 degrees from that of the combs they had previously built, the exact angle by which the magnet deflected the magnetic field.

EATING

How do insects respond to **hunger**?

Not surprisingly, hungry insects behave differently from insects that have recently fed. Hungry insects do things that will increase the probability of finding food. They are likely to move about more than well-fed individuals and to be more sensitive to stimuli, especially stimuli that are associated with food. The behavioral response to hunger differs from species to species. Caterpillars deprived of food wander incessantly. The tendency for migratory locusts to move upwind in response to the odor of food, grass in this case, increases as the duration of their separation from food lengthens. Cutworm caterpillars, which come out to feed on plants at night and hide in the soil during the day, are usually photonegative, that is, they move away from light. But when they are hungry they become less photonegative and are, therefore, more likely to search for food during the day.

What do insects **eat**?

Taken as a group, insects eat virtually everything organic. Well over half of the known insects feed on plants. They will eat roots, stems, wood, blossoms, pollen, nectar, seeds, the fleshy parts of fruits, and leaves. Many insect are predators that capture and eat insects, other arthropods, and even small vertebrates. At least 115,000 species of insects, about 13 percent of the known species, are parasites that live within or on the bodies of insects or other arthropods. Some insects are parasites that live in or on the bodies of vertebrates. Lice live among the feathers of birds or the hair of mammals; some suck blood and others eat feathers or dander. The maggots of certain flies live within the bodies of mammals and other vertebrates. The blood of vertebrates is food for piercing-sucking insects such as fleas, bed bugs, mosquitoes, black flies, and horse flies. Insects are among the most important of the scavengers that eat dead plants and animals. Fly maggots, burying beetles, hide beetles, and clothes moths consume the flesh, hair, hide, and other parts of the carcasses of dead birds, mammals, and other animals. Many insects eat dead plant material; among them are beetles, maggots, a cockroach that consumes the wood of fallen trees, and a variety of insects that eat fallen leaves, fruits, and other plant debris. Maggots and various kinds of beetles, especially scarabs, eat the droppings of elephants, zebras, cows, and most other vertebrates.

A horse fly finds a meal. (Photo by Edward S. Ross.)

What do mosquitoes of the **genus *Harpagomyia*** eat?

These mosquitoes of Africa and Asia steal food from ants, as described by C. O. Farquharson:

> You know how worker ants stop each other and exchange a little regurgitated food, a momentary transaction almost, both passing quickly on their way. The mosquitoes do exactly the same. They will drop downwards just over an ant that is hastening along in the usual way. The ant may stop and give an alms to the beggar, passing on a moment or two later as if it had just met a friend, and the mosquito flies up and down again till another obliging ant is met.

How do mosquitoes **locate their victims**?

Locating a bird or mammal from which to suck blood is a problem that only female mosquitoes face. Male mosquitoes do not take blood meals; they eat only plant fluids such as nectar. Mosquitoes in search of a blood meal locate their victims by responding to a sequence of cues that they recognize innately. The sequence begins when a searching female notices and then flies to a large, dark object that contrasts with the background. It might be an animal, but it could also be something else. She just moves on if the object does not emit additional cues that identify it as a living animal. If it gives off heat, as do the warm-blooded birds and mammals, she will land on it. If it also gives off carbon dioxide, as do all animals, she will not immediately leave, and if its smell and taste suit her, she will insert her piercing-sucking mouthparts and suck its blood.

Are **plant-feeding insects** indiscriminate in their choice of plants?

Some are but many are not. No known insect will feed on all the different kinds of plants that are available to it. But there are insects that are more or less indiscriminate feeders, such as cutworm caterpillars that will feed on almost any non-woody plant, and adult Japanese beetles, which are known to feed on about 350 different species of taxonomically unrelated plants, including both woody and herbaceous species. Many insects are said to be "host specific," that is, they feed on only a few closely related members of one family of plants. Caterpillars of the monarch butterfly feed only on plants of the milkweed family. The silkworm of commerce will eat the leaves of only a handful of plants of the mulberry family. A few species of beans, among them garden beans and soybeans, are the only food plants of the Mexican bean beetle.

Why have some insects been **compared to botanists**?

Plant-feeding species whose menus include only plants that belong to the same family or genus have been referred to as the botanical taxonomists of the insect realm because they can distinguish between the plants of their chosen family or genus and all other plants. They have, in other words, an innate "botanical sense" by which they can recognize plants as being closely related. Human plant taxonomists acquire this ability only through extensive training in botany.

How do insects **recognize their food plants**?

An insect recognizes the plants that it is willing to eat by means of its chemical senses: smell and taste. Related plants, generally speaking, have similar and distinctive odors and flavors. For example, caterpillars of the cabbage white butterfly, which primarily feed on kale, cabbage, broccoli, turnips, and other members of the mustard family, recognize these plants by the flavor of the mustard-oil glucosides that they all contain. (Interestingly, they'll also eat two plants that are not in the mustard family, nasturtium and spider plant, because these plants also contain mustard-oil glucosides.) The many different odors and flavors of plants are caused by the non-nutritive secondary substances that they contain. Unlike primary substances that all plants need to survive (such as proteins, carbohydrates, vitamins, and minerals), secondary substances are not necessary for a plant's survival. But if plants contained only the primary substances, they would all taste pretty much the same. Of the thousands of different secondary plant substances, only a tiny fraction of them occur in any one plant species. Related plants often contain the same or similar secondary substances, they have similar flavors and odors. By distingusihing between these flavors and odors, insects (and humans, too) identify what they're willing to eat.

Do insects steal food from other insects?

Animals that steal food from other animals are known as kleptoparasites. The most widely known of the kleptoparasites are the jaegers, marine birds that harass gulls to get them to drop or disgorge food. Only a few insects are kleptoparasitic. Among them are the death's head moths that sneak into the nests of honey bees at night to steal honey, and scorpionflies that steal insects that are trapped in the silken webs of spiders. The scorpionflies are adept at walking on a web without getting entangled, but if they do get trapped in the sticky web, they free themselves by regurgitating a fluid that dissolves the silk that entangles them.

Can **leaf-feeding insects** be tricked into eating paper?

A Canadian entomologist did just that. He found that the cabbage-eating diamond back moth caterpillar and other insects that specialize on eating plants of the mustard family will try to eat filter paper that has been coated with mustard oil glucosides, the nonnutritive substances that give cabbage and the other plants of the mustard family their distinctive flavor and odor.

REFLEXES

What is a **reflex**?

It is an involuntary and instinctive response to a stimulus. An example familiar to people is the instantaneous withdrawal of the hand when it touches something painfully hot. Another example is the righting reflex, which beetles and other insects exhibit when they are turned over on their backs.

What is the **tarsal reflex**?

If a winged insect's tarsi (feet) lose contact with a surface, it immediately begins to fly by reflex. This has been demonstrated with winged insects, like adult cockroaches or flies. One end of thin string is attached to the upper side of its thorax. If the insect sits on a smooth surface and is then pulled up by the string, it will begin to fly as soon as its tarsi lose contact with the surface. It will continue to fly as long as it remains suspended. It will stop when lowered back to the surface or allowed to grasp something with its tarsi.

How do dragonflies maintain their **equilibrium in flight**?

When a dragonfly in flight begins to tilt to one side or the other, its head, which can swing from side to side like a pendulum, tilts slightly in the direction of the roll. Hair-like sensors on the neck perceive this tilt and translate it into the direction and degree of the roll. The dragonfly rights itself with compensating changes in the beat and the angle of attack of its wings. It "knows" that it is once again in equilibrium when the head hangs vertically, not tilting to either side.

Are **reflexes involved in feeding** by insects?

The extension of the sucking proboscis in response to the taste of sugar is a reflex that has been observed in the honey bee, several flies, and various moths and butterflies. All of these insects have organs of taste on their feet (tarsi), and if their feet touch something sweet, they extend the proboscis by reflex. You can demonstrate this reflex to yourself by holding a butterfly by its wings and touching its front tarsi to a piece of paper tower that is wet with a solution of sugar and water. The butterfly's long proboscis, the "soda straw" that it uses to suck up nectar, will immediately uncoil from beneath the head and extend forward.

ARCHITECTS

Are insects good **architects**?

Some of them certainly are. A few examples will make the point. Bald-faced hornets make their own paper and use it to build large, football-shaped aerial nests that consist of a tier of combs surrounded by an outer covering. Female potter wasps build little pot-shaped nests of tiny pellets of clay or mud that they collect from the soil and carry to the nest site one at a time. Cecropia caterpillars spin intricate silken cocoons in which they spend the winter. The cocoon consists of an inner envelope suspended within a tough outer envelope by a loose mesh of threads. A valve at one end of the cocoon allows the moth to emerge in spring. Antlions excavate a conical pit in the soil, a pitfall that traps unwary crawling insects. The aquatic larvae of some caddisflies live in portable shelters that they build of tiny pebbles, sand grains, or bits of thin plant stems. Depending upon the species, the shelters may be tube-like, conical, or have the spiral shape of a snail shell.

Which insects are the **best architects**?

The termites win hands down! Although termites of the north temperate zone are relatively modest builders, some tropical species build truly imposing structures that

Antlion pits awaiting unwary insects. (Photo by Edward S. Ross.)

may house a population of over a million. The nests of some species consist of chambers excavated in the soil and topped by mounds or variously shaped towers that may rise as much as 27 feet above the ground. These towers are marvels of insect engineering that, at least in some species, regulate the temperature of the nest. The mound of a fungus-growing African termite is an air conditioner. The metabolism of the huge colony and its fungus gardens heats the air in the core of the nest. The hot air rises by convection to a chamber above the core of the nest and then passes into a network of chambers adjacent to the wall of the mound. After the air is cooled by its passage through these outer chambers, it sinks downward to a large chamber below the occupied core of the nest.

TRAVELLING

How do ants **locate and exploit a source of food**?

New sources of food are located by wandering scouts. On her way back to the nest, the scout marks her route by dabbing the ground with a pheromone. Other workers then follow this odor trail to the source of food. If the source is productive, they reinforce

Why are there so many flying insects around lights at night?

They are not attracted to lights from a distance, as is often said. Flying insects accumulate at artificial lights because they come too close and are trapped there by their own innate navigation system. Night-flying insects, moths for example, use the moon as an aid to navigation. The moon is so far away that its rays are practically parallel to each other when they reach earth. Thus, an insect can keep itself on a straight-line course if it always keeps the rays of the moon at the same angle to its eye. But artificial lights, newly arrived on the evolutionary scene, confound this instinctive behavior because they are so close to the insect that their rays are not parallel but, rather, radiate in all the directions of the compass. An insect trying to fly a straight-line course can keep the rays of the artificial light at a constant angle to its eye only by flying around the light in a spiral pattern, which it repeats time after time.

the odor trail as they make their way back to the nest. This reinforcement is necessary because the pheromone is volatile and soon dissipates. It is a good thing that the pheromone does not persist indefinitely. Otherwise, the ants' territory would be laced with many no longer useful odor trails that lead to places where the supply of food has been exhausted.

How do **scout ants find their way back to the nest** from a newly discovered food source?

The scout does not return by retracing the wandering and convoluted path that she described as she conducted her search. On her return trip to the nest she takes the shortest route, a "beeline" that leads directly to the nest. She manages to do this by using the so-called "sun compass." She knows the direction of the nest with respect to the position of the sun, and finds her way back by moving in a direction that is at the appropriate angle to the direction of the sun.

Has there been an **experimental demonstration of the use of the sun compass** by an insect?

The existence of sun compass orientation has been demonstrated by using mirrors to change the apparent position of the sun and thereby tricking ants to change the direction in which they are moving. When the sunward side of an ant's course is shaded while the sun is reflected by a mirror on the other side of its course, the ant reverses its direction by 180 degrees.

Do insects compensate for the **ever-changing position of the sun**?

At least some insects, including certain ants, do compensate for the changing position of the sun by changing the angle between their straight-line course and the line from their position to the sun. If they did not do so they would not arrive at their intended destination. Early in the morning, a course 20 degrees to the right of the sun goes toward the southeast; early in the afternoon a course 20 degrees to the right of the sun goes toward the southwest. The ability to compensate for changes in the position of the sun implies the ability to tell time, the existence of an biological clock within the insect. The existence of such an internal clock is shown by the fact that insects kept in the dark will continue to follow the same day-night rhythm that they follow when they are kept outdoors. If a diurnal insect becomes active at dusk, say at 8:00 p.m., it will become active at 8:00 p.m. even when it is kept in constant darkness.

How do honey bees use their **internal clocks**?

Like ants and some other insects, they use them as an aid in navigation and to maintain their day-night rhythm. Amazingly enough, they also use their time sense to keep "scheduled appointments." Bees that visited a sugar source that was available only at midmorning and at tea time in the afternoon soon learned this daily routine and showed up only at the correct times. They came searching for the sugar source at the appropriate time even on days when it was not present.

What is **phoresy**?

Phoresy has been likened to hitchhiking. A phoretic insect uses an animal of another species to provide transportation, and although it is an unbidden guest, it does not otherwise parasitize its living conveyance. Among the phoretic insects are certain lice that parasitize birds. Being permanently wingless, the lice have few opportunities to move from one bird to another. They can crawl to a new host only when two birds are in close contact, as when copulating or brooding their young. But some bird lice broaden their horizon by hitching rides on the bodies of hippoboscid flies, louse-like flies that are blood-sucking parasites of birds. Some hippoboscids, also know as louse flies, are wingless, but the ones that carry lice as passengers are winged, fly in search of birds, and are large enough to accommodate several of the little lice.

Do burying beetles **transport phoretic passengers**?

Yes, and they do so willingly. Life would be difficult for them if they didn't. The passengers are tiny mites that clamber onto the bodies of newly metamorphosed burying beetles about to leave the chamber in the soil in which their attentive parents raised them on a diet of carrion. These newly matured beetles form pairs, locate the carcass

Where do monarch butterflies spend the winter?

There are two separate populations of monarchs in North America, one west of the Rocky Mountains and another east of the Rocky Mountains. Western monarchs migrate to the coastal strip of California between Monterey and Los Angeles, where they spend the winter in large aggregations of thousands of individuals clustered on Monterey pines or eucalyptus trees. Eastern monarchs fly to the mountains of the Transverse Neovolcanic Belt west of Mexico City, a journey of over 2,000 miles for individuals from Canada. The migrants congregate in fir forests at twelve known sites at elevations of from about 9,800 feet to about 11,000 feet above sea level. They form astonishingly dense aggregations that are far larger than the winter aggregations in California. At one of the Mexican sites, over 14 million monarchs were crowded into an area of less than 14 acres. The trees at this site looked orange rather than green, because their foliage was all but obscured by roosting monarchs.

of a small animal such as a mouse, bury it in the soil, and raise a family of their own. The mites, which are members of a species found only in association with burying beetles, move from the beetle's body to the carcass. They do not feed on the carrion. Instead, they eat the eggs and newly hatched maggots of carrion flies that arrive at the carcass at about the same time as the burying beetles. The mites serve the beetles well by killing the maggots that would, if unchecked, consume the carcass before the beetles could raise their young.

MIGRATION

Do insects **migrate**?

If migration is defined in a broad sense—as an active mass movement or, as one entomologist put it, "adaptive traveling"—many insects qualify as migrants. Some insects make a one-way migration that, depending upon circumstances and the species involved, may be short range or long range. The most famous of the long range, one-way migrants are several species of migratory locusts of Western Asia and North and East Africa. Great flying swarms of these destructive grasshoppers, which may include many millions of individuals and cover hundreds of square miles, often move cross country for hundreds of miles. Other insect migrants make a return trip, just as do many birds. The most famous of these round-trip migrants is the monarch butterfly of North America.

Do locusts make regular **yearly migrations**?

They do not. They migrate only when they become crowded and food is likely to run short. Migratory locusts occur in two different forms that are anatomically and behaviorally clearly distinct, although they are only phases of the same species. Individuals of the *solitary phase* are relatively short-winged, inconspicuously colored, quite inactive, not in the least gregarious, and choosy about their diet, which includes only grasses. When a locust population becomes crowded, the solitary phase is replaced by the swarm-forming *migratory phase.* Crowded locusts acquire the characteristics of the migratory phase as they mature. They become long-winged, conspicuously colored, extremely active, highly gregarious, and indiscriminate feeders that will eat any green plant. Even as wingless nymphs they form swarms and march cross country. When they are mature and have fully developed wings, they form the vast flying swarms that are so destructive.

What is the **climate** like in the Mexican sites where **monarchs spend the winter**?

Although these sites are in the tropics, they are at such a high elevation that their climate is much like that of the coniferous forests of the northern United States and Canada. In winter it is usually cold, there are often frosts, and it even snows occasionally. But the monarchs are somewhat protected from the weather by the dense stands of trees in which they congregate. It is usually too cold for them to become active and use up their energy reserves, but not cold enough to kill them by freezing or to cause them to lose their grip and fall from the trees.

Do the **overwintering monarchs** in Mexico feed?

Practically none of them feed. On warm days, they leave the trees to drink water, but the few flowers near the overwintering sites are sucked dry of nectar by the first few monarchs that find them.

How do the overwintering monarchs in Mexico **survive without feeding**?

They survive on large stores of energy-rich body fat that they acquired as they migrated south. When the migrating monarchs get to Texas and northern Mexico, they slow their journey as they make stops to fill up on nectar from fall-flowering plants. By the time they get to the mountains where they will spend the winter, most of them are fat enough to survive the winter without feeding. On average, their bodies consist of about 50 percent fat. Their fat supply lasts through the winter because, inactive in the cold climate of the high mountains, they use up very little energy.

The praying mantis is an ambusher of prey that uses its grasping, raptorial front legs (seen here in the seemingly prayerful position) to catch its meals, usually other insects. (Photo by Edward S. Ross.)

The green June beetle is a common beetle that feeds on ripening fruits and corn. The larvae of the June beetle, called white grubs, often feed on and kill turf grass. (Photo by Edward S. Ross.)

Mites, like this red velvet mite, are the smallest of the arachnids, and can be found virtually anywhere on Earth, from the dust in our homes to the wilds of Antarctica. (Photo by Edward S. Ross.)

The female black widow, the dangerous sex, is shiny black with red markings, usually in the shape of an hourglass on the underside of her abdomen. (Photo by Edward S. Ross.)

Tarantulas, large, hairy spiders of the tropics and subtropics, are among the largest of the arachnids. (Photo by Edward S. Ross.)

More than half of the world's insectivorous insects are beetles, like the ladybird beetles (also called ladybugs) seen here swarming on a daisy. (Photo by Edward S. Ross.)

Adult dragonflies are easily recognized by their compound eyes, their long, slender abdomen, and four elongated, membranous, and many-veined wings. (Photo by Edward S. Ross.)

Adult weevils look like most other beetles except for their long proboscis-like snouts, which, as in this rose weevil, bear chewing mouthparts at their tips. (Photo by Edward S. Ross.)

The Madagascar Croecus moth (*Chrysiridia madagascariensis*) is considered by some, including this book's author, to be the world's most beautiful insect. (Photo by Edward S. Ross.)

All centipedes, like this African species, are predators that eat small animals, usually earthworms or insects, but some of the tropical species are large enough to capture and eat small lizards or mice. (Photo by Edward S. Ross.)

Woolybears, also known as woolyworms, are the large and very hairy caterpillars of tiger moths. (Photo by Edward S. Ross.)

Although the literal meaning of the word millipede is one thousand legs, none of them has as many as that. Some millipedes have as few as 80 legs, and others have as many as 400 legs. (Photo by Edward S. Ross.)

The egg, larva (far right), and adult stages of the Colorado potato beetle. (Photo by Edward S. Ross.)

Dog-day cicadas, like the one seen here, make shrilly, high-pitched mating sounds that can be heard during the hot summer days of July and August. (Photo by Edward S. Ross.)

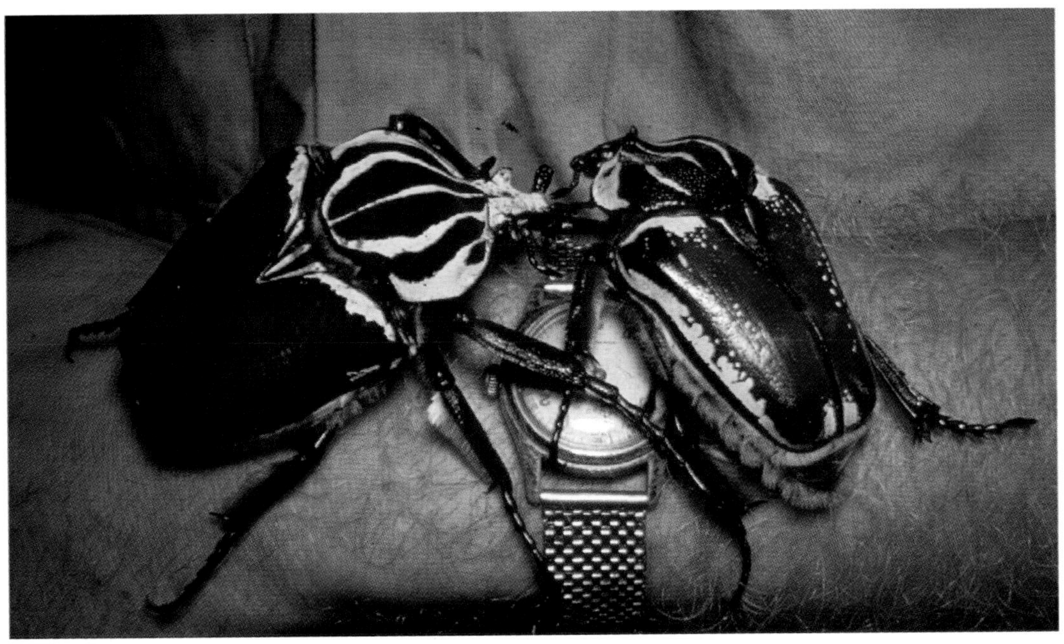

Goliath beetles are the world's heaviest insects, sometimes weighing up to a quarter of a pound. (Photo by Edward S. Ross.)

Mating butterflies. (Photo by Edward S. Ross.)

Some tropical species of termites build structures that may house a population of over a million and may rise as much as 27 feet above the ground. (Photos by Edward S. Ross.)

1. The larva (or caterpillar) stage of the Monarch butterfly.

2. The larva spins a pad of silk from which it will hang as a pupa.

3. The pupal, or resting, stage of the Monarch butterfly.

4. The adult Monarch visible through its pupal skin.

5. The adult Monarch leaves its pupal skin as a mature adult.

Photos 1–5 by Edward S. Ross.
Adult Monarch photo (right) by Robert J. Huffman

The *Kanchong,* a superbly camouflaged, bright pink praying mantis found on the Malay Peninsula, deceives its victims by blending in—almost to the point of invisibility—with the bright pink blossom of the *Sendudok*, on which it waits in ambush. (Photo by Edward S. Ross.)

A tropical katydid, member of the order Orthoptera. (Photo by Edward S. Ross.)

Grasshoppers and other insects can use flash colors to confuse a would-be predator. (Photo by Edward S. Ross.)

Because insects are so abundant (and nutritious), many predators, including other insects, fish, birds, and lizards, rely on them as a food source. (Photo by Stephen Dalton. Courtesy of Photo Researchers, Inc.)

Cockroaches, like this brown-banded one, are deft runners, and have been clocked at almost two miles an hour, or 32 inches a second. (Photo by Edward S. Ross.)

Silkworms feed ravenously on Mulberry leaves prior to spinning the cocoons that will eventually become the silk used in fabrics. (Photo by Edward S. Ross.)

Antennae, like that of the luna moth pictured here, may be sensitive to odors, tastes, touch, heat, moisture, and wind currents. (Photo by Edward S. Ross.)

Caterpillars grow tremendously before pupating to adulthood, many of them increasing their body weight by thousands of times. (Photo by Edward S. Ross.)

A beetle's elytra (hard, rigid wing covers) are held out of the way above the thorax while the membranous hind wings do the flying. (Photo by Edward S. Ross.)

Many species of wasps are expert hunters, catching and killing other insects to provide food for themselves and their young. (Photo by Edward S. Ross.)

The body hairs of bees are branched or feather-like to retain pollen grains that the bee brushes against as it moves about on a flower. (Photo by Edward S. Ross.)

Some species of crab spiders, like the one pictured above, have evolved the capacity to change their color like chameleons to match the color of the different kinds of blossoms on which they wait for prey. (Photo by Edward S. Ross.)

Leaf-cutter ants of the New World tropics eat a fungus that they grow on a mulch of leaves in large underground chambers. (Photo by Edward S. Ross.)

Ant colonies usually consist of three castes: workers, soldiers, and a queen. All but the winged queen are sterile. (Photo by Edward S. Ross.)

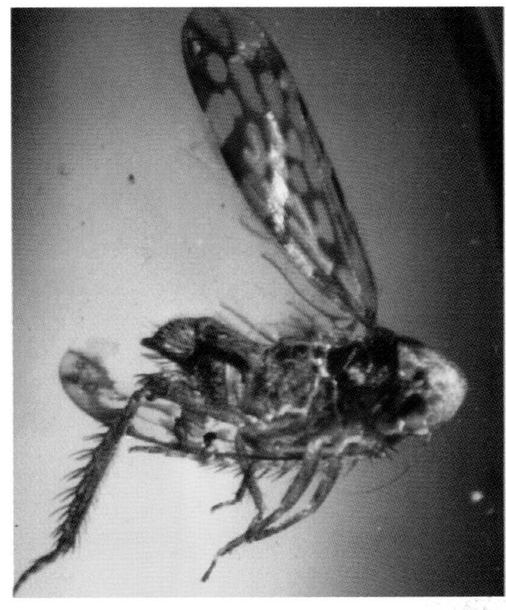

Amber, the fossilized resin of ancient trees, sometimes contains beautifully preserved insects and other organisms. (Photo by J. Koivula. Courtesy of Photo Researchers, Inc.)

The blood of vertebrates is food for piercing-sucking insects such as fleas, bed bugs, mosquitoes, black flies, and horse flies like the one pictured here. (Photo by Edward S. Ross.)

SOCIAL INSECTS

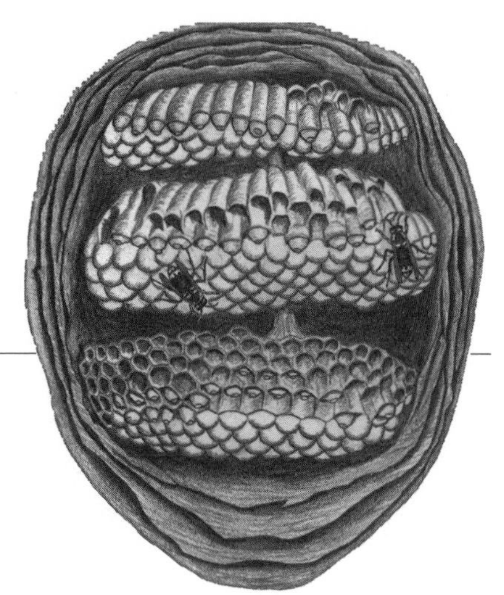

Do insects **cooperate** to raise their progeny?

Some species form social groups that care for the young. Such a society may be small and simple, perhaps consisting of no more than the two parents. Other societies are large and complex, consisting of anywhere from dozens to hundreds of thousands of individuals that belong to different specialized castes. Simple societies are said to be subsocial, and complex ones are said to be eusocial.

How do **horned passalus beetles** care for their young?

These shining black beetles, sometimes more than an inch and a quarter long, are also known as bessbugs or patent leather beetles. A male and a female join forces to dig tunnels in the decayed wood of fallen trees and, together with their 20 to 60 larvae, form an integrated community. The adults prepare meals for the larvae by chewing up wood and treating it with their saliva. Adults and larvae stay in constant communication by means of sound signals; they are said to have a repertoire of fourteen distinct signals, more than most birds have. Both larvae and adults make squeaky sounds by stridulating, or rubbing two body parts together. The adults rub a roughened area on the hindwings against a roughened area on the upper side of the abdomen. The larvae scrape their greatly shortened hind legs against the file-like bases of the middle legs.

What are the characteristics of a eusocial species?

In a eusocial, or "truly" social, species, individuals of two or more generations live in the Isame nest and cooperate in caring for the brood. They are divided into at least two castes: a reproductive caste and a sterile worker caste that cares for the offspring of the reproductive caste. The eusocial insects include all of the termites and ants, and the

Soldier termites. (Photo by Edward S. Ross.)

most highly organized bees and wasps. Among the latter are the North American bumble bees, the honey bee, hornets, yellowjackets, and the paper wasps, or polistines.

TERMITE COLONIES

What is the structure of a **termite society**?

The members of a termite society, or colony, belong to one of four castes, each one consisting of specialized individuals that have different forms and that perform different functions. All termite castes consist of both sexes, unlike wasp, ant, and bee societies in which the soldier and worker castes consist only of females. Members of the *primary reproductive caste* are dark in color, have a somewhat hardened cuticle, and are the only members of a colony that have fully developed wings. Their functions are to found new colonies and to carry on reproduction within the colony. *Secondary reproductives* are paler than primary reproductives and never have fully developed wings. If the primary reproductives die, the secondary reproductives assume the duties of reproduction. *Workers* are small, pale, soft-bodied, sterile, and make up most of the population of a colony. As their name indicates, they do most of the work: building and repairing the nest, foraging, and feeding and grooming the members of the other castes. Members of the *soldier caste* have greatly enlarged heads and large, strong mandibles, formidable weapons used to defend the colony against invaders such as ants.

How are **termite colonies founded**?

New colonies are founded by a pair of primary reproductives, a king and a queen. In spring or summer, termite colonies produce large numbers of primary reproductives that leave the colony as a swarm. After flying for some distance and mixing with swarms from other colonies, they alight on the ground, shed their wings, and form pairs. Each pair then searches for a suitable place to found a colony, which in many species is a place where wood is in contact with the moist soil. They remain together and mate repeatedly throughout their lives. The queen's abdomen swells to accommodate her large ovaries; she becomes an egg laying machine. In some tropical species, her abdomen, grossly swollen to accommodate her ovaries, may be two inches long, while her relatively tiny head and thorax may be only about a quarter of an inch long.

How do termite soldiers **defend their colony**?

The soldiers of most species use their powerful mandibles to wound, dismember, or even behead attackers, which are most often predatory ants. Some termites use a chemical defense instead. The mandibles of the soldiers of these species are not enlarged, but the head is elongated to form a forward-pointing nozzle that can expel a sticky substance that will disable an enemy.

WASP COLONIES

How do eusocial wasps **found new colonies**?

Wasps of the temperate zone found colonies only in spring. The wasps survive the winter only as mated queens that shelter in crevices, hollow trees, or other protected places. Generally speaking, each new colony is founded by just one queen. Throughout the summer, the workers keep busy feeding larvae and enlarging the nest as the population increases. In late summer, when the colony has reached its maximum size, it produces large females destined to be queens and the first and only males of the year. The queens mate before entering their winter quarters, and the males die with the onset of cold weather.

How do eusocial wasps **care for their young**?

When she founds her colony in spring, the queen builds a small paper nest that contains only a few cells, in each of which she lays a single fertilized egg that will become a sterile female, a worker. She feeds and otherwise cares for this first group of workers, but when they mature, they assume all the work of the colony, including the feeding and care of the next group of larval workers. This leaves the queen to do nothing but lay eggs. When a larva is ready to pupate, the workers cap its cell with a layer of paper and give it no further care. Soon after it emerges from its cell as an adult worker, it assumes the duties of its caste.

What do eusocial wasps **feed their larvae**?

They feed them soft-bodied insects. A Eurasian species feeds its larvae mainly honey bees, but others use a variety of insects, including caterpillars, moths, butterflies, bees, and flies. The adults chew the prey into a pulp before feeding it to the larvae. Sometimes, especially when dealing with caterpillars, they discard the intestines of the prey insect.

HONEY BEE COLONIES

How many species of honey bees are there?

There are four, the only members of the genus *Apis.* All are eusocial, and all construct combs of wax secreted by the workers. The familiar domesticated honey bee (*Apis mellifera*) originally occurred only in Western Asia, Europe, and Africa, but people have introduced it to virtually all parts of the world. *Apis cerana,* the Indian honey bee, smaller than *Apis mellifera* but similar to it in behavior and appearance, has been domesticated throughout much of its native range in tropical Asia. The dwarf honey bee (*Apis florea*), another native of tropical Asia and the smallest of the honey bees, constructs a single naked comb that is no more than ten inches in diameter and hangs from the underside of a branch of a tree. Although it is not generally domesticated, its honey is much prized in Asia. The largest of the honey bees is *Apis dorsata,* the giant honey bee, yet another native of tropical Asia. It constructs a single naked comb that may be more than a yard in diameter and that hangs beneath a shelter such as an overhanging cliff, the roof of a building, or a large tree branch. It has not been domesticated, but its combs are regularly collected for their honey.

What do honey bees **feed their larvae**?

They feed the larvae bees' milk, which is secreted by glands in the heads of workers that are less than eighteen days old. The raw material for its production is pollen,

What do adult honey bees eat?

As do all other bees, including the solitary, subsocial, and eusocial species, adult honey bees eat pollen, nectar, and occasionally the honeydew produced by aphids and other species of Homoptera. They store both pollen and nectar, the latter in the form of honey, in their nests for future use. Pollen is their source of proteins, fats, vitamins, and minerals, all of which are essential for reproduction and growth. Nectar is largely a source of the sugars that provide the energy bees require.

which these young workers eat in large quantity. The bees' milk is supplemented by matter, mainly carbohydrates, that the workers regurgitate from their stomachs.

How do honey bees **regulate the production of castes**?

Although the queen lays the eggs, the workers determine how many she lays and whether they become workers, drones, or queens. The queen lays only one egg per cell and will not lay at all unless she comes upon an empty cell. Consequently, the workers can control the number of eggs that she lays by increasing or decreasing the number of cells that they make. The queen lays unfertilized eggs, which will become males, or drones, only in cells that are somewhat larger than the cells that house larval workers. The workers determine how many drone cells they build. Fertilized eggs become females, and it is the workers that determine whether an egg will become a sterile worker or a fertile queen. Fertilized eggs that are laid in small cells become workers; those that are laid in large pendulous cells become queens. The great majority of females become workers. Raised in small cells, they are fed royal jelly on their first three days and ordinary bees' milk. Larvae destined to become queens are fed only royal jelly throughout their lives.

Queen honey bee surrounded by workers. (Photo by Edward S. Ross.)

What is **royal jelly**?

Royal jelly is nothing more than bees' milk that has been fortified with extra sugar. It does not contain some wonderful substance—other than sugar—that causes a larva to become a queen rather than a mere worker. The extra sweetness of the royal jelly stimulates the larva to eat more and thus grow larger. The fact is that any larva that grows large enough will secrete in its own body a hormone that causes it to become a queen. Although royal jelly is nutritious for humans, it does not enhance femininity as the advertising for some food additives and cosmetics seems to imply.

Why do honey bees **dance**?

The waggle dance communicates the direction and distance of a resource such as water, a patch of flowers, or a source of plant gum for sealing cracks in the nest. When a scout returns from a worthwhile resource—a nectar-yielding patch of flowers, for example—she does the waggle dance on the vertical surface of a comb hanging in the nest. As she dances, other bees crowd in close and follow her through the pattern of the dance as they touch her with their antennae. The dance is in the form of a compressed figure eight. The dancer first runs in a straight line, the cross bar of the eight; then she turns right and loops back to her starting point. Then she repeats the straight-line run, but this time she loops to the left to return to the starting point. As she makes each straight-line run, she waggles her abdomen from side to side and makes a high-pitched hum. She repeats this dance over and over again. The distance to the patch of flowers is indicated by the duration of the waggle phase of the dance: the longer its duration, the greater the distance to the flowers. The direction is indicated by the bearing of the straight-line waggle run with respect to the vertical axis of the comb. Just as people follow the convention that the top of a map is north, honey bees understand that the top of the comb indicates the direction of the sun. Thus, if the direction of the flowers is directly toward the sun, the waggle run is directed straight up the comb. If the direction of the flowers is sixty degrees to the right of the line from the nest to the sun, the waggle run is directed sixty degrees to the right of the vertical axis of the comb. How persistently the dancer performs indicates the quality of the resource: the longer the dance lasts, the better the quality. The scent of the nectar and pollen that the bees bring back to the nest indicates the identity of the flowers.

How have people used **robots to communicate** with honey bees?

A peppermint-scented robot bee supported by a small arm protruding through a comb was manipulated so that it danced like a bee indicating a source of nectar at a certain distance in the direction of the sun. Some bees followed the dancing robot and responded by flying to a container of peppermint-scented sugar water at the indicated distance and direction. Very few bees came to other baits that were at the same distance from the hive but in different directions.

How do honey bees **found new colonies**?

Honey bee nest. (Photo by Edward S. Ross.)

They can be founded only by a large swarm of workers accompanied by a queen, never by a lone queen, as with ants, wasps, and bumblebees, or by a royal pair, as with termites. When a honey bee colony becomes congested, the workers construct several queen cells. A few days before the first new queen is due to emerge, the old queen leaves the nest with a swarm of thousands of workers that have engorged on stored honey. The swarm flies to a temporary resting site on a tree or a bush and forms a tight cluster around the queen. Scouts then fly off in search of nesting sites. Those that find a suitable site—perhaps in a hollow tree—return and perform a waggle dance that indicates the direction and distance to the site. Workers in the cluster follow the scout as she dances and then leave to see the site for themselves. If they consider it to be good, they recruit more workers by repeating the same waggle dance when they return to the swarm. The better the quality of the site that she has found, the more persistently the worker dances. In this way, the dancers eventually reach a consensus. When all of them are performing the same waggle dance, almost always the one that indicates the best of the available nesting sites, they fly off en masse to move into their new home.

Where and when do **queen honey bees mate**?

They mate only during the first few days after they emerge as adults. Virgin queens fly to trysting sites where drones from several colonies congregate for the purpose of meeting a mate. As the queen flies over the trysting site, she releases a pheromone that soon attracts an entourage of males that follow behind her. She mates with one or more of them in flight. She may return on succeeding days to mate again. But she soon settles down in the hive and will never mate again.

How do honey bees **survive the cold of winter**?

Unlike other insects, they do not go into diapause and become inactive. Instead, they keep themselves warm by producing heat. When the temperature drops to about 55 degrees Fahrenheit, all the workers in a nest form a cluster that surrounds the queen, the brood, and a store of honey. The workers at the cluster's periphery crowd closely together to form a living blanket that is two bees thick and that insulates the rest of the cluster. Bees within the cluster are less densely packed and can move about. Bees move back and forth between the periphery and the inner cluster. Those in the inner cluster eat honey and convert its calories to heat by vigorously vibrating their wing muscles without moving their wings. Even when the outside temperature is far below freezing, the bees can keep the cluster at a comfortable temperature between 68 degrees Fahrenheit and 86 degrees Fahrenheit.

Do honey bees **cool their nests**?

Yes, and they do a good job of it! Air conditioning is a necessity because the brood survives and grows only within the narrow range of temperatures between about 90 degrees Fahrenheit and 97 degrees Fahrenheit. When the air temperature is cool, the workers cluster around the brood to keep it warm, but when it is too hot they disperse about the nest and fan their wings to circulate fresh air. If this does not lower the temperature enough, they resort to evaporative cooling. They bring in drops of water and make them evaporate by fanning. This system works amazingly well. Even when the air temperature is far above 100 degrees Fahrenheit, the bees keep the temperature in the nest below 97 degrees Fahrenheit as long as they can get water.

Who discovered and deciphered the **waggle dance**?

Karl von Frisch, an Austrian entomologist, won the Nobel Prize for this discovery. By marking foraging bees that found a dish of sugar water and then watching them dance when they returned to a glass-sided observation hive, he and his helpers showed that the form and pace of the waggle dance corresponded to the direction and distance from the hive to the dish of sugar water.

ANT COLONIES

How are **ant colonies founded**?

They may be founded by "budding," the division of an existing colony into two independent parts, but are more often founded from scratch by lone queens. Mature colonies produce swarms of winged queens and winged males that usually mate with ants from other colonies. Mated queens go off on their own and shed their wings, using their legs to snap them off at fracture points near the bases of the wings. They then prepare a nest, in many species a burrow in the soil, in which they lay their first batch of eggs, all of which are destined to become sterile workers. The queen feeds and otherwise cares for these first workers until they mature and assume the work of the colony, relieving the queen to do nothing but lay eggs. Unlike colonies of wasps and bumble bees, ant colonies can survive the winter and may persist for many years.

What do founder queen ants **feed their first larval offspring**?

Queens of primitive species leave the nest open and go out to hunt for insects that they feed to their larvae. Queens of the more evolutionarily advanced species seal their nests shut and feed their larvae with nutrient substances that they themselves produce by metabolizing their fat bodies and wing muscles, the latter now useless because the wings have been shed. These nutrients are presented to the larvae in one of two forms, or a combination of both: as special, edible secretions of the salivary glands, or as "trophic" eggs that cannot develop and are used only as food.

How do worker ants **care for immature ants**?

Adult workers of even primitive species give lavish care to all of the immatures in the colony: the eggs, larvae, and pupae that are their sisters. They lick and carry immatures of all stages; they feed them insect prey or other food that they gather; they regurgitate nutrients for the larvae or lay infertile eggs for them to eat; they help the larvae to shed their skins; they pile soil around the larvae to facilitate cocoon spinning; and, finally, they remove the empty cocoons after the adults have emerged from them.

What are **driver ants and army ants**?

In his 1910 book, *Ants,* W. M. Wheeler wrote of the driver ants and the army ants, also known as legionary ants, in the lyrical prose of his day:

> The driver and legionary ants are the Huns and Tartars of the insect world. Their vast armies of blind but exquisitely cooperating and highly polymorphic workers, filled with an insatiable carnivore appetite and a longing for perennial migrations, accompanied by a motley host of weird myrmecophilous [ant-loving] camp-followers and concealing the nuptials of their strange, fertile castes, and the rearing of their young, in the inaccessible penetralia of the soil—all suggest to the observer who first comes upon these insects in some tropical thicket, the existence of a subtle, relentless and uncanny agency, directing and permeating all their activities. These marvelous insects have been studied by many travelers—for they are among the most conspicuous creatures in the tropics—but although our knowledge of them has been

How do soldier ants defend the nest?

Although they occasionally assist at other tasks, the main function of the soldiers is to defend the nest against aggressors, which are often other species of ants. Soldiers are sterile females. Their heads are usually enlarged, sometimes almost grotesquely so, and many of them have large, powerful mandibles. Soldiers defend the colony in three basic ways: 1) Some may use their strong mandibles to shear off the appendages of enemies or otherwise wound them. 2) The soldiers of some species have long, sickle-shaped mandibles that they use to pierce the body of an enemy. 3) Some species have soldiers that plug the entrance to the nest with their heads, which are shaped accordingly, like a plug in some species or like a shield in others.

> notably increased within recent years, we still have much to learn concerning their habits and development.

Today much more is known about these ants than was known in Wheeler's day, but every study of them raises new questions. Finding the answers is a fascinating adventure in biology.

How do army ants **hunt**?

These aggressive ants of the lowland forests of Central and South America hunt in large swarms that fan out over the ground and even up into trees as they seek their arthropod prey. They have even been known to kill vertebrates such as lizards, snakes, birds, and small mammals. In science fiction, army ant swarms may be a mile wide and pose a serious threat to humans, but this is a gross exaggeration. Swarms are no more than sixty feet wide and move so slowly that people can easily avoid them.

Where do army ants live?

Army ants have no permanent nest. They form "bivouacs" in sheltered places, sometimes under the trunk of a fallen tree. A bivouac consists of a tightly packed mass of from 150,000 to 700,000 workers that surrounds the queen and that may be as much as a yard in diameter. During its two- to three-week nomadic phase, the colony is on the move and forms a new bivouac each night. Stationary phases of about the same duration alternate with nomadic phases. During a stationary phase, swarm raids go out each night but return to the same bivouac. It is only during this phase that reproduction occurs, as the queen lays from 100,000 to 300,000 eggs in an extraordinary burst of effort. The immature stages are cared for within the mass of bivouacking

Do ants enslave other ants?

Quite a few species do. Some capture ants of other species and use them as "domestic animals," a practice that entomologists rather ambiguously refer to as slavery. Only two closely related species of honeypot ants are known to practice slavery in the strict sense of the word. They enslave ants of their own species, but only individuals from a foreign colony.

workers, and when the immatures have become adults, the colony switches back to the nomadic phase.

How do **driver ants differ from army ants**?

Like the army ants of the New World, the driver ants of Africa move cross country in devastating swarms that destroy virtually all of the arthropods and other animals in their path. They differ from army ants in that they live in secure nests in the soil. They will remain in a nest anywhere from a week to three months, sending out huge raiding parties almost every day. From time to time the colony must move on and excavate a nest in a new area in which they have not exhausted the food supply.

What are **fire ants**?

These ants are named for their painful, fiery stings, delivered as an ant sinks its powerful mandibles into its victim's flesh to gain leverage. Birds and small mammals are sometimes killed by these stings. The imported fire ant, the most troublesome of the fire ants in the United States, occurs throughout most of the southern states. Its mounds may be as much as three feet tall, and there may be as many as one hundred nests per acre in crop fields and pastures. It is a serious agricultural pest that attacks the young and tender plants of many crops.

What are **honey pot ants**?

These ants of the desert, hunters of insects and collectors of nectar, live in nests in the ground that may extend as much as twenty feet beneath the surface. Since they cannot build storage cells, as do bees, they store honey in the bodies of a special caste of workers known as repletes, or honey pots. The honey pots, their abdomens grotesquely swollen with honey, hang from the ceilings of chambers in the nest—sometimes as many as 1,500 honey pots in a single colony. When temperatures are moderate and the ants have a low metabolic rate, foraging workers pass nectar to the honey pots, but

Army ant swarm. (Photo by Edward S. Ross.)

when it gets to 90 degrees Fahrenheit or above, workers solicit honey from the honey pots to fuel their more active metabolism.

What are **weaver ants**?

These ants, predators of other insects, live in arboreal nests that are made of leaves fastened together with silk. Adult ants do not secrete silk, but use their larvae—which do secrete it—as "sewing machines" to fasten together leaves. As some workers pull two leaves together, others fasten them together with silk exuded by larvae that they hold in their mandibles.

What are **leaf-cutter ants**?

These ants of the New World tropics eat a fungus that they grow on a mulch of leaves in large underground chambers. Long files of these ants returning to their nests are a common sight, each of them holding in its mandibles a large piece of green leaf.

What are **ant plants**?

Ants and plants are associated in various ways, but one of the most complex and intimate of these relationships is the one between acacia trees and acacia ants. The trees, known as bull's horn acacias, provide the ants with all the necessities of life. The ants nest in large, swollen, hollow thorns that are arranged in pairs along the branches and twigs of the tree. The tree provides both nectar and solid food. At the base of the stem of each of the large compound leaves is an extrafloral nectary, a nectary that is not associated with a flower. At the tip of each leaflet of the compound leaf is an edible structure known as a Beltian body, which is rich in the fat and protein required by the ants. The ants reciprocate by protecting the plant that houses them against insect and mammalian herbivores, and against other competing plants that sprout nearby. The ants cut down the plants, kill infesting insects, and drive away large herbivores with their powerful stings.

EATERS OF INSECTS

In what ways are **insects attacked** by other organisms?

The organisms that "eat" insects can, generally speaking, be divided into three groups: predators, which kill and devour their prey; parasites, which live in or on the bodies of their hosts; and pathogens, which cause diseases.

PREDATORS

What is a **predator**?

A predator is an animal that makes direct attacks on other animals, killing them more or less immediately and eating all or most of their bodies. A predator kills and consumes several or many animals during its life.

What **kinds of organisms** prey on insects?

Many different species of invertebrates, vertebrates, and even a few plants have evolved the ability to prey on the insect bounty all around them. Insects are, after all, nutritious, abundant, and virtually ubiquitous on land and in fresh water. Among the predators that feast on insects are centipedes, scorpions, spiders, mites, insects, fish, frogs, salamanders, lizards, snakes, turtles, many kinds of birds, and a diversity of mammals ranging from mice and bats to anteaters and bears. Some of these predators, among them ladybird beetles and anteaters, eat virtually nothing but insects; and others, among them jays and mice, make insects only a part of their diet.

A crab spider catches a bee. (Photo by Edward S. Ross.)

What are the most **important predators** of insects?

The most important predators of insects are insects and other arthropods such as spiders. It has been said that insects are their own worst enemies. There are many thousands of insect-eating insects. They belong to several orders and so many different families that it would be impractical to list them all here. More than half of these insectivorous insects are beetles, notably ladybird beetles, fireflies, tiger beetles, ground beetles, and water tigers. Many ants are insect eaters as are all of the social wasps and most of the solitary wasps other than the parasitic ones. Although most of the true bugs are vegetarians, some, among them the ambush bugs and the assassin bugs, use their piercing-sucking mouthparts to suck their insect prey dry. Without exception, all of the dragonflies and damselflies are insectivores both as nymphs and adults. Robber flies, many hover flies, green lacewings, and antlions are among the many other insects that prey on insects.

How do insects **capture prey**?

In general terms, insects use three major strategies for capturing prey: searching, ambushing, or trapping. Dragonflies cruise the air as they search for mosquitoes and other flying insects. Praying mantises wait in ambush for a victim to come within striking distance. Antlions dig steep-sided pitfall traps and wait at the bottom for any unwary insect to stumble in.

Ground beetle with captured caterpillar. (Photo by Edward S. Ross.)

How do **ground beetles capture prey**?

Most of them are searchers that crawl on the ground or even climb trees as they hunt for insects. The fiery searcher, a ground beetle of the genus *Calosoma,* is one of the largest beetles at a length of nearly an inch and a quarter, and, with its bluish-black body and shiny green wing covers margined with red, is also one of the most beautiful. Both larvae and adults are active runners and climb trees as they search for the caterpillars that are their favorite prey. During its two-week period of development, a *Calosoma* larva was observed to eat fifty full-grown gypsy moth caterpillars, each about two and a quarter inches long. The adults may survive as long as three or four years, during which time they eat several hundred large caterpillars. A closely related species, the caterpillar hunter, was introduced into the United States as an aid in controlling gypsy moths.

How do **tiger beetles catch insects**?

Adult tiger beetles are searchers that pursue insects by flying or running swiftly over the ground. You have probably seen the adult six-spotted tiger beetle: as you walk along a woodland path in summer, you are likely to see a brilliantly iridescent green beetle about a half inch long sitting on the ground. When you get within a few feet, it flies a few yards down the trail and lands on the ground. The beetle will do this repeatedly as you walk on and disturb it. Tiger beetle larvae, sometimes known as doodlebugs, are difficult to find and seldom seen. They live in burrows in the ground that may be from a few inches to several feet deep and are usually in hard-packed earth in open, sunny places. If they are undisturbed, the larvae sit at the opening of the burrow watching for walking insects to come near. If an insect comes close enough, the tiger beetle larva dashes out to grab it and drags it back to its burrow to eat it.

What are **robber flies**?

They are large, insect-eating true flies that may be as much as an inch and a half long. The larvae live in soil or decaying logs. Not much is known about their feeding habits, but some are known to feed on larval insects. The adults are voracious predators that feed mainly on flying insects. Much like the birds known as flycatchers, robber flies dash out from a perch to intercept flying insects. You can see them on perches that give a clear view of the surrounding air space, often the tip of a twig or the upper surface of a leaf. A robber fly that has caught an insect returns to its perch or a nearby shady place to eat it. It pierces its prey with its sharp beak and injects powerful digestive enzymes that liquefy the prey's internal tissues. The fly then sucks up its fluid meal.

What are **hangingflies**?

Hangingflies are not true flies but are a subgroup of the order that also includes the scorpionflies. They are unique in that their hind legs rather than their front legs are modified for grasping prey. Their feet, or tarsi, do the grasping. The terminal (fifth) segment of the tarsus has a single very large and sharp claw and can grasp tightly by snapping shut like the blade of a jackknife against the preceding (fourth) segment of the tarsus. These insects hang by their front legs from a plant, usually in a dank, shaded area. When an insect, which may be as large as a small moth comes close enough, they swiftly grasp it in their raptorial hind tarsi. Hangingflies may be three-quarters of an inch long and, because of their narrow wings and long, spindly legs, resemble crane flies.

What is a **beewolf**?

The beewolf is one of the predaceous solitary wasps. The female stocks her nest, a burrow in the soil, with paralyzed bees, which are the food of her larval offspring. A female hunting for bees flies from flower to flower. In this phase of the hunt she will respond only to the sight of a bee. Amazingly, she pays no attention to the odor of bees unless she has an insect of about the size of a bee in view. If she spots such an insect, she hovers downwind of it at a distance of about five inches. If it does not have the scent of a bee, she immediately moves on. But, as experiments with dummy bees have shown, if a dummy has the odor of a bee, the wasp quickly pounces on it. Although she readily grabs dummy bees, she does not sting them. If she determines her prey to be a real bee, she will sting it and carry it back to her nest.

How did mantispids get their name?

This name—with its Latin ending—means "like a mantis." An apt name for this insect, which looks like a mantis, hunts like a mantis, but is not related to the mantises. It has the giraffe-like "neck" of a mantis and its raptorial front legs, but is a relative of the green lacewings, the antlions, and the dobsonflies. Like a mantis, it waits in ambush on a plant, often on a blossom, for its insect victims to come close. This is a striking example of convergent evolution: two organisms, independent of each other, evolving almost identical ways of solving the same problem.

What is a ***Kanchong***?

Kanchong is the Malay name for a superbly camouflaged praying mantis found on the Malay Peninsula. This bright pink mantis deceives its insect victims by blending in—almost to the point of invisibility—with a bright pink blossom of the *Sendudok,* on which it waits in ambush. Not only is its color a perfect match for the blossom, but it also has on its middle and hind legs thin, wide flanges that look like pink petals of the *sendudok* blossom. When an insect comes to the blossom, the mantis strikes out with its raptorial front legs to capture its next meal.

What are **water striders**?

They are predaceous true bugs that have staked out an unusual ecological niche. They literally walk on water and prey on insects that land or fall onto its surface. These long-legged insects, light enough to be supported by the water's surface film, dimple the film with their feet as they skate along. On sunny days the shadows of these dimples move across the bottom as the water strider glides over the surface of a quiet, shallow pond. The ripples caused by an insect that falls onto the surface are perceived by sense organs on the water strider's legs. Guided by the ripples, it skates to the fallen insect, grasps it with its front legs—which are not used in locomotion—and pierces its body to suck its juices.

Is there an insect that subdues its prey with a **tranquilizer**?

There is at least one—an ant-eating assassin bug in Java. The hungry bug stations itself along a trail that runs from an ant nest to a "herd" of aphids that the ants keep for the honeydew that they excrete. When an ant comes along, the assassin bug rears up to expose a bright red spot on the underside of its abdomen that secretes a substance, presumably sweet, that the ants eat. But the bug's sugary secretion contains a powerful tranquilizer that causes the ant to collapse. The bug then grasps its helpless prey and sucks it dry.

Insects make up an important part of a bird's diet. (Photo by Kenneth H. Thomas. Courtesy of Photo Researchers, Inc.)

Do insects prey on **insect eggs**?

Some do. Among them are several kinds of blister beetles that in the larval stage eat grasshopper eggs. Adult blister beetles are strict vegetarians that browse on the foliage of many different kinds of herbaceous plants. They lay their eggs in the soil in several masses, each containing from 100 to 200 each. The tiny, long-legged larvae that hatch from the eggs disperse and run around on the ground searching for a place where a pod of grasshopper eggs is buried. The larva makes its way through the soil down to the eggs and begins to feed. With the first molt it becomes short-legged, and sluggish, and continues to feed on the grasshopper eggs until it is full grown. Then it molts to an inactive pupa-like stage, which has been called a pseudopupa, in which it spends the winter. In spring it molts to once again become an active larva. This final larval stage pupates, and the adults emerge in midsummer.

How important are insects in the **diets of birds**?

Very important. The great majority of birds, even some hawks, gulls, and sandpipers, make insects at least a part of their diet, and almost all insects are preyed upon by birds. Some seed-eating birds, such as grosbeaks, finches, and certain sparrows, eat very few insects. Other birds, among them chickadees, jays, and woodpeckers, take mixed diets that include many insects. Cuckoos, flycatchers, swallows, vireos, warblers, and tanagers are exclusively or mainly insectivorous. The great majority of songbirds, even most of those that as adults eat practically nothing but seeds or other plant matter, feed their nestlings a high protein diet that usually consists mostly of insects. Josselyn van Tyne, an ornithologist, watched a male cardinal as it put down a beakful of caterpillars at a feeder, cracked and ate some seeds, and then retrieved the caterpillars and left to deliver them to his nestlings.

In what ways do **birds exploit** insects?

In almost every conceivable way. Since they first appeared on earth about 150 million years ago, birds have become ever more specialized to exploit insects wherever they are to be found. Some birds, among them warblers and vireos, are leaf gleaners that pick small caterpillars and other insects from foliage. Bark gleaners, such as creepers and nuthatches, search for insects such as beetles and springtails that live under loose flakes of bark or in crevices. Woodpeckers dig in wood and bark to expose beetle larvae, sawfly larvae, ants, or other insects that tunnel in bark or wood. Flycatchers and other birds such as cedar waxwings and Townsend's solitaires sally forth from a perch to snatch insects that fly by. Swallows, swifts, and nightjars course and swoop through the air as they scoop up flying insects and ballooning spiders. Even aquatic insects have avian enemies such as ducks that use their bills to strain insects such as mayfly nymphs, dragonfly nymphs, and caddisfly larvae from the bottom muck; and dippers, also known as water ouzels, that walk under water in swift-flowing streams to pluck stonefly nymphs, black fly larvae, and other aquatic insects from the rocky bottom.

What do **woodpeckers** have to do with the **worm in the apple**?

The worms that make such terrible messes inside apples are codling moth caterpillars. When the caterpillars are full grown, they tunnel out of the apple and crawl down to the trunk of the tree, hide under a loose flake of bark, and spin the cocoon in which they will pass the winter. In winter, hungry downy woodpeckers, opportunistic and ever searching, discover the hidden caterpillar and reach them by pecking holes, centered on the caterpillars, through the flakes of bark that cover them.

How do **woodpecker finches** catch insects?

The woodpecker finch of the Galapagos Islands has, in the absence of woodpeckers, evolved to occupy the woodpeckers' feeding niche. It and the mangrove finch are the only wood probers in the Galapagos. They, like woodpeckers, use their strong bills to dig into wood in search of insects but lack the long, barbed tongue that woodpeckers use to spear insects that are out of reach of their bills. The finches compensate for their short tongues by using a twig or a cactus spine to probe for wood boring insects that are out of reach. The woodpecker and mangrove finches are among the few tool-using birds in the world.

What is **aerial "plankton"**?

The aerial plankton, named by analogy for the planktonic organisms that float in sea water, consists of the myriad insects and other arthropods, mostly spiders, that fly or float in the air. Ten cubic yards of air, a space about the size of a small clothes closet, is likely to contain about 10 arthropods, mostly insects. Samples taken by insect traps under the wings of an airplane showed that a volume of air a mile square and extending above the ground to a height of 20 feet contained over 32 million insects and other arthropods. Among them were mites, spiders, and well over 700 species of insects belonging to 18 orders. Birds have taken advantage of this bounty. Swifts are almost constantly on the wing and feed only on the aerial plankton. Swallows spend almost as much time in the air and subsist largely on the aerial plankton. Bats, whip-poor-wills, and other nightjars take over the night shift.

Why do **birds** associate with **army ants**?

Birds follow swarms of these insect-eating ants not to feed on the ants but to eat the myriad insects, including cockroaches, beetles, bugs, moths, flies, and others, that flush as they try to escape from these voracious New World ants. A swarm of army ants, consisting of thousands of individuals advancing on a front as much as 60 feet wide, may be accompanied by as many as 50 birds of 20 or more species, among them motmots, puffbirds, cuckoos, woodcreepers, tanagers, and some species of the antbird family.

What are **honeyguides**?

These African birds feed on the wax combs of honey bees. Since they are neither large enough nor strong enough to break into a nest of honey bees in a hollow tree or some similar shelter, they enlist the help of a person or a honey badger. Constantly calling loudly and fanning its tail and ruffling its wings to reveal white tail feathers and yellow shoulder patches, a honeyguide leads a person or a honey badger to a colony of bees. After its follower has broken into the nest and eaten its fill, the honeyguide feeds on the leftovers: wax, honey, and bee larvae.

What do **bats eat**?

In other parts of the world there are fruit-eating, fish-eating, and even blood-sucking bats, but the North American species eat virtually nothing but night-flying insects. Their prey includes insects of all kinds, ranging from mosquitoes to large moths.

Do **anteaters** eat only ants?

These toothless South American mammals do eat ants, but termites—sometimes called white ants—are probably a more important part of their diet. Anteaters have on their front feet large powerful claws for tearing open the nests of their prey. Their long tongues, coated with sticky saliva, are only about a half inch in diameter but can be extended as much as two feet into a nest to pick up ants or termites.

How voracious are **shrews**?

Shrews, which are almost entirely insectivorous, are certainly the most voracious of the mammals. They have very high metabolic rates and must eat almost constantly—both day and night. They generally eat their own weight in food in a day and may eat three times as much. Shrews are quite tiny. The masked shrew, common in Canada and much of the northern United States, weighs only about an eighth of an ounce.

PARASITES

What is a **parasite**?

A parasite is an organism that lives on or within the body of an animal, its host, and depends upon it for nutriment. The association between host and parasite is more or less prolonged. The parasite does not benefit the host but usually does not kill it.

What kinds of animals parasitize insects?

The great majority of the parasites of insects are other insects, at least 115,000 known species. The only other arthropod parasites of insects are mites. Among the nonarthropod parasites of insects are certain of the flatworms known as flukes, a few tapeworms, some spiny-headed worms, certain nematodes (roundworms), and some of the hair worms, which are also known as horsehair worms.

What are the **life histories** of insect-parasitizing "worms" like?

Some are simple, wherein the insect occupies only one host, an insect, during its lifetime. Others are quite complex. The parasite occupies a sequence of hosts that are not necessarily taxonomically related and are likely to belong to different phyla. Some hair worms parasitize two different species of insects in sequence. But in most cases, an insect is only one of a sequence of hosts. One of the flukes, for example, first para-

Caterpillar killed by wasp-larva parasites. (Photo by Edward S. Ross.)

sitizes a snail, then moves on to an aquatic insect, and finally ends up in a vertebrate such as a snake or bird.

What kinds of insects do **roundworms** parasitize?

Among them, various species of roundworms parasitize many different kinds of insects, including grasshoppers, aphids, beetles, ants, midges, fungus gnats, and black flies.

What is a **roundworm's** life like?

The life histories of most roundworms are unknown or poorly understood, but that of *Agameris decandata,* a species that parasitizes grasshoppers, has been thoroughly studied. The adult worms live in cavities a short distance below the surface of the soil, coiled in groups that include several males but only one female. The eggs are laid in the cavity during summer and fall but do not hatch until the following spring. The newly hatched worms, less than a quarter of an inch long, move up to the surface of the soil and climb up onto plants that are wet with rain or dew. When and if the opportunity arises, they penetrate the body wall of a newly hatched grasshopper nymph and remain in the body cavity. They ultimately fill its body and do great damage to the internal organs. After one to three months, the full-grown worms emerge from the host by making a hole in its body wall and enter the soil.

How did hair worms get their name?

These parasitic worms, which live in fresh water during the adult stage, are dark brown, very thin and hair-like, and may be as much as a yard long. They sometimes occur in farmyard watering troughs, which gave rise to the erroneous idea that horse hairs that drop into the trough are transformed into worms. The adults do not feed, but they copulate and the females lay a million or more eggs. Larval worms emerge from the eggs and form cysts (protective structures). If the cyst is ingested by an insect, often a cockroach, a cricket, or a grasshopper, the larval worm is released from the cyst and makes its way to the blood in the insect's body cavity, where it absorbs nutrients through its body wall and grows to its full size. The full-grown worm escapes from the insect and enters the water to begin the cycle again.

How do **roundworms that are not parasitic** make use of insects?

Certain roundworms of the genus *Rhabditis* live in dung and take advantage of flying, dung-inhabiting insects such as flies or beetles to transport them to a fresh pile of dung when the old pile is no longer a satisfactory source of food. In some cases the roundworms have become intimately dependent upon the insects that transport them. In one species of roundworm, hundreds of juvenile worms board a dung-inhabiting scarab beetle to be carried to a fresh pile of cow manure. They have become so totally dependent upon the beetle that they cannot continue to grow and develop unless they are transported to fresh dung by one of these beetles.

What is the life history of the **dog tapeworm**?

This tapeworm requires two hosts, a flea and a dog. The adult tapeworms, which are hermaphroditic (having both male and female reproductive organs) and about a foot long, live in the intestines of a dog. Their eggs are passed out with the dog's feces and survive only if they are ingested by a flea larva. They develop into the infectious stage in the flea and continue their development to the adult stage if the adult flea is ingested by a dog.

Do **flukes** parasitize dragonflies?

Dragonfly nymphs are one of the sequence of three hosts that a fluke of the genus *Plagiorchis* must occupy during its life if it is to survive. The fluke's eggs pass out with a snake's feces. Eggs that are fortunate enough to be ingested by a snail hatch to produce *miracidia* which metamorphose to become *redia*. The *redia* bore in the snail's tissues and feed on its cells. They ultimately produce *cercaria,* which leave the snail

Are any insects "true parasites" that do not ultimately kill their hosts?

There are very, very few. As R. R. Askew pointed out in *Parasitic Insects,* a few insects are very nearly, but not quite, true parasites. Among them is a tiny chalcid wasp that parasitizes scale insects but does not kill them until they have laid some eggs. Some ichneumonid wasps that parasitize adult beetles fit the definition of a true parasite. After the larval parasites complete their development and emerge from the beetle's body, the beetle may survive to feed and lay eggs.

and swim about. Most *cercaria* perish, but some enter the body of a dragonfly nymph and become *metacercaria.* If the dragonfly nymph is eaten by a snake, the *metacercaria* become adults and the cycle is complete.

How many insects parasitize other insects?

At least 115,000 of the 900,000 known species of insects live by parasitizing other insects. About 100,000 of them, or 87 percent, are wasps of one sort or another—often tiny creatures that most people would not recognize as wasps. Most of the rest of them are flies, about 11,000 or somewhat less than 10 percent. Most of these insect-parasitizing flies belong to one family, the Tachinidae. The remaining 4,000 parasites are scattered among various orders including Lepidoptera (moths and butterflies), Coleoptera (beetles), and Strepsiptera (the stylopods).

What is a **parasitoid**?

Many of the insects that parasitize other insects should really be referred to as parasitoids, because, unlike the "true parasites," parasitoids more or less immediately kill their hosts. Most of the parasitic wasps, for example, live as true parasites during the first part of the larval stage, absorbing nutriment from the host's blood and doing little or no damage to its vital organs. But when these larvae are nearly full grown, they show themselves to be parasitoids, killing the host by devouring it in its entirety or at least destroying its inner organs.

What is an **endoparasite**?

An endoparasite lives within the body of its host. Most insects that parasitize other insects are endoparasites.

What is an **ectoparasite**?

An ectoparasite lives on the outside of the host's body. Only a few insects are ectoparasites of other insects.

How do endoparasites **get inside their hosts**?

In one of two ways. In most species, including the great majority of parasitic wasps, the parasite mothers use their piercing ovipositors to place an egg or several eggs inside the host's body. In some other species, including many of the parasitic flies, the parasite mothers do not put their eggs inside the host but stick them to the outside of its body. It is up to the newly hatched larva to burrow into the host's body. Some parasitic wasps have extremely long ovipositors. For example, *Megarhyssa,* an ichneumonid wasp that parasitizes the wood-boring larvae of sawflies, has a long, thread-like ovipositor about three inches long, about twice the length of her body. She uses this formidable organ to drill deep into wood to reach the tunnel of a host. Flies that place their eggs—sometimes actually a tiny, newly born larvae—outside of a host may place them directly on the host's body or on vegetation near a host. Flies that lay their eggs on caterpillars place them just behind the caterpillar's head, where it can't reach them with its mandibles.

Are insects parasitic **in all life stages**?

Insect parasites of mammals and birds—lice, for example—are parasitic in all of their life stages, but this is never the case with insects that parasitize other insects. With just a few exceptions, only larvae parasitize other insects. Eggs and pupae may be in the host's body, but they do not take nourishment from the host. Most adult insects are also not parasitic. They are free living and can thus carry out the essential role of delivering their eggs to a host.

What do the **parents of larval parasites eat**?

They sip nectar from flowers and consume honeydew, the sweet, watery excrement of aphids and other Homoptera. They also feed on the body fluids of the host, a source of the protein required to develop eggs. Some adults drink the fluid that exudes from the wound made by the ovipositor. This is no problem if the host is exposed but is difficult if the host is covered—hidden within a cocoon or kernel of grain. A parasite of the Angoumois grain moth has solved this problem. After piercing the kernel of wheat or corn in which the host larva is hidden, the parasite female withdraws her ovipositor part way, until its tip is just inside the hollow in which the larval host lies. Then she secretes a viscous fluid from the tip of her ovipositor and forms it into a tube that connects with the ovipositor wound in the host. This done, she carefully withdraws the ovipositor and turns around to suck fluid from the tube.

Are parasites fussy about what species of hosts they use?

Parasitic insects are generally fussy about their choice of hosts; in other words, they tend to be host specific. Some are very specific. Certain tiny parasitic wasps insert their eggs only into the eggs of moths and butterflies. Some wasps parasitize only aphids, and some flies parasitize only caterpillars. Among the most specific parasites is a tiny fly that attacks only scale insects of one family. No parasitic insect is more specific than a blow fly that is known to use only one species of land snail as a host. Some parasitic insects use hosts of several species but are specific to certain characteristics: insects that feed on certain plants, for example, or that bore in twigs, or that live under the bark of trees.

What **life stages** do parasitic insects attack?

All of them. Most parasitic insects live within the growing stage of the host: nymphs in insects with gradual metamorphosis or larvae in insects with complete metamorphosis. The only insects known to parasitize insect eggs are various wasps. Some egg parasites complete larval development within the egg, and others enter the embryo and continue to develop in the larva after it hatches. Parasites that develop only in the egg are, of course, very tiny. The adults of one such species, a trichogrammatid wasp, are only about 0.007 inch long. Some wasps and some flies parasitize adult insects such as true bugs, beetles, ants, wasps, and bees. The thick-headed flies, Conopidae, parasitize large adult wasps and bumble bees by laying an egg inside the host while in flight.

How do parasites **find their hosts**?

Much remains to be learned, but we do have some answers to this question. With few exceptions, the mother locates the hosts that her larval offspring will parasitize. Some mothers first orient to the plants that the hosts eat, and then search for hosts that may or may not be there. Among them is a wasp whose larvae parasitize caterpillars that feed on pines. Females whose ovaries are not mature are actually repelled by the odor of pine oil, but when their ovaries mature and they are ready to lay eggs, they are strongly attracted by it. Recent evidence shows that plants that are under attack by insects send out a call for help from parasites. For example, plants that are being chewed on by armyworm caterpillars release volatile chemicals that attract certain parasites of the caterpillars. A plant that has been artificially wounded with a razor blade attracts no parasites, but if the artificial wound is smeared with regurgitant from a caterpillar, parasites are attracted. Some parasites find their hosts by following the host's sex attractant pheromone. Certain tiny wasps, for example, are attracted from a distance to pheromone-releasing scale insects, the hosts that their larvae parasitize.

What are **hyperparasites**?

A hyperparasite, sometimes referred to as a superparasite, is a parasite of a parasite. Hyperparasitism is most frequently seen among the smaller parasitic wasps. Sometimes hyperparasites are themselves the victims of parasites. Thus, there may be parasites of parasites of parasites. As Jonathan Swift wrote:

> So naturalists observe, a flea
> Hath smaller fleas that on him prey;
> And these have smaller still to bite 'em;
> And so proceed *ad infinitum.*

A chain of parasite upon parasite cannot, of course, be infinitely long as Swift imagines, but chains of parasites with four links are known. A cecropia caterpillar may be parasitized by an ichneumonid wasp, which may be parasitized by a second species of ichneumonid; and the second ichneumonid may be parasitized by a chalcid wasp, which may be parasitized by a second chalcid.

What is **polyembryony**?

Polyembryony is a strange and uncommon form of reproduction practiced by certain parasitic wasps. It is the insect equivalent of twinning—the development of more than one individual from a single egg. The parasite inserts one or a few eggs into the host. At the very beginning of its development, when it has reached the four-cell stage, the embryo divides and redivides until it has split into anywhere from eight to two thousand identical replicas of itself. The replicas are, of course, all of the same sex as the original embryo. This horde of parasitic larvae ultimately consume all of the soft parts of the host and pupate within its skin, in many species completely filling the host's skin as a sausage is stuffed with meat. This often happens to cabbage looper caterpillars, which you may find on the cabbages in your garden.

Can insects **defend themselves** against parasites?

Insects have evolved many ways to foil parasites, ranging from trying to drive off egg-laying females to using physiological methods to destroy parasites that have actually invaded their bodies.

How do **Mexican bean beetle larvae** fend off parasites?

The leaf-eating larvae of the Mexican bean beetle—yellow, spiny, and soft-bodied—are easily observed pests of garden beans throughout most of the United States. They are not immune to parasites, but the multibranched spines that cover their bodies probably ward off many egg-laying parasites. These spines are not only a physical barrier. When insects as small as ants brush against them, the fragile tips of the spines break

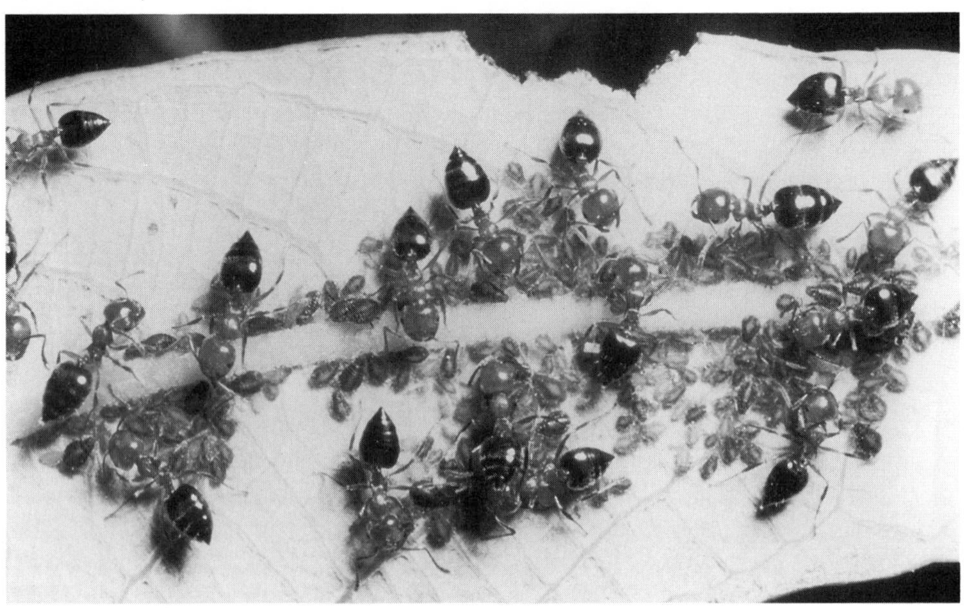

Ants herding aphids. (Photo by Edward S. Ross.)

and ooze a sticky fluid that gums up the intruder's body. The intruder, which is likely to be a parasite, limps off and attempts, not always successfully, to clean its body.

How do **leaf-cutter ants** drive away parasites?

These ants are plagued by parasitic flies that lay eggs on their necks. The larvae that hatch from these eggs burrow into the fly's head and ultimately kill it by eating its brain. Worker ants carrying large pieces of leaf in their mandibles as they return to the nest cannot defend themselves against these parasitic flies. But these workers are often accompanied by a guard, a smaller worker that rides shotgun as it sits on the leaf-piece carried by its larger sister. The guard snaps at approaching flies and often succeeds in driving them off.

How are **aphids** protected against parasites?

They are often protected by ants that collect the sweet honeydew that aphids excrete. Honeydew is an important part of the diet of some species of ants. Much as people keep dairy cows, some ants maintain herds of aphids that they "milk" for honeydew. To varying degrees, ants protect their aphids against predators and parasites—sometimes going so far as to build shelters over the aphids or to maintain permanent populations of root-feeding aphids in their nests.

Ant "milking" a caterpillar. (Photo by Edward S. Ross.)

What is **honeydew**?

Honeydew is the sweet excrement of aphids, scale insects, leafhoppers, and other Homoptera. These piercing-sucking insects drink large quantities of sap from the phloem tubes of plants, the tubes that carry sugars and other nutrients manufactured by the leaves down to the stems and roots. These insects take in more phloem sap than they can use and excrete the excess as honeydew. Honeydew is mostly water but contains significant amounts of nutrients required by insects: small quantities of amino acids (the building blocks of proteins) and much larger quantities of sugars. Trehalose, the blood sugar of insects, makes up about 35 percent of the sugars in honeydew.

Do **ants protect caterpillars** against parasites?

Caterpillars do not excrete honeydew, but some butterfly caterpillars, such as hairstreaks and silvery blues, have "honey glands" that secrete a sweet and nutritious "honey" that is prized by ants. Ants tend these caterpillars and protect them against parasites. Observations have shown that these caterpillars receive significant protection from the ants that tend them. Only 26 percent of the caterpillars tended by three or more ants were parasitized by insects, but a whopping 63 percent of those left untended or tended by only one ant were parasitized by insects.

What are the tiny white things clustered on the backs of the big green caterpillars that feed on my tomato plants?

The caterpillars are either tobacco or tomato hornworms, and the dozens of white things are cocoons spun by tiny larvae that lived as parasites in the caterpillar's body until they emerged through the skin of its back. Caterpillars with cocoons on their backs are still alive, but are paralyzed and neither can move nor feed. Do not remove these parasitized caterpillars from your plants. The adult parasites that emerge from the little white cocoons are your allies. Each one will lay a batch of eggs in several caterpillars.

How are the **eggs of some walkingsticks** protected against parasites?

Walkingsticks, which feed on the leaves of trees, simply let their eggs fall to the ground, where they are easy victims for parasitic cuckoo wasps that lay their eggs in the much larger walkingstick eggs. But many walkingstick eggs are rescued by ants that carry them back to their underground nests. The ants do not eat the hard-shelled walkingstick eggs, but they do eat a large edible appendage of the egg that is known as the capitulum. The eggs are not injured by the ants and the ants do not interfere with the tiny, newly hatched walkingsticks as they make their way from the nest up into the trees.

Do insects **flee areas infested with parasites**?

In a sense they do. The females of many species disperse widely, sometimes a matter of miles, before or while they lay their eggs. If their home area is heavily infested with parasites, the only eggs that will survive to become adults are those that are laid elsewhere. The population then shifts to a new habitat, which—if they are lucky—has not yet been occupied by their parasites. Ecologists refer to such insects as "fugitive species," because their populations "flee" to new areas from time to time.

Can insects **destroy parasites** that have already invaded their bodies?

Insects have a last line of defense that they use against parasites that have penetrated their bodies. They can encapsulate the parasite by covering it with blood cells. Blood cells migrate to the parasite, flatten themselves against its body, and ultimately form a thick capsule that smothers the parasite by cutting off its access to oxygen. This tactic is often successful against generalist parasites, but parasites that specialize on one or a few hosts can often protect themselves against being encapsulated.

Do **house flies** have parasites?

These pestiferous flies would be more numerous if they were not parasitized by almost thirty species of wasps. Among them are chalcid wasps that spend the larval stage in the pupae of flies. The adult female parasite must laboriously perforate the fly's cocoon-like puparium with her ovipositor before she can inject an egg into the pupa within. The pupa is ultimately killed by the parasite.

INSECT-EATING PLANTS

Are there many **insect-eating plants**?

Worldwide there are 538 known species of carnivorous plants —many of them mainly insect eaters—belonging to eight different families. This is only a tiny fraction, about two-tenths of a percent, of the more than 250,000 known species of plants, but a rather surprisingly large number considering how anomalous it is for a plant to eat an animal.

Where do insectivorous plants occur?

Geographically speaking, they occur in almost every region on earth except for the seas, extremely dry deserts, Antarctica, and the high Arctic. Ecologically speaking, they are generally found only in nutrient-poor habitats such as bogs, peat, sand, or decaying sandstone.

How do insect-eating plants **attract their prey**?

Terrestrial insect-eating plants attract nectar-seeking insects by their vivid flower-like colors, by emitting a honey-like odor, and by actually secreting nectar.

How do carnivorous plants **capture insects and other arthropods**?

They do so in several different ways. The pitcher of the pitcher plant is a slippery-sided pitfall trap. The aquatic plants of the tropical genus *Genlisea* have traps that work like a lobster pot or eel trap. Tiny insects and crustaceans easily enter the chamber of the trap but are prevented from leaving by inward pointing hairs that line the tunnel-like entrance. The familiar sundew plant has specialized sticky leaves that work like flypaper. The highly specialized leaves of the Venus flytrap work like a

Venus flytrap. (Photo courtesy of Photo Researchers, Inc.)

spring trap. The two sides of the leaf, hinged and fringed with incurving spines, are held open like the jaws of a trap. When an insect lands on the leaf, it quickly snaps shut, the fringes of spines interlocking to trap the insect. The bladders borne on the leaves of the aquatic bladderworts are sophisticated traps that capture tiny insects and crustaceans. There is a partial vacuum within the closed bladder. If some tiny swimming creature brushes against fine hairs on the outside of the bladder, the bladder suddenly opens and the creature is sucked in by the vacuum.

How does a **pitcher plant's pitfall** trap work?

The trap, actually a modified leaf, is about a foot tall, pitcher-like in shape, open at the top, and partially filled with water. Insects are attracted to it by nectar, its presence advertised in some species by the brilliant coloration of the pitcher. Nectar is secreted most abundantly just inside the mouth of the pitcher and, except in the common pitcher plant of the eastern United States, is protected from being evaporated by the sun or diluted by rain by an overhanging hood. Just below this nectar-secreting area, the inner walls of the pitcher are slippery— unsure footing for insects that wander away from the nectar source. Unfortunate nectar seekers that lose their footing plummet down into the water at the bottom of the pitcher. They are prevented from escaping by the slippery, vertical walls of the pitcher and a blockade of downward pointing hairs. In some pitcher plants the fluid in the pitcher contains a substance that paralyzes insects.

Do any carnivorous plants **specialize in ants**?

Some pitcher plants seem to be designed to attract and capture ants. These plants are traversed by a trail of nectaries (nectar-producing organs) that leads from the ground up to the mouth of a pitcher. Flying insects are attracted by the color of the pitcher, but ants, which are wingless, cannot see this color as they crawl on the ground. It is very likely that the trail of nectaries is an "ant-trail" that leads ants to the rich source of nectar that is located just inside the mouth of the pitcher. Ants are frequent visitors to the pitchers. Some lose their footing and fall into the water at the bottom of the pitcher, but most of them collect a load of nectar and leave without a mishap. It has been suggested that the relationship between ants and pitcher plants is mutualistic. The few ants that are trapped probably provide the plant with enough mineral nutrients to more than offset the "cost" of producing nectar. The ant colony's loss of an occasional worker is probably more than offset by the calorie-rich nectar that it gains.

Do **plants benefit** from trapping insects?

Experiments done both in nature and in the laboratory leave no doubt that insect-eating plants benefit from being carnivorous. Carnivorous plants that were fed artificially improved in both growth and reproduction, while those that were deprived prey decreased in growth and reproduction. Since these plants grow on nutrient-poor soil—soil lacking in minerals such as nitrogen—it is highly probable that their insect prey provide them with the lacking minerals. It may well be that insect-eating plants can survive on nutrient-poor soil only because of their carnivorous diet.

How do insect-eating plants **digest their prey**?

Most of them, with the exception of certain pitcher plants, have special glands that produce enzymes that digest insects —that break them down to molecules that the plant can absorb. But what about the pitcher plants that have no enzyme-producing glands? It seems that the insects that fall into the water at the bottom of the pitcher are digested for the plant by bacteria and protozoa that live in the water.

Do **insects exploit carnivorous plants**?

Very few insects feed on carnivorous plants. A few aphids, caterpillars, and weevils feed on the leaves, and a type of caterpillar that burrows in underground stems. In Florida, plume moth caterpillars crawl about on the leaves of sundew, eating trapped insects and also feeding on the leaves. Some insects live in the water in the pitfalls of pitcher plants, but do the plant no harm greater than appropriating for themselves some of the plant's prey. Among them are the larvae of a midge, a mosquito, and a

Who was Agostino Bassi?

Agostino Maria Bassi (1773–1856) was the first person to demonstrate conclusively that a microorganism is the cause of an infectious disease of an animal: specifically, that a fungus causes the muscardine disease of silkworm caterpillars. Louis Pasteur's discovery of the cause of pebrine disease of silkworms (1870) is usually credited as laying the foundation of the "germ theory of disease," which ultimately revolutionized the practice of human medicine. But that honor should really go to Bassi, whose publication on the muscardine disease of silkworms predates Pasteur's publication by 35 years.

flesh fly. Certain spiders that live on the walls of the pitcher seize insects as they enter the pitcher.

Do **mosquito larvae** live in North American pitcher plants?

The larvae of the pitcher plant mosquito (*Wyeomyia smithii*) live nowhere except in the water in pitcher plants. After taking a meal of blood, adult females lay their eggs inside young pitcher leaves just as they are opening and usually before water has accumulated in them. The larvae feed on bacteria, protozoa, and small organic particles at the bottom of the pitcher. Larvae that are late to mature spend the winter in the pitcher, often frozen in the water. In 1901, J. B. Smith wrote as follows about lumps of ice taken from pitcher plants that he had moved to a warm room:

> Long before the lumps were completely melted those [larvae] first released were moving about actively . . . Soon after the ice had melted and the debris had settled, the insects were busily engaged in apparent feeding.

PATHOGENS

What kinds of microorganisms cause **diseases** in insects?

A great many different species of pathogens—organisms that cause disease—occur in insects. Among them are various kinds of viruses, bacteria, fungi, and protozoa. People have been aware of insect diseases for centuries, but it was not until well into the

19th century that scientists began to discover the pathogenic organisms that cause diseases of insects.

How did Agostino Bassi prove that a fungus causes **muscardine disease**?

Bassi found that the fungus, today known as *Beauveria bassiana,* grows in the living silkworm and eventually causes its death. With the help of a botanist, Bassi isolated and characterized the fungus. He demonstrated that healthy silkworms came down with muscardine disease after being inoculated with the fungus, and that in a colony of silkworms the disease is transmitted by contact and contaminated food. He also discovered that the disease can be controlled by disinfecting the area where silkworms are raised and the associated equipment with lye, wine, brandy, boiling water, and exposure to sunlight.

What is **pebrine disease**?

It is another disease of silkworms—but caused by a protozoan (a relative of the amoeba) rather than a fungus. The deadly pebrine disease was devastating the French silk industry in the 19th century. In 1853 France produced 57 million pounds of silk. By 1865, production had fallen to less than nine million pounds per year due to pebrine disease and some less important associated diseases. Louis Pasteur was called on to solve the problem. He eventually discovered the causative agent of the disease, the protozoan, and found that it was spread not only by contamination but also through the egg. Thus a culture of silkworms started with infested eggs was doomed. Pasteur's solution was to eliminate all eggs that carried the protozoan. This was accomplished by examining the egg-laying moths under a microscope to determine if they harbored disease-causing protozoa. If they did, all of the eggs that they had laid were destroyed by burning. Eggs that had been laid by moths that contained no protozoa were retained and used to start healthy silkworm cultures.

What causes **honey bee paralysis**?

It is caused by a virus. Bees infected with this virus become lethargic, weak, and reluctant to fly. Even in the early stages of the disease, other bees in the colony recognize infected individuals, tugging at them and finally driving them out of the hive. In the advanced stages of this disease, its victims become helpless, may lose their hair, have dark, greasy-looking abdomens, and soon die.

What is **milky disease**?

This bacterial infection kills several kinds of insects but is best known in the Japanese beetle. Larval beetles become infected by ingesting bacterial spores as they feed on

Grasshopper infected with milky disease. (Photo by Edward S. Ross.)

the roots of grass in the soil. The spores germinate, and the active bacteria make their way through the walls of the gut into the body cavity. There they multiply until they turn the insect's blood milky white. At this point, infected larvae, which will soon die, can be recognized by their milky white color.

ESCAPING FROM PREDATORS

What is the **first line of defense** of most insects?

Camouflage—blending in with their surroundings so that predators tend not to notice them. Tree-dwelling katydids have broad, green wings that look like leaves, and in some species have markings that resemble disease spots, insect nibbling, or other blemishes that are commonly seen on leaves. Nocturnal moths that rest motionless on the trunks and branches of trees during the day are deceptively colored and patterned like bark. Most of them are brown and gray to match the dark bark of oaks, maples, and other trees on which they rest. A few species that habitually rest on the trunks of white-barked birches are colored in matching white.

How good are **camouflaged moths** at selecting matching backgrounds on which to rest?

A controlled experiment done by Theodore Sargent showed that they are very good at it. Several species of moths with wings of different colors and shades were placed at night in a glass-covered box whose inner walls were painted four shades of gray ranging from light to dark. The box was placed in a shaded woodland, and the next morning the backgrounds that the resting moths had selected were noted. Most of the moths had selected a shade of gray whose light reflectance, measured with a spectrophotometer, matched the light reflectance of their wings. Interestingly, dark and light forms of the same species selected different backgrounds that matched their own shade.

What are **stick caterpillars**?

Some of the inchworms—the caterpillars of geometrid moths— are known as stick caterpillars because they are deceptively camouflaged to look like twigs. They feed on

Leaf katydid. (Photo by Edward S. Ross.)

leaves at night, but during the day they sit frozen on a branch with their bodies jutting straight up so that they look like a short stubby twig. Different species are amazingly well attuned to the appearance of the twigs of their host plants. A stick caterpillar that feeds on birch has a slender and rather smooth body, like a birch twig. A species that feeds on oaks has a thick, bumpy body that looks like an oak twig. Both species match the color and pattern of the twigs of their respective host plants.

Are some camouflaged insects **polymorphic**?

Some are. That is, members of the same species come in different forms—morphs in the parlance of biology—that are camouflaged in different ways. This is probably an evolutionary strategy that is equivalent to not putting all of the eggs in the same basket. The caterpillars of a hawk moth of the Galapagos Islands are a good example. When young, these caterpillars are green, and when not feeding, rest on the undersides of the green leaves of their food plant. The older caterpillars can be green, brown, or gray. The green ones continue to rest on green leaves, but the brown and gray ones prefer to rest on twigs when they are not feeding.

What is **counter shading**?

As you have probably noticed, many animals, including many insects, are dark on the dorsal (upper) surface, and pale on the ventral (lower) surface. This pattern of col-

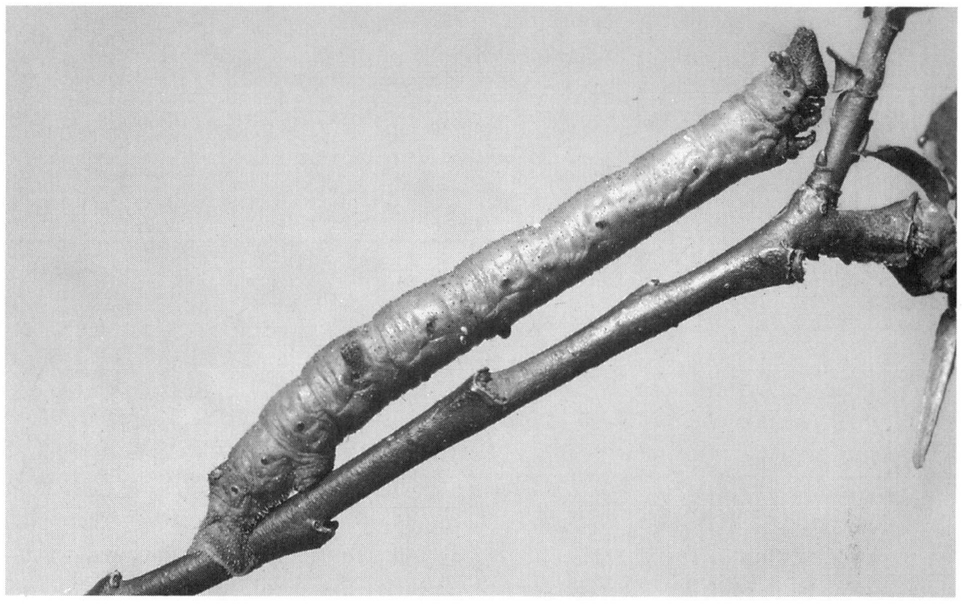

Stick caterpillar. (Photo by Edward S. Ross.)

oration, known as counter shading, tends to obscure the three dimensional form of a camouflaged animal's body. When light, which usually comes from above, falls on the body of an animal or any other rounded object, it lights the upper side but leaves the lower side more or less shaded. The contrast between the lighted and the shaded areas reveals the rounded form of the animal, making it stand out from its background and thereby attracting the attention of predators. Counter shading tends to eliminate this contrast. Most camouflaged caterpillars are counter shaded in the usual way, dark on top and light on the bottom, but those that habitually rest upside-down, as by clinging to the underside of a twig, have reversed counter shading. They are dark on the lower surface, which, in their position, is uppermost, and pale on the upper surface, which, in their position, is lowermost.

How did natural selection affect the **peppered moth's camouflage**?

These moths are superbly camouflaged when they rest motionless during the day on the trunk or a branch of a tree. They match its light-colored bark and even have markings that look like lichens that grow on the tree's bark. This ruse worked well until early in the nineteenth century, when the smoke and soot from factories blackened the bark and killed the lichens on trees near industrial cities such as Manchester in England. Light-colored moths were conspicuous when they rested on these blackened trees and were picked off, as has been demonstrated experimentally, by insect-

Do camouflaged insects always remain motionless?

Not always. Movement may enhance camouflage under certain conditions. Walkingsticks, which live among twigs and leaves and masquerade as twigs, mask their movements by walking very slowly and rocking from side to side on their long, threadlike legs so as to resemble a twig swaying in the wind. Similarly, dead leaf butterflies perched on a twig may enhance their superb camouflage by swaying gently from side to side to simulate movement in the breeze.

eating birds. A few black mutant peppered moths had probably been appearing all along from time to time but were quickly eliminated because they were conspicuous to birds. But after the trees had been blackened, the dark moths were much less conspicuous than the light ones and were, therefore, more likely to survive. The survivors were, of course, the parents of the next generation, and since the black mutation is a heritable trait, black moths soon virtually replaced white ones near industrial cities. This was, of course, an obvious example of natural selection and evolution in action. Natural selection is now having the reverse effect. As England eliminates air pollution and as tree bark becomes light in color and once again lichen-covered, white moths are replacing black moths in industrial areas.

How did scientists prove the **peppered moths theory**?

During the day, both light and dark moths were placed on tree trunks; some of each type on trees that matched their color and others on trees that contrasted with their color. The following night many of these moths were recaptured. Moths that had been placed on bark that matched their color were more likely to be recaptured than moths that had been placed on bark that did not match their color. Clearly, moths that were not well-camouflaged were disappearing, presumably because they were more often captured by birds.

How do we know that **insect-eating birds are the selective agents** that favor well-camouflaged peppered moths?

The important role of birds was demonstrated by a simple experiment done in the field. Black and light-colored moths were placed on matching or contrasting tree trunks and watched from blinds. Birds were often seen to capture moths that contrasted with the bark on which they sat, but they very seldom captured moths that sat on bark that matched their color.

Do insects fool birds by **resembling inedible objects**?

Yes, some insects look like inedible objects. For example, some insects and even some spiders look deceptively like bird droppings, as is graphically expressed in Colonel A. Newnham's account of an experience that he had in India:

> I came across the larva in question in the month of August or September 1892, at Ahmadabad on a bush of *Salvadora* . . . I was stretching across to collect a beetle and in withdrawing my hand nearly touched what I took to be the disgusting excreta of a crow. Then to my astonishment I saw it was a caterpillar half-hanging, half-lying limply down a leaf. [A] thing that struck me was the skill with which the colouring rendered the varying surfaces, the dried portion at the top, then the main portion, moist, viscid, soft, and the glistening globule at the end. A skilled artist working with all materials at his command could not have done it better.

What are **flash colors**?

Flash colors are those that are suddenly revealed and likely to distract a predator. A common grasshopper of North America, the Carolina grasshopper, is a familiar example. It is so well camouflaged when it rests on the ground that it is all but invisible. If we come too close to one as we walk along a path, it bursts into flight, revealing its conspicuous black and yellow hind wings as it makes a loud crackling sound. A few yards down the path it lands, folds its wings, and once more becomes invisible. A bird that flushes and chases one of these grasshoppers is likely to be deceived. It has a "search image" for something yellow and black and will probably not notice the camouflaged grasshopper after it lands on the ground.

What are **underwing moths**?

They are large, handsome moths called underwings because their brightly colored hind wings are, when the moth is at rest, concealed by their somber front wings. There are many species, and all are beautifully camouflaged when they rest motionless on the bark of a tree during the day. Most have front wings deceptively patterned with gray and brown to blend in with dark-colored bark, but the front wings of a species that habitually rests on white-barked birches are white with fine black markings. The conspicuous hind wings of underwings are black and banded with white, red, or yellow. Underwings "flush" only when they are touched or very closely approached. If touched with the point of a pencil, or presumably by the bill of a bird, they suddenly lift the front wings to reveal the brilliantly colored hind wings. This probably startles the attacking bird—perhaps only momentarily—but gives the moth precious extra seconds in which to escape. If the bird chases the moth, it may not notice the moth

How can I observe underwing moths?

They are almost impossible to find during the day. But they can be attracted at night by using a technique that entomologists call "sugaring." The "sugar" is a frothing, fermenting mixture of beer, sugar or molasses, and fruit—canned peaches are good. During the day, paint this mixture on the trunks of several trees in a woodland. Come back on succeeding nights to check your trapline of trees with a flashlight. You will probably find many different kinds of moths drinking your intoxicating bait, some so drunk that you can pick them up in your fingers. With a bit of luck, you will find some underwings among them.

when it lands on the bark of another tree and covers the bright colors—the bird's search image—to once again become invisible.

Is there any evidence that underwing moths **actually do startle birds**?

A graduate student at the University of Massachusetts used blue jays and "artificial underwings," to explore this question. An artificial underwing consisted of a triangular piece of cardboard to which were attached plastic "wings" that on some models had been painted to look like the conspicuous hind wings of an underwing. A pinyon nut was attached to the underside of the model. When a model was inserted into an opening in a board, the cardboard body was visible, but the plastic "wings" were hidden. When a blue jay withdrew the model to get the pinyon nut, the plastic "hind wings" were suddenly revealed. The jays were clearly startled by the appearance of the unfamiliar and conspicuous hind wings. Startled jays dropped the model without removing the pinyon nut, raised their crests, sounded alarm calls, and retreated to the far side of the cage.

Do insects **mimic snakes**?

This would be a good way to scare off insect-eating birds, but at first thought it seems impossible for an animal as small as an insect to pass for an animal as large as a snake. But a large caterpillar, such as the large South American hawk moth caterpillar described by the Rev. A. Miles Moss, can resemble the head and neck of a small snake. The resting caterpillar hangs motionless from a small branch and is so well camouflaged that it looks like nothing more than a broken, lichen-covered branch. But when disturbed it turns into a snake before your eyes. As the Rev. Moss described, the snake-like effect is produced by:

False eyespots can frighten potential predators away. (Photo by Edward S. Ross.)

the creature turning itself over and exhibiting its ventral area, which is adorned by a broad band of dark olive-green with the three anterior sets of claspers completely withdrawn and scarcely visible. The thoracic segments, which are always swollen, become puffed out laterally to an exaggerated extent; a pair of [false] black eyes on segment 4, hitherto concealed and situated behind the now recumbent and wholly inconspicuous legs, open out; the cheeks appear to be adorned by yellow scales with black edges; and the fraudulent notion that one is beholding merely the head and neck of a formidable, if small, snake is carried to a nicety by the rigidity of the curve adopted. Then, as if to mesmerize, a swaying side-to-side motion is kept up for an appreciable number of seconds, before the creature, seeming to realize that an attack is no further contemplated, gradually closes its false eyes and relapses once more into diurnal slumbers.

Do the large **eye-like patterns** on the wings of some moths have a function?

The certainly do. They startle predators such as birds and may even scare them off. These patterns, generally referred to as eyespots, may be only crude imitations of the eyes of vertebrates, but those of some moths are convincingly realistic imitations that even have a highlight on the "pupil" of the "eye." In either case, they are on the upper surface of the hind wings, are usually covered by camouflaged front wings, and, if the moth is disturbed, are suddenly revealed by lifting the front wings. A large moth with its wings spread wide to reveal its eyespots can look like the face of a glowering owl, an apparition that will, at the least, startle an attacking bird and give the moth a few extra seconds to make its escape.

Is there any concrete evidence that **large eyespots frighten birds**?

There is convincing experimental evidence that at least some birds are frightened by large eyespots. A. D. Blest rubbed away the eyespots on the hind wings of some peacock butterflies and did not disturb the eyespots on the wings of others. Attacking yellow buntings were often startled by butterflies with intact eyespots but not by butterflies from which the eyespots had been removed. In another experiment, he trained birds to take insects from a piece of frosted glass onto which he could project images from below. When a chaffinch, a great tit, a yellow bunting, or a reed bunting was about to pick up an insect from the blank glass, he projected an image on either side of the insect. The birds were greatly startled by the sudden appearance of eye-like patterns but were little affected by the appearance of crosses or other images that did not resemble eyes.

Do the **tiny eyespots** on the wings of some insects have a function?

The available evidence indicates that they serve to deflect a bird's peck away from a vital area of the insect's body. When birds seize an insect, they aim for the head end rather than the tail end. That way they may disable the insect and it will be less likely to escape. One of the best ways to tell the head from the tail is to look for the eyes. A. D. Blest did a simple experiment that showed that birds actually do aim for the eyes. He painted tiny eyespots on the tail ends of some mealworms (succulent beetle larvae that are a treat for birds). When yellow buntings were offered these mealworms, most of them misdirected their pecks at the tail end. But when they were offered mealworms that had no painted eyespots on their tail ends, they directed most of their pecks at the true head end. Knowing this, it comes as no surprise that many insects have tiny eyespots on nonessential parts of their bodies, such as the tips of the hind wings.

Do insects have **dummy heads**?

Some do, and their function is probably to deflect a bird's attack away from the vulnerable true head. Many of the hairstreak butterflies, including some North American ones, have false heads at the ends of their hind wings. The false heads are adorned with tiny eyespots and long, thin, antenna-like projections of the wing. When a hairstreak is perched or sitting on a flower, it holds its real antennae motionless, and moves it hind wings just enough to make the false antennae wiggle. When a certain South American hairstreak lands from a flight, it swiftly flips around so that the false head on its tail end is where its true head was an instant before. A bird that pecks at a false head makes only a superficial wound and gets only an expendable fragment of wing rather than the whole insect. Furthermore, when the insect makes its escape, it confuses the attacking bird by flying off in a direction opposite to what the bird expects.

Do insects have **defensive weapons**?

As anyone who has been stung by a bee or a wasp knows, some insects have potent defensive weapons. Insects have other weapons too. Certain caterpillars are covered with fine, venom-filled hairs that break off in the mouths of birds or other predators. Some insects discharge sprays of noxious chemicals much as do skunks. Beetles with powerful mandibles bite in defense, and predaceous robber flies and true bugs often stab with their sharp beaks. Cockroaches, grasshoppers, and other large insects may drive away a predator by kicking with powerful legs armed with sharply pointed spines.

Do insects give **warning** of their defensive capabilities?

The great majority of them do. It is safer to warn away a predator than to be attacked and forced to use a defensive weapon. The warning signals that insects give are many and varied. The great majority of insects with potent defensive weapons are brightly colored—often with combinations of black, red, and yellow—and stand out conspicuously against their backgrounds, the exact opposite of camouflage. They may enhance the effect of their warning colors with attention-grabbing movements such as spreading their wings, wagging them, or rocking from side to side. Like rattlesnakes, some insects make warning sounds.

What is the **lubber grasshopper's defense** against birds?

It's a very effective chemical defense accompanied by an unmistakable warning. This large, slow-moving, flightless grasshopper of the southeastern United States is conspicuously marked with yellow and black—a striking contrast to the camouflage of most other grasshoppers. If an intruder approaches, it raises up on its legs and partly reveals its short but brilliantly red front wings. If it is then touched by a pencil point—or presumably by a bird's beak—it raises its red wings the rest of the way and discharges a noxious substance that smells like creosote. Predators usually back off in response to this display, but birds that happen to eat a lubber vomit and will thereafter stay away from these insects.

How do **bombardier beetles** protect themselves?

If a predator doesn't get the message conveyed by their orange and blue warning colors, they bombard it with a spray of noxious, irritating chemicals. The beetle's chemi-

How potent are the venoms of stinging ants, wasps, and bees?

The sting of a female—only females sting—may be mild and cause little pain, or it may be very painful to people and may be even more painful to smaller animals such as birds, toads, and lizards. As Justin Schmidt wrote, the sting of a tiny fire ant, which weighs in at about three billionths of an ounce, can have a terrific impact on a comparatively huge person that weighs about ten million times as much as the ant. The ability to sting has obviously been useful to the Hymenoptera (ants, wasps, bees, and relatives), since about 70,000 of them out of a world total of about 108,000 species can sting.

cal discharge, although on a smaller scale, is probably more potent drop for drop than a skunk's discharge. If a bird, a toad, or some other predator threatens it, the beetle raises its hind end, aims it at the predator, and sprays it with boiling-hot defensive chemicals produced by an explosive chemical reaction in a special chamber in the beetle's body. Toads that make the mistake of trying to snap up a bombardier beetle are sprayed in the mouth. The toad's discomfort and disgust are obvious. It gags, sticks out its tongue, and rubs it against the ground to get rid of the noxious chemicals.

Why are the **venoms** of some stinging insects more painful than venoms of others?

Generally speaking, there is a correlation between a stinging insect's life style and the painfulness of its venom. The more an insect's life style predisposes it to attacks from vertebrates, the more painful its sting is likely to be. Colonies of social insects constitute such a big meal that they are likely to be raided by animals as large as bears. It is thus fitting that social bees and wasps generally have painful stings. A few solitary wasps that are almost constantly exposed to vertebrate predators also have painful stings. Among them are tarantula hawks—large wasps that spend most of their time running around on the ground looking for spiders.

How are **monarch butterflies** protected against predators?

Most of them, like many other insects, are poisonous and make any animal that eats them ill. While some insects synthesize their own poisons, monarchs sequester poisons, cardiac glycosides, from the milkweed plants that they eat in their caterpillar stage. Cardiac glycosides, which are related to digitalis, a drug used to treat heart problems, are deadly poisons. But, fortunately for the predator that eats a monarch, the dose that causes vomiting is a little lower than the deadly dose. Thus, the predator is sickened but eliminates the cardiac glycosides from its body before they do any serious harm.

How was the effect of **toxic monarch butterflies** on birds demonstrated?

In a series of masterful experiments, Lincoln Brower and his colleagues proved that monarchs obtain poisons (cardiac glycosides) from their food plants, that these poisons make birds ill, and that birds that have been sickened by eating a monarch thereafter reject monarchs on sight. He raised some monarchs on a species of milkweed that does not contain cardiac glycosides and others on a species that does. Blue jays that had been kept in captivity long enough to forget previous experiences with monarchs eagerly consumed monarchs that had been raised on the milkweed that does not contain cardiac glycosides. They continued to eat nontoxic monarchs until they were given monarchs that had been raised on the species of milkweed that does contain cardiac glycosides. Shortly after eating a toxic monarch, they showed obvious signs of distress and then vomited and retched. Thereafter these bluejays rejected both toxic and nontoxic monarchs, and some retched at the sight of a monarch.

How do **poisonous butterflies benefit** when they must be eaten before their poison has an effect?

The individual that is eaten does not, of course, benefit directly from its toxicity, but other members of a victim's species do benefit from its sacrifice. Poisonous species are generally warningly colored, as is the orange and black monarch butterfly, and may present other warning signals that predators learn to associate with an unpleasant experience with a toxic insect. Since birds and other predators rarely die from eating a toxic insect, the other members of a victim's species benefit from the sacrifice of their relatives, because their potential predators have been taught not to attack them. Even the victim benefits indirectly, because many of its genes will survive in its relatives, thus increasing the victim's "inclusive fitness." The idea of inclusive fitness can be understood if we think of an organism as a gene's way of making and passing on copies of itself—an idea not unlike Samuel Butler's aphorism that "a hen is only an egg's way of making another egg."

What is **Batesian mimicry**?

Batesian mimicry, named in honor of its discoverer, the 19th-century English naturalist Henry W. Bates, is the close resemblance of an edible animal (the mimic) to a venomous, toxic, or otherwise noxious animal (the model). In this form of mimicry, the mimic tries to bluff its way past predators by falsifying the warning signals of the model. Some flies look like wasps; some edible butterflies look like poisonous butterflies; some hairy flies look like bumblebees.

An ant-mimicing spider. (Photo by Edward S. Ross.)

How close can the **resemblance between a mimic and a model** be?

Sometimes the resemblance is only approximate, but in other cases, it is uncannily close. A harmless hover fly, for example, looks so much like a viciously stinging yellowjacket wasp that entomology students have been known to put them with the wasps in their collections. The fly looks like the wasp in shape and color pattern, and also mimics it in more subtle ways. The wasp has long, black antennae that it waves in front of its head. The fly has short, barely visible antennae (as do most flies), but it gives a convincing imitation of the wasp's antennae by waving its long, black front legs in front of its head. When a yellowjacket sits on a flower, it holds its tinted wings out to the side and folds them lengthwise so that they look like a narrow, brown band. The fly holds its wings out to the side but cannot fold them. Nonetheless, a brown band along the leading edge of the fly's otherwise colorless wing looks like the wasp's folded wing. The wasp advertises its presence by constantly rocking from side to side. The fly does not rock but imitates that motion by wagging its wings. Finally, if a person, or presumably a bird, grasps a wasp, the wasp makes a loud squawk. If the fly is similarly handled, it makes a squawk that is almost identical in acoustic properties to the sound made by the wasp.

Is there any **proof** that Batesian mimicry actually works?

A number of experiments done with various kinds of predators, models, and mimics have proved that Batesian mimicry does indeed work. In one of these experiments, inexperienced birds readily ate harmless flies that mimic bumble bees. When these same birds were offered real bumble bees, they tried to eat them but were stung in the mouth. Thereafter, they did not even attempt to eat either real bumble bees or their mimics.

What is **Müllerian mimicry**?

Like Batesian mimicry, Müllerian mimicry involves a close resemblance between two different kinds of animals—almost always insects. But in Müllerian mimicry, both insects gain by resembling each other. As pointed out by Fritz Müller, two or more poisonous and warningly colored insects will tend to evolve to resemble each other since all will benefit by adopting the same "advertising logo." Even in the most toxic species, some individuals will be killed in the process of educating and reeducating predators. If two noxious species use the same warning signal, the predators need learn only one signal rather than two, and fewer individuals will have to be sacrificed.

What is an **example of Müllerian mimicry**?

There are many, but the stinging wasps and bees constitute an astonishing example that often goes unremarked. There are tens of thousands of these stinging insects, but the great majority of them share the same warning signals. They are barred with yellow and black and make similar buzzing noises.

Is the **viceroy butterfly** a Batesian or a Mullerian mimic of the monarch?

The monarch and the viceroy look so much alike, nearly impossible to distinguish on the wing, that there is no doubt that one of them is mimicking the other. The viceroy has for many decades been held up as the classical example of a Batesian mimic. But, strictly speaking, it could be considered a Müllerian rather than a Batesian mimic. Laboratory tests show that viceroys are somewhat noxious to birds, but not nearly as noxious as monarchs. Can we really consider two such unequally noxious insects to be Müllerian mimics of each other? In other words, does the monarch gain by sharing the same "advertising logo" with the far less noxious viceroy? Think about it this way: Would a manufacturer of powerful batteries benefit by using the same brand name as a manufacturer of less powerful batteries?

What is **aggressive mimicry**?

An aggressive mimic resembles another organism in order to take advantage of it or some other organism. A female firefly that flashes false signals to attract and devour males of some other species of firefly is a practitioner of aggressive mimicry. The wasp and bee orchids of Europe and Australia use a cruelly deceptive form of aggressive

How do we know that some moths respond to the cries of bats?

We know this from a fascinating series of observations and experiments done by Kenneth Roeder. In one of these experiments, he observed the responses of moths flying near and around a light in his backyard to recorded ultrasonic sounds. Many of the moths responded by making evasive maneuvers. Some moths, species that do not have ears, did not respond at all.

mimicry to attract pollinating insects (in this case male wasps or bees) to their blossoms. These orchids derive their common name from the resemblance of their blossoms to a wasp or a bee. The resemblance is far from perfect, but close enough to deceive a sex-starved male of the species. The orchid blossoms also give off scents that mimic the sex-attractant pheromones of wasps or bees. Since the blossom smells, looks, and feels like a female, a male who has taken the bait tries to copulate with it. He may be quite persistent, but after several futile attempts to accomplish coitus, he becomes discouraged and flies away—not before two pollinia, bundles of pollen grains, have stuck to the front of his head. These pollinia will fertilize the next wasp or bee orchid blossom that tricks the hapless male.

Why do some **moths have ears**?

This is a good question. With very few exceptions, moths are mute, incapable of making sounds. What, then, are they listening to if not to each other as do singing insects such as crickets, katydids, and cicadas? The answer is that they are listening for the ultrasonic cries of hunting bats. The bats, which are nocturnal, locate their insect prey through echolocation, also known as sonar. The ultrasonic cries of bats, too high pitched for the human ear to hear, bounce off flying insects as well as obstacles such as branches or telephone wires. By hearing these faint echoes, the bats "see" what is around them, including the insects on which they prey. When moths hear the cries of a bat, they take evasive action. If the bat is far away, they change their course to get away from it. If the bat is nearby, some moths fold their wings and drop to the ground, and others make a power dive into the vegetation.

How do **tiger moths** respond to bat cries?

Certain species of Arctiidae, the tiger moth family, can make ultrasonic sounds, and when they hear a bat, they respond by making sounds of their own. Tame bats refuse to eat arctiid moths, as do birds and other insectivores. It seems likely, therefore, that the sounds made by these moths, which are in the hearing range of bats, are a warning of their noxiousness.

Do **mute insects** other than moths have ears?

Some do. Praying mantises have a single ear between their hind legs, and green lacewings have an ear on each forewing. The fact that these two insects have such different ears tells us the ability to listen for bat cries evolved independently at least twice. Actually it evolved at least four times, since owlet moths have a pair of ears on the thorax, and hawk moths have ears on their heads.

BENEFICIAL INSECTS

Just how **beneficial are insects** for people?

Immensely so! As a matter of fact we could not survive without them—certainly not as a population that even approaches in size the current human population and surely not in what we now consider to be comfort. Most of us focus on the tiny handful of insects that we consider pests and ignore the vast majority of insects that, considered as a whole, are important and often essential members of all of the world's ecosystems except for the seas. These are the ecosystems in which we live and that provide us with food, medicines, fiber, lumber, and recreation. Without their insects virtually all of these ecosystems would disappear or become something different that would probably be less hospitable to humans.

In what ways are insects **important in ecosystems**?

In many different ways. Insects pollinate the great majority of flowering plants. They are important scavengers, second only to bacteria as decomposers of dung and dead plants and animals. Those that prey upon or parasitize plants, insects, and other animals help to keep their burgeoning populations in check. Insects are essential or important food for many animals ranging from toads to bears. Finally, they are second only to earthworms as tillers and aerators of the soil.

How important are insects as **pollinators**?

Insects are by far the major pollinators of flowering plants, the angiosperms. Pollination is the transfer of pollen (the flowering plants' equivalent of sperm) from the male structures of a blossom to the female structures of a blossom. It is accomplished for some plants by the wind and certain kinds of birds and bats, but about 80 percent of the world's flowering plants are wholly or partly pollinated by a great variety of insects,

Long-horned beetle eating pollen. (Photo by Edward S. Ross.)

among them beetles, tiny gnats, various flies, bees, ants, butterflies, and moths. Considering just a few of the plants that provide food or drink for people, without pollinating insects there would be no chocolate, coffee, tea, pumpkins, squash, melons, cucumbers, onion, sunflowers, figs, peaches, plums, apricots, cherries, strawberries, raspberries, blackberries, blueberries, cranberries, kiwis, citrus fruits, pears, or apples.

Why did Charles Darwin say that **old maids are the mainstay of the British Empire**?

Darwin's jocular argument is that old maids keep cats, that cats eat field mice that destroy bumblebee nests, that bumblebees pollinate clover, that clover makes good beef, and that good beef makes the soldiers who extend and defend the Empire. Darwin's view that insects are essential for clover was confirmed when it was discovered that red clover grown in New Zealand, where it does not occur naturally, did not bear seed until bumble bees were introduced.

How important are **insect-pollinated plants**?

They are very important. Green plants, the only organisms that can harness the energy of the sun to produce food, are the foundation of virtually all ecosystems, the first link in almost all food chains. Insect-pollinated plants are a dominant element in practical-

Are insects important decomposers of dead plants and animals?

Yes, they are. For one thing, insects that eat dung, dead plants, or dead animals are extremely abundant. A square yard of ground litter in a forest, for example, may contain about 30,000 insects, most of them decomposers of dead plant and animal matter. One pat of cow dung is likely to be inhabited by hundreds of insects, mostly various species of maggots and beetles. A dead animal is fed on by a succession of many different insects, the species inhabiting the corpse changing as it decomposes—ranging from blow flies that lay their eggs or larvae on the body within minutes of death, to hide beetles and moths that appear only when nothing but bones, dry skin, and hair are left.

ly all terrestrial ecosystems. Of the approximately 250,000 known species of plants, at least 195,000 of them, about 78 percent, are flowering plants or *angiosperms*. About 80 percent of the flowering plants are more or less dependent upon insects for pollination—about 156,000, or well over 60 percent of the known plants.

Are pollinating insects **economically important**?

Very much so. Insect pollinated crops constitute about 15 percent of the American diet. In 1988 the total value of the insect-pollinated crop plants in the United States was about 24.6 billion dollars.

How are **lady's slippers** pollinated?

Through deceit. Lady's slippers, the showy native orchids of North America, are among the few flowering plants that do not reward the insects that pollinate them. They produce no nectar, and their pollen is not available to the insects. The largest and showiest part of their blossom is a balloon-like pouch, the "slipper." The pouch, which functions as a pitfall trap, has a slit-like opening on its upper surface. A nectar-seeking bee or fly that lands on the colorful "slipper" slides down into the pouch through a slippery-sided opening. The only way it can get out of the slipper is to crawl through a narrow opening, unavoidably brushing against the stigma, the female organ of the flower, and against masses of pollen that stick to its back. If the insect is trapped by another lady's slipper, the pollen rubs off on its stigma as it crawls out of the trap.

What are **carrion flowers**?

The blossoms of a few plants stink of carrion and are pollinated by flies that lay their eggs on the rotting carcasses of animals. An African carrion flower is dark red and even looks like rotting meat. Carrion flies that are fooled by the deceptive blossom will actually lay their eggs on it. They pollinate the blossom as they walk about on it, but for them the experience is a catastrophe. The larvae that hatch from their eggs will starve to death.

How do we know that insects are **important decomposers of dead plant material**?

The experimental elimination of insects and other arthropods that feed on plant litter significantly reduced the rate at which it decomposes. When the arthropod decomposers were killed with insecticides, the rate at which plant litter decomposed was reduced by as much as 53 percent. Arthropods facilitate the action of fungi and bacteria, which are the ultimate decomposers, largely by increasing the surface area of the litter by chewing it up and converting it to feces.

Why were **dung beetles** introduced in Australia?

When cattle were first raised in Australia, their droppings accumulated on the ground and did not decompose for months, thus choking off forage plants and seriously impairing the productivity of pastures and range land. This was because there were no dung-eating beetles in Australia capable of coping with wet, sloppy cow pats. Australian dung beetles were adapted to utilize only the small, dry dung pellets of kangaroos, the only large grazing animals of the native Australian fauna. The problem was solved by introducing from Africa and Europe scarab beetles that are evolutionarily adapted to utilize the wet droppings of cattle, buffalo, and other large bovine grazers.

What is the ecological function of **parasitic and predaceous insects**?

By killing their hosts or their prey they help to maintain the "balance of nature." The insects and other animals of an ecosystem are in an approximate state of balance. Populations increase and decrease, but rarely does a population grow so far out of bounds that it seriously disrupts its ecosystem. Parasitic and predaceous insects are important factors in restraining population growth. Any animal population has the potential to increase astronomically, because it normally produces an excess of offspring. A female house fly, for example, lays about 500 eggs during her life If just two of them survive to become reproducing adults, she will have replaced herself and her mate. If this keeps up, the house fly population will neither increase nor decrease from year to year. But what if in each succeeding generation 20 out of the 500 eggs survive because the population of an important predator or parasite of house flies is at low ebb? By the end of seven house fly generations (the usual number in a growing season), the descendants of a single pair will be 10 million pairs, or 20 million flies.

How important are insect parasites and predators to **maintaining the "balance of nature"**?

More important than any other group of animals. The great majority of parasitic and predaceous animals in the world are insects, a total of over 400,000 known species. That's close to 50 percent of the known insects and over 30 percent of all of the known animals. According to R. R. Askew, about 115,000 species of insects are parasites, and according to H. H. Ross, over 300,000 are predators in at least one of their life stages. Most of these parasites and predators attack other insects and, with the possible exception of disease-causing microbes, are the major biotic check on the growth of insect populations. A few insects are parasites of animals other than insects, ranging from earthworms to mammals, and as transmitters of disease-causing organisms are a significant check on the increase of bird and mammal populations.

Are parasites and predators as **important as the weather** in keeping insect populations in check?

Both are important, but over the long haul parasites and predators are much more important. Indeed, they are essential. If a storm or a severe winter decimates an insect population, the cause-and-effect relationship is obvious and makes a big impression. But unfavorable weather is sporadic and may not occur when the population of some insect is on the increase and needs to be checked. Parasites and predators may not be conspicuous but they are always there—at least generally speaking. Not only are they there, but they will increase as their food source, their hosts or prey, increases. Thus, unlike storms or severe winters, their controlling effect escalates as the population that needs to be controlled increases.

How do we know that parasitic and predaceous insects are essential to the **smooth running of ecosystems**?

Their importance becomes obvious when an insect is introduced into a new area unaccompanied by its usual parasites and predators or when parasite and predator populations seriously decline in an insect's native habitat. When an insect that is innocuous in Australia, the cottony cushion scale, was unintentionally brought into California, its population grew out of bounds and it became a destructive plant pest and threatened to destroy the citrus industry. When a scale-eating ladybird beetle from Australia was brought to California, cottony cushion scale populations plummeted and the scale was no longer a pest. When DDT was sprayed in apple orchards to control the codling moth, it did not kill a caterpillar known as the red-banded leaf roller, but it did kill parasites and predators of this caterpillar. Leaf roller populations burgeoned and this once innocuous insect became a serious pest.

Are insects important **links in food chains**?

They are important and often essential links in almost all terrestrial and fresh water food chains. Insects are the main eaters of plants—the first to convert plant material into animal (insect) tissue, which is, in turn, eaten by such other animals as other insects, fish, frogs, toads, salamanders, lizards, snakes, turtles, many different kinds of birds, and mammals such as bats, shrews, moles, mice, anteaters, and even bears. At first glance it may seem that such grazing mammals like bison and moose must eat more plants than insects do, but a closer look shows that this is not so. A thorough search that extracts insects from the soil and flushes them from their hiding places shows that, as tiny as they are, in the aggregate they outweigh the mammals in ecosystems on a per area basis.

Are insects important in the **diet of fish**?

Both aquatic insects and terrestrial insects that fall onto the surface of the water are very important in the diet of fish. Trout, for example, feed heavily on aquatic insects that live in streams, especially mayflies, stoneflies, alderflies, and caddisflies. The importance of these insects in the diet of trout is exemplified by the artificial "flies" that anglers use as lures for trout. Made mainly of feathers, hair, and wool tied to a hook, artificial flies are, to varying degrees of faithfulness, made to resemble the adult stage of the stream-dwelling insects that trout eat.

What good are **mosquitoes**?

Although mosquitoes are annoying pests and, in the case of malaria-transmitting species, the most dangerous insect enemies of people, they do have useful ecological roles. They have a significant role in many aquatic food chains, bridging the size gap between fish and the tiny, near-microscopic organisms that are too small for the fish to eat or even notice. Mosquito larvae are filter feeders that strain tiny organic particles such as unicellular algae from the water and convert them to the tissues of their own bodies, which are, in turn, eaten by fish. The role of the mosquito larva is to combine tiny particles of food into a package—its own body—that is large enough to be food for fish (when it's still a larva) and for birds (after it has emerged from the water as an adult).

Are **soil-dwelling insects** ecologically important?

It has been said that insects are second only to earthworms as creators of humus and "tillers" of the soil. Insects help to form humus by eating organic litter, mainly fallen leaves and other vegetable debris, and excreting it as fecal material, which is then further decomposed by fungi and bacteria. What is left is humus, the all-important organic constituent of fertile soils.

Soil-dwelling beetle larva. (Photo by Edward S. Ross.)

Why are burrowing insects important in **soil formation**?

By burrowing in the soil, or "tilling" it, insects aerate the soil and increase the depth of the fertile top soil by bringing to the surface relatively sterile and infertile inorganic subsoil, which becomes mixed with the humus. Insects, especially ants, are prodigious burrowers. When an abandoned field in Michigan was sampled, it was found that just one species of ant had brought to the surface 750 pounds of excavated soil per acre. On the Great Plains another species of ant builds conical mounds of excavated soil that, on average, weigh 170 pounds each. There may be as many as twenty of these mounds per acre, or about 1.7 tons of subsoil per acre.

What **insect products** do people use?

The commonly used insect products are silk, honey, beeswax, shellac, and cochineal. Insects also have medicinal value in treating infected wounds.

What insects have people truly **domesticated**?

Only the silkworm and the honey bee have been domesticated, but the cochineal insect comes close. Honey bees and cochineal insects can survive on their own in the wild, but the silkworm is so thoroughly domesticated—much more so than any of our domesticated mammals—that it cannot possibly survive unless it is cared for by people.

Silk moth on its cocoon. (Photo by Edward S. Ross.)

SILK

What are **silkworms**?

These wonderful domesticated creatures, which secrete the silk that is woven to make neckties and lingerie, are certainly not worms and bear no resemblance to earthworms or to worms of any other kind. They are caterpillars, the immature growing stage of the silk moth. But the name silkworm has been in use for so long that we are stuck with this misnomer. Even my Oxford dictionary uses it. The domestic silkworm, whose cocoons yield almost all of the silk of commerce, belongs to the family Bombycidae. Small quantities of commercial silk are produced by several wild Asiatic species that belong to a different family, the Saturniidae, sometimes known as the giant silkworm moths. Attempts, some of them successful, have been made to rear giant silkworms, but with little commercial success. Several giant silkworms that are native to North America are well known to naturalists, among them the cecropia moth, the promethea moth, and the beautiful luna moth.

How are silkworms **raised**?

With difficulty and much hand labor. That is why silk is expensive. So domesticated that they no longer exist in the wild, silkworms need help from humans at every stage of

Young silkworms feeding on mulberry leaves. (Photo by Edward S. Ross.)

the life cycle. The females, scarcely able to fly and having lost the instinct to place their eggs on plants, stick their eggs to paper provided for this purpose. The eggs are in a state of hibernation (diapause) and must be stored in a cold place during winter. In spring, the newly hatched silkworms, which emerge from the eggs after about 10 days, are placed in trays with finely chopped white mulberry leaves—the only thing that they will eat except for the leaves of a few trees related to white mulberry. As the silkworms grow, their appetites increase prodigiously and the leaves are more coarsely chopped. Each silkworm eats about 3.2 ounces of leaf as it grows from its initial weight of about one milligram to its ultimate weight of about 3,850 milligrams, or about thirteen hundredths of an ounce. The caterpillar stage lasts about 28 days, and during the last six days, which the Japanese call the period of great voraciousness, the silkworm consumes about 80 percent of its lifetime intake of food. When they are full grown, the silkworms spin their silken cocoons on loose bundles of straw that are placed on the trays in which they were raised. A few of these cocoons are set aside. The adults that emerge from them after 10 or 12 days are the breeding stock that will produce the next generation of eggs. The rest of the cocoons are the harvest that will be processed to yield silk fiber.

How is the silkworm cocoon **converted to silk fiber**?

The cocoon is made of a single strand of silk that must be unwound, often as a continuous filament that may be as much as 3,600 feet long, almost seven-tenths of a mile.

After the cocoons have been cleaned by picking off bits of leaf and other debris, they are steamed to kill the pupae within them. The silk is ruined if a moth emerges from the cocoon. Some time later, the cocoons are put in boiling water to loosen the silk by dissolving the fiber's outer coating. Then, with patience and keen eyesight, the loose end of the fiber is found and attached to a reel to be unwound. When all of the silk of a cocoon has been reeled up, nothing is left but the bare pupa, which is not wasted. (The Chinese have recipes for making them into tasty dishes.) Two or more fibers are twisted together to form the threads that are woven into fabrics.

How much is **silk worth**?

In 1988, raw silk sold for about $17.60 per pound. The world production of silk in that year was about 75 million pounds, which had a total value of more than 1.3 billion dollars. That was the value of the *raw* silk. After being woven into fabrics and made into clothing and other items, its total value was far greater.

HONEY

What is **honey**?

Honey is the nectar of flowers that has been converted by bees to a concentrated and nutritious substance. Honey is a large and important part of the diet of honey bees and their larvae, the other part being pollen. The nectar that a bee obtains from a flower is mixed with saliva, swallowed, and carried back to the hive in the crop, or honey sac. At the hive the nectar is regurgitated into a waxen cell and mixed with more saliva that contains enzymes that convert the sugars in the nectar into the more digestible sugars of honey. Much of the water is evaporated from the nectar by air currents produced over the honey cells by worker bees rapidly beating their wings. When a cell is full of ripened honey, the workers cap it with wax. Honey keeps almost indefinitely.

What is **mead**?

Mead is an alcoholic drink made from honey. It is made by fermenting a mixture of honey and water, sometimes with yeast added to speed up the process. At one time mead was the common alcoholic drink among Scandinavians, Britains, and other peoples of northern Europe, where grapes for producing wine did not grow well. But by the 16th century, mead was well on the way to being replaced by beer, ale, and wine imported from France and other grape-growing areas.

What is **beeswax**?

Beeswax is a natural secretion of worker honey bees from glands that open on the underside of the abdomen. The bees use the wax to make the combs of hexagonal cells in which larval bees grow and honey is stored. Well over three million pounds of beeswax are produced in the United States each year. About a million pounds are pressed into foundation and returned to bee hives as a base for building combs. It is also used to make candles, shaving cream, cosmetics, and many other products.

Beekeeper collecting honey and beeswax. (Photo by Edward S. Ross.)

OTHER INSECT PRODUCTS

What is **shellac**?

Shellac is the partially purified form of lac, a natural resin secreted by certain scale insects of India and Burma as a protective covering for their colonies. Colonies form on small branches or twigs and may be very large. An encrustation of lac on a twig may be several inches long and almost three quarters of an inch in diameter. After harvesting this *stick lac,* people grind it into granules that are soaked in water and trodden underfoot to crush them and flush out their wine-colored pigments. After drying and bleaching in the sun, the lac is put into cloth bags, heated over a fire, and squeezed out of the bags as it melts. The soft lac is stretched into thin sheets by hand and foot. The dried sheets are broken into small, thin flakes and shipped to market. These flakes are used in the manufacture of many products, and are dissolved in alcohol to form the varnish that is usually called shellac.

How are maggots used to **cure infections**?

When surgery and antibiotics fail to cure a deep-seated infection such as osteomyelitis, placing certain carrion-eating maggots in the wound is the last resort, and the alternative to amputation. Improbable as it may seem, this technique usually works and is very simple to use. Maggots of several species will eat the dead, putrefying tissue in the wound but will not eat living tissue. They are meticulous and thorough feeders that

What is cochineal?

Cochineal, one of the most beautiful and permanent of the red dyes, is the dried, pulverized bodies of a particular species of mealybug, an insect related to the scale insects. This New World insect, native to Mexico and part of the southwestern United States, feeds only on certain species of prickly pear cactus. Long before Europeans arrived in the Americas, the Aztecs and the Pima Indians of Arizona cultivated cochineal insects and used them as a dye. The usefulness of cochineal was first reported to Europe by Hernando Cortez, who found the Aztecs of Mexico using it in 1518. It soon became one of most widely used dyes in Europe. It was largely replaced as a dye for fabric by synthetic aniline dyes discovered early in the 19th century. But even today, cochineal and one of its derivatives, carmine red, is used as a natural coloring agent in beverages, confectionery, cosmetics, and pharmaceuticals. In the United States, both cochineal extract and carmine red must be pasteurized to destroy the *Salmonella* with which it is sometimes contaminated.

remove every last bit of dead tissue. In addition, they secrete an antibiotic, allantoin, into the wound, quite possibly to kill bacteria that are their main competitors for dead tissue. When the maggots are full grown and ready to pupate, they leave the wound. In nature they drop to the soil, but when used as maggot therapy, they gather under the dressing that covers the wound and are easily removed. There is evidence that maggot therapy is an ancient tradition of certain tribal people, but its recent history goes back to World War I, when army physicians noticed that wounded men who were not quickly rescued and had maggots in their wounds seldom developed infections, but that wounded men who were quickly rescued and had no maggots in their wounds very often developed infections. Maggot therapy was quickly adopted and widely used but was all but abandoned when the first antibiotics were discovered. Even today, however, some physicians resort to maggot therapy when all else fails.

What is **forensic entomology**?

Forensic entomology is the application of entomological knowledge and techniques to the investigation of crimes. It is often used to determine the time of death of a corpse. As a corpse decomposes, it is inhabited by a succession of different insect species—from maggots that may appear on the corpse within minutes of death, to hide beetles that arrive when there is nothing left but bones, hair, and scraps of dry skin and flesh. The sequence in which these insects appear and how long they are present is so precise and predictable that the time of death can be established by determining what kinds of insects are present and how old they are. This is quite accurate if air temperatures, usually available from weather records, are taken into account. Since insects are cold-blooded, the rate at which they grow and develope varies with the temperature.

INSECTS THAT PEOPLE EAT

Do people really **eat insects**?

Most of the people of the world include insects in their diets, sometimes as just a tasty gourmet treat and sometimes as a significant source of nourishment. But members of Western societies, Europeans and transplanted Europeans—a minority among the six billion people of the earth—are an exception. Americans, for example, eat lobster, shrimp, and other insect relatives, but have a strong aversion to eating insects except for the occasional chocolate-covered ant or some other jocular novelty. On the other hand, Africans, Asians, Native Americans, and almost all other non-Western peoples do not have a prejudice against eating insects, and often include them as an important part of their diets.

Do Americans consume insects **without knowing it**?

Yes, we certainly do. It can't be avoided. Because it is impossible to totally exclude insects as a food is grown, harvested, and shipped, most of the foods we eat contain small quantities of insects or insect fragments. It might be possible to produce a bottle of ketchup that contains not even one insect or insect fragment, but it would take a huge effort that would raise the price of a bottle of ketchup to astronomical levels, perhaps even hundreds of dollars. Recognizing this problem, the United States Food and Drug Administration does not make a futile effort to keep foods completely free of insects. Instead, they set a maximum legal limit on how many insects or insect parts can be contained in a food that is to be sold. These limits, or tolerance levels, are regularly published in *Food Defect Action Levels* by the Department of Health and Human Services. For example, a hundred grams (about 3.5 ounces) of frozen broccoli is not permitted to contain more than 60 aphids and/or thrips and/or mites. Peanut butter is allowed to contain up to 30 insect fragments per 100 grams.

Giant water bugs for sale as people-food. (Photo by Edward S. Ross.)

Are insects **kosher**?

Most are not, but a few are. Leviticus 11:20 warns the people of Israel that insects are unclean and not to be eaten: "All winged creeping things that go upon all fours are an abomination unto you." The warning is reiterated in Deuteronomy 14:19: "And all winged creeping things are unclean unto you: they shall not be eaten." But Leviticus 11:21-22 specifically exempts locusts and other leaping Orthoptera: "yet these may ye eat of all winged creeping things that go upon all fours, which have legs above their feet, wherewith to leap upon the earth . . . the locust after its kind, and the bald locust after its kind, and the cricket after its kind, and the grasshopper after its kind." The specification of creeping things that go on *all fours* is a bit confusing. Insects have six legs. But the author of Leviticus seems not to have noticed that. Excluding locusts from the list of unclean creatures makes good nutritional sense. They often overrun the lands of the Mideast in astronomical numbers and are an abundant and protein-rich source of food too good to pass up.

Are insects **nutritious**?

Insects are a good source of energy, protein, vitamins, and minerals. The pupae of silkworms, commonly eaten in Asia, consist of about 79 percent water (about the same as the water content of most fish), 2.8 percent fat, 13 percent proteins, plus minerals and vitamins. Some termites are about 14 percent protein, and certain caterpillars may contain as much as 28 percent protein. These protein values are comparable to those of many of the foods that we consider to be good sources of protein: beef, 26 percent; fish, from about 14 percent to 18 percent; lobster, 16.2 percent; and kidney beans, 23 percent.

Are **silkworm pupae** a popular food in China?

They are a welcome and widely eaten food in silk-producing districts such as the province of Kwangtung (Guandong) in Southern China. As F. S. Bodenheimer reports, the cocoons are dropped into very hot water before the silk is reeled, and the reeling fac-

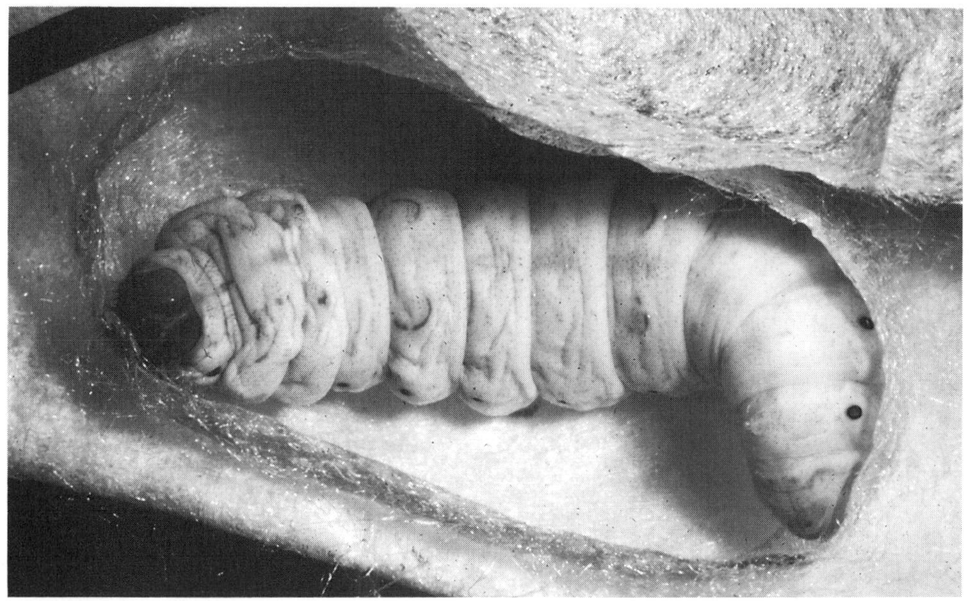

Silkworm pupa. (Photo by Edward S. Ross.)

tories have the pleasant odor of food being cooked. The girls who unwind the silk from the cocoons "have a plentiful supply of freshly cooked food before them all day long. They eat pupae on and off all day long and take more of them home." Roasted pupae are sold in food stalls throughout the silk district and are also available elsewhere.

Do people eat **termites**?

In many African cultures, termites are an important food and are relished as delicacies. They are often very abundant, especially in the rainy season when immense swarms of winged termites, the reproductive caste, leave the nests to mate and found new colonies. One writer compared "the welcome of the rainy season with its termite flights in Central Africa to the hailing of the advent of the Oyster season by the British gourmets." In nutritional value they are comparable to most foods that people eat. Termites are abundant and are easily harvested in large quantities. Who can deny, assuming no prejudice against the eating of insects, that they are a valuable food resource that is well worth exploiting?

How are **termites harvested**?

The most abundant harvest comes when immense numbers of the reproductive caste swarm en masse from the nests. One way to capture these swarming insects is to place containers of water around the termite mound. Many members of the chaotic

Is there an insect food that is fit for a king?

Properly prepared, palmworms, *con-duong ch-la* in Vietnamese, were at one time reserved for the royal table in Annam, the central region of Vietnam. These beetle larvae are collected from the roots of certain palms, and then inserted into stalks of sugar cane. When sufficiently fattened, they are marinated in *nuoc-mam,* the favorite sauce of the Vietnamese, wrapped in a flour paste, and fried in lard. When thusly cooked, they smell like hazelnuts.

swarm fall into the water, drown, and are skimmed off when the container is full. F. S. Bodenheimer, an Israeli entomologist, described another and probably more productive way in which people harvest swarming termites: "They tightly enfold the termite mound in several layers of the broad leaves of a . . . reed, the interstices soon being closed by the termites, which usually join the inner leaves to the nest. A projecting pocket, built on one side of the leaf cover, serves as a trap; for when the winged termites begin to swarm, they find no egress and finally drop in masses into the pocket from which they are scooped out." Termites can be caught, albeit in smaller numbers, even when they are not swarming. When a palm leaf is poked into a hole in a nest, defending soldier termites clamp onto it with their formidable mandibles and can be withdrawn with the leaf. Chimpanzees, probably the most intelligent of the primates other than humans, have discovered and regularly use a similar technique. They strip a twig or a stem of grass of its leaves and then poke it into a hole in a termite mound. Shortly thereafter, the stem is withdrawn, covered with termites that are licked off.

Are insects eaten in **Mexico**?

About 57 insect species, including the the eggs of water bugs known as water boatmen, plus grasshoppers, beetles, ants, wasps, flies, mosquitoes, dragonflies, and butterflies are eaten in Mexico. Insect eating goes back to the Aztecs, and even today most Mexicans have little or no prejudice against this practice. Insects are a staple protein source in much of the country, and in Mexico City, some of the finest restaurants serve maguey worms, ant eggs, the eggs of water boatmen, and other insects as gourmet dishes. When the National Autonomous University of Mexico polled residents of Mexico City on the question of eating insects, they found that the majority of those polled would be willing to include insects in their diet.

How do Mexicans **harvest the eggs of water boatmen**?

These aquatic insects, abundant in the lakes near Mexico City and in other areas, lay prodigious quantities of eggs that are collected in very large quantities by removing them from the stems of the water plants on which they are laid. Bundles of rushes that are attractive to egg-laying females are placed in the water, and after some weeks are removed, dried, and beaten on cloths to separate the eggs. The eggs are then cleaned, sifted, and ground into a flour that is used to make cakes known as *hautle*.

Do people eat **insect products** other than honey?

Yes. In the Mideast, people eat a confection made from the honeydew of aphids. Honeydew, the sweet excrement of aphids, is what's left over after these insects have extracted their required nutrients from the sap that they suck from plants. It is essentially a solution of sugars in water, but also contains small amounts of other nutrients, among them amino acids, proteins, vitamins, and minerals. In Hebrew, honeydew is call *man*. In Arabic, honeydew is also known as *man,* and *man-es-simma* is the honeydew that falls from the sky—the manna from heaven. Some believe that honeydew is the biblical manna that sustained the ancient Israelites as they crossed the Sinai desert in their flight from Egypt. Today, the Kurds of Turkey and northern Iraq collect large quantities of honeydew from aphid-infested oaks. Branches cut in early morning—before ants appropriate the honeydew for themselves—are beaten to knock off the honeydew, which soon hardens into a rock-like mass in the dry air of the region. The rock-like masses of honeydew are sold to confectioners, who dissolve it in water and strain it through a cloth to remove leaf fragments and aphids. The purified honeydew is mixed with eggs, almonds, and seasonings and then boiled and allowed to solidify. The solidified confection is ready to eat after it has been cut into pieces and coated with powdered sugar. It is said to be delicious, and that, once tasted, its flavor is never forgotten.

PEST INSECTS

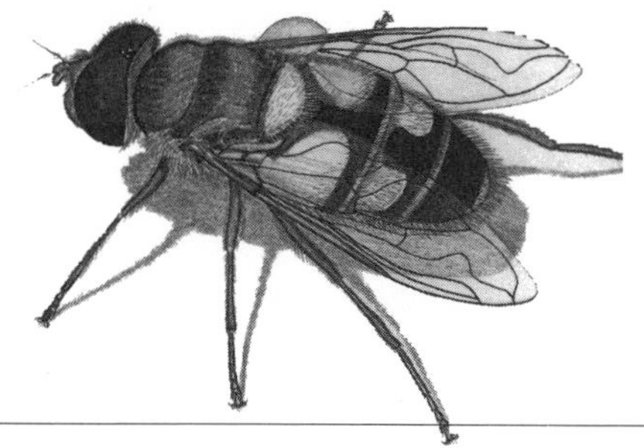

How many insects are actually **destructive**?

Economic entomologists, the people who make pest insects their business, often say that about 10 percent of the insects in the United States are destructive to crops and otherwise inimical to people. That would be about 8,800 species of pests. But that is surely a grossly inflated figure. The real figure is less than 2 percent, no more than 1,500 species—and that includes some very trivial pests. This is based on the number of insects that the Entomological Society of America includes on its list of approved common names. The list consists mostly of pest species, but also some useful insects and some showy ones that are not pests but are noticed by people. That means that only about 1,500 North American insects are considered important enough to merit common names, and surely any significant pest would have been assigned a common name.

How much do insects **cost the United States' economy** each year?

According to *Destructive and Useful Insects* by R. L. and R. A. Metcalf, the "bible" of economic entomology, in 1988 insects cost the people of the United States at least 14.4 billion dollars. That is a lot of money and justifies spending many millions of dollars on entomological research. But let's keep it in perspective! According to Metcalf and Metcalf, in 1988 insects benefited the American economy by over 24.6 billion dollars—and that includes only the most important items.

What are the **most destructive insects** in the world?

Without doubt they are the *Anopheles* mosquitoes that transmit the *Plasmodiums* (amoeba-like protozoans) that cause the four forms of human malaria. Malaria is one of the most prevalent of the infectious diseases of humans, and the most important of

In addition to being annoying pests, mosquitos are transmitters of disease. (Photo by Edward S. Ross.)

the arthropod-transmitted ones. In 1990 there were about 270 million cases and about two million deaths, mostly in the tropics—especially Africa.

How many kinds of **lice** live on humans?

There are three different species. The head louse, which—as its name indicates—lives in the hair of the head and glues its eggs, or nits, to the hairs; the body louse, which actually lives in the clothing; and, finally, the pubic louse, or crab, which lives in the course hair of the body—mainly the pubic hair. All of these lice are in the order Anoplura and all have piercing-sucking mouthparts that they use to suck blood.

Do lice **transmit diseases**?

Yes, several of them do. The most important of them is louse-borne, or epidemic, typhus—a debilitating and sometimes deadly disease that was particularly prevalent in Europe. It becomes epidemic when people can't keep themselves clean, as in prisons, concentration camps, armies in the field, and bombed-out cities. Napoleon's catastrophic losses in Russia were due more to disease, especially louse typhus, than to battle casualties or the cold Russian winter. Napoleon invaded Russia with about 453,000 men in June of 1812. When his defeated army limped out of Russia the following December, only 20,000 men were left. The last great epidemic of louse typhus

How are lice transmitted?

Lice are transmitted only through close contact between people, because they are wingless and soon die if they are not on a person. You can get head lice if you wear the hat of an infested person, and you can get body lice by wearing infested clothing. Crab lice, which live mainly in the pubic hair, are almost always transmitted during sexual intercourse. You can't catch lice from an animal. Piercing-sucking lice are very fussy about their hosts; they live on only people. The crab louse does, however, have a close relative that lives on gorillas.

occurred in 1943 and 1944 in Naples during World War II. The epidemic was stopped,—the first time this was ever accomplished — by dusting the three million inhabitants, both civilians and occupying troops, with DDT and other insecticides.

What is the **lead cable borer**?

Inorganic substances, such as metals, are generally ignored by insects because they are not good to eat. But not always! The lead cable borer, a beetle that normally burrows in wood, sometimes bores holes through the lead sheathing that covers aerial telephone cables. Moisture enters these holes and causes short circuits that are very troublesome to telephone companies. The beetles cannot profit from this behavior and no one has figured out why they do it.

What are **horn flies**?

Horn flies are blood-sucking pests of cattle. They suck blood but do not injure the horns. They get their name from their habit of clustering about the base of the horns when they rest. They are not all bad, though, because their maggots help to decompose cattle dung. The eggs are laid only in very fresh dung. The females dash out from their position on the cow just when dung is dropped, and deposit their eggs on its surface. Within two minutes, the dung loses its attraction for egg-laying females.

What are **deathwatch beetles**?

They are tiny beetles that burrow in the wood of buildings. Although they damage the wood, they are best known for the sounds that they make by banging their heads against the side of their burrow. The beetles probably perceive this sound as a vibration in the wood, but one assumes that it is "music to their ears," because it brings the sexes together. It is not music, however, to the ears of superstitious people who think

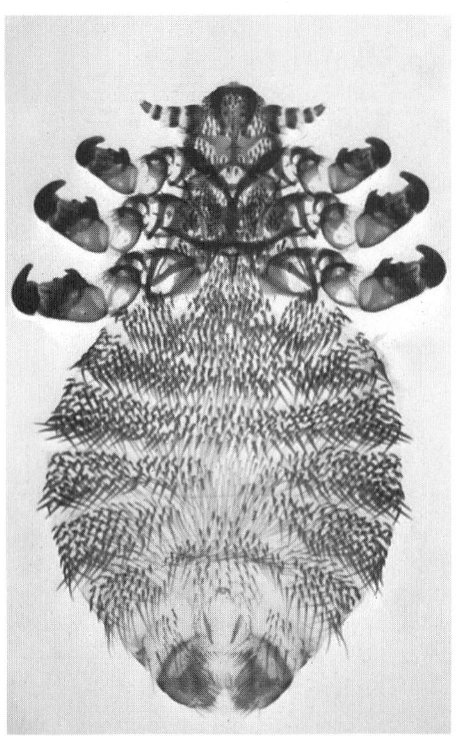

Louse viewed through a microscope. (Photo by Edward S. Ross.)

that it presages the death of a person in the house. As J. H. Comstock wrote, "This belief probably arose from the fact that the sound is most likely to be heard in the quiet of the night, and would consequently be [heard] by watchers by sickbeds."

What are **earworms**?

Contrary to what the name implies, they do not get into people's ears. They live in ears of corn. Sometimes when you peel back the husks from an ear of sweet corn you expose a big caterpillar, brown, green, yellow, or sometimes even salmon pink, that is at the tip of the ear and has eaten a few of the kernels and excreted a mass of soft fecal material. Except under very rare circumstances, there will be only one caterpillar; corn earworms are ravenously cannibalistic. Don't discard an infested ear. The caterpillar won't have eaten much, and the damaged kernels and excrement can be gotten rid of by cutting off the tip of the ear. This is a difficult insect to control, because the caterpillar is exposed to insecticides for only the short time it spends crawling from its egg on the silk at the tip of the ear to safety beneath the husks. Usually no attempt is made to control this insect on corn grown for grain. But farmers who grow sweet corn, mindful of their squeamish customers, spray their fields every two or three days! It would surely be more economical and environmentally sound to leave the crop unsprayed and let the customer remove the earworms.

Where do the red and black bugs that **invade houses in fall** come from?

They are box elder bugs and come from box elder maples that grow near the house. They feed mainly on box elder seeds, and are, consequently, found only on female box elders. In fall, the adult bugs seek winter quarters in such places as hollow trees and buildings. There they will hibernate until spring. They can be a minor annoyance, but they neither bite people nor damage the building or anything in it. You can spray to kill these bugs, but a far simpler and permanent way to get rid of them is to cut down any female box elder trees in the vicinity of the house.

Do carpenter ants eat wood?

No, they do not. They only nest in wood, hollowing out broad galleries. They usually nest in stumps and tree trunks but are not averse to carving out nests in telephone poles and the timbers of buildings. Since they do not eat wood, their damage is minor compared to that of termites. They forage for insects outdoors, but will also enter homes to feed on sweet things.

What are those **brown, spindle-shaped bags** that hang from the branches of ornamental trees and shrubs?

They are the homes of the caterpillars that weave them. These silken bags are festooned with small bits of stems or leaves and may be as much as two inches long. The caterpillar, properly known as the evergreen bagworm, sticks its head and thorax out of the front end of the bag as it crawls about and feeds ravenously on the leaves of trees and shrubs. The other end of the bag tapers to a sleeve-like valve through which the fecal pellets are expelled. When the caterpillar is ready to molt, it fastens the front end of its bag to a twig with silk. Before it molts to the pupa in late fall, it turns around in the bag so that it can later emerge head first through the valve. Bagworms attack many kinds of woody plants, but their favorites are evergreens, especially junipers, or red cedars. If left uncontrolled they may completely defoliate and kill junipers.

What is the best way for a homeowner to **control bagworms**?

The simplest and most thorough method is to pick the bags in late fall or winter and destroy them. If you do this every year and don't let an infestation grow, there will be very few bags the following year. To understand why this method works, we need to understand the life cycle of the bagworm. You can begin by carefully snipping open several winter bags lengthwise. If the bag housed a male, it will be empty except for the wadded molted skin of the full-grown caterpillar and perhaps the empty pupal skin still protruding from the lower end of the bag. The male emerged and mated the previous fall. If the bag housed a female, it will be all but filled by her pupal skin. If you open the pupal skin, you will find a mass of eggs, as many as two thousand, at its back end and a wad of light yellow hairs at its front end. The females are wingless and leave the bag only after they have laid all their eggs and are ready to die. Bagworms survive the winter only as eggs, and by destroying them you break the life cycle. If you keep tropical fish, the eggs are a bonus. Fish love them and flourish on this nutritious live food. Eggs can be stored in a refrigerator for at least a year.

How did gypsy moths get to North America?

They were brought here purposely in 1869 by Leopold Trouvelot, an artist and astronomer who was interested in silk culture. He intended to cross silkworms with gypsy moths or other moths to produce a hardier and more disease-resistant strain of silkworms. He was, of course, not successful, but some gypsy moth caterpillars escaped from breeding cages in the backyard of his home at 27 Myrtle Street in Medford, Massachusetts. Knowing that they were destructive, he searched for the escapees but could not find them. He then published a notice of what had happened, but little attention was paid; unfortunate because it might then have been possible to nip the infestation in the bud. By 1889 the gypsy moth had become a serious pest around Medford. It has since spread through New England, the north and south central states, and even to the Pacific Coast.

What are **gypsy moths**?

Gypsy moth caterpillars, which are about two inches long when full grown, are extremely destructive defoliators of forest and shade trees. By late May and early June, large areas of forest may be so completely defoliated that the only green to be seen are the stubs of leaf stems that the caterpillars left behind. They will feed on almost all deciduous and evergreen trees and shrubs. When they are close to full grown they often switch from deciduous to evergreen trees and they grow better on this mixed diet than on a diet of only deciduous foliage. The gypsy moth is a native of Europe that was accidentally released in the United States in Massachusetts in 1869.

What is the most **universal** of the household insect pests?

It is surely the common house fly. This fly may well be the most cosmopolitan of the insects, occurring virtually everywhere on earth except for Antarctica. It is a rare home that is not at least occasionally invaded by houseflies, and, in some parts of the world, homes sometimes swarm with them. Generally speaking, houseflies constitute about 98 percent of the flies caught in human dwellings.

Why are **house flies** objectionable?

For two reasons: they annoy us by lighting on our persons and speckling our walls and ceilings with their excrement; and they are likely to be transmitters of pathogenic microbes that cause diseases such as bacterial dysentery, cholera, and typhoid fever. House flies are simple, mechanical carriers of pathogens that contaminate their bod-

The house fly. (Photo by Edward S. Ross.)

ies. House flies can transmit pathogens on the hairs of their bodies, on their sticky feet, by the regurgitation of vomitus, and through their feces. There is little direct evidence that house flies are disease carriers, but the circumstantial evidence is abundant and compelling. For example, during the Spanish-American War in 1898, about a fifth of the soldiers in encampments contracted typhoid fever. This disease was responsible for about 80 percent of the deaths among soldiers. It is very likely that it was at least in part transmitted by house flies, contaminated by excrement in latrines, that swarmed in the mess tents and crawled over food. The flies often had traces of lime on their bodies, which they could have picked up only in a latrine.

Who is responsible for the **greatest reduction ever** of the house fly population in North America?

It has to be Henry Ford. His mass production of the first inexpensive automobiles, first the Model T Ford and then the Model A Ford, led to the near demise of the horse as a significant means of transportation. Before his automobiles, almost every home had its own stable and accompanying manure pile. House flies, which breed in manure, were distressingly abundant. One of the first forest rangers in the United States told the story (perhaps only a little exaggerated) of an experience he had in 1905 in a small restaurant near the Deer Lodge National Forest in Montana. After finishing his meal, he pointed and said, "I'll have a piece of that blueberry pie." The wait-

What is the TV cockroach?

TV cockroach is another name for the brown-banded cockroach, which likes warm places and aggregates in electric clocks, television sets, and other appliances that generate mild warmth. A person who had watched television in a badly infested apartment reported seeing a brown-banded cockroach walk across the screen. A western was on, and he said that the cockroach looked like just one more cow in a herd of cattle.

ress swished her hand over the pie and said, "Shoo! That's not blueberry; that's apple." With the disappearance of manure piles, their main breeding areas, the house fly population dropped and is now only a tiny fraction of what it once was.

Do **coffin flies** live as their name suggests?

Yes, they do. These little flies can live through many successive generations on bodies in coffins that have been in the ground for a year or more. The adult flies can make their way down to the coffin through several feet of soil and can make their way back up again. All stages of the fly can live in the coffin, getting air through natural cavities in the soil and completing whole life cycles. But are these creatures really pests? Some think of them that way, but others think of them as a natural agent of decomposition, a recycler that returns our bodies to the earth.

What is a **cheese skipper**?

Cheese skippers are tiny maggots that sometimes burrow in cheese. They are called skippers because they can leap two or three inches into the air by bending their bodies nearly double and then straightening. They do little harm to cheese, but can cause intestinal upsets if they are eaten along with the cheese by gourmets in ill-advised excesses of gastronomic enthusiasm. One of the symptoms is the passing of live maggots with the stool.

Are **waterbugs** different from **cockroaches**?

They are the same thing. Waterbug is just a euphemism for cockroach. It is most often applied to the little German cockroach, which likes to inhabit kitchens and is usually the most numerous of the pest cockroaches.

How can Dutch elm disease be controlled?

The progress of this disease can be slowed, often to such an extent that a healthy population of white elms can be maintained, by following good forestry practices. Pruning dead branches from otherwise healthy trees, and promptly removing and burning all dead or diseased trees, eliminates the sources of both the Dutch elm fungus and the bark beetles that transmit it. It is very difficult to stop the spread of this disease by spraying the trees with an insecticide. A tree will sicken and die if it is inoculated by only one beetle or by many beetles. Thus, the insecticide must prevent even one bark beetle from feeding on a healthy tree. Insecticides are good at reducing large insect populations to small ones, but they generally cannot eliminate an entire population.

Do all **moths** damage clothing or other fabrics?

Definitely not. Of the over 10,000 species of moths in North America, only three attack fabric. The casemaking and the webbing clothes moths are the most common. The third species, the carpet moth, is much less common in North America. The moths themselves, buff colored and with a wingspan of about a half inch, are harmless, but the tiny caterpillars eat holes in woolen cloth, furs, hair, and feathers. The eggs, 100 to 150 per female, are laid on cloth. The white larvae, which attain a maximum length of about a third of an inch, mature in about six weeks at optimal conditions, but may take as much as four years to mature under poor conditions. They pupate in tough cocoons on the cloth and emerge as adults in from one to four weeks.

What are all those big caterpillars that are **stripping the leaves from my catalpa tree**?

They are the larvae of the catalpa sphinx, a nocturnal, narrow-winged moth that has a wing span of from 2.5 to 3 inches. They lay their eggs in masses of as many as 1,000 on the undersides of catalpa leaves. Thousands of the dark or black caterpillars are often present on a single tree and may completely defoliate it. When full grown, they descend to the ground to burrow in the soil and pupate. There are two generations per year, and the insects of the second generation survive the winter as pupae in the soil.

What is the **Dutch elm disease**?

This fungus disease, transmitted from tree to tree mainly by the European elm bark beetle, is deadly to the native American white elm, probably the most magnificent of all the streetside shade trees. The adult beetles transmit the fungus. When they emerge from their burrows in the bark they have spores of the fungus on their bodies. Although they lay their eggs in tunnels in the bark of sick or weakened trees, they take their meals from the bark of the twigs of trees that are often healthy. In so doing they inoculate the healthy tree with spores. Both the fungus and the beetle were imported into the United States from Europe on elm logs to be used for furniture veneer. The disease and the bark-burrowing beetle spread quickly and now occur as far west as Colorado and Wyoming, and inhabit most of the eastern part of the United States. In many areas, white elms have been all but eliminated. The streets of Champaign-Urbana, Illinois, for example, were once lined with thousands of magnificent white elms. Now all but a dozen or so are gone.

How do **corn root aphids** and **cornfield ants** gang up on farmers?

Cornfield ants do not feed on corn, but they do keep corn root aphids, which suck sap from the roots of corn and other plants, as domestic animals that provide them with the honeydew that is an important part of their diet. The aphids are completely dependent on the ants, and cannot survive on their own. In winter, the ants store the aphid eggs in their underground nest, moving them from place to place to keep them at a suitable temperature and humidity. In spring, the ants move newly hatched aphids to the roots of corn or other plants. In July and August, winged aphids appear. Most of them stay put in the ants' nest, but a few fly off to other places. Aphids on the ground cannot find a place to feed and will perish unless they are found by a cornfield ant. An ant that finds a corn root aphid on the soil surface picks it up, carries it down into its nest, and places it on a root.

How did the **Hessian fly** get its name?

This tiny fly, one of our most destructive pests of wheat, was introduced from abroad, as were so many of our pest insects. Its original home was in Europe. It was first noted in North America in 1779 on Long Island not far from the 1776 encampment of Viscount William Howe, the British general who fought the Americans during the War of Independence. Howe commanded German troops, Hessian mercenaries who had been hired to fight for the British. The fly that is now known as the Hessian fly was probably introduced into North America in straw bedding that the Hessians brought from Europe.

Why is the **Mediterranean fruit fly** important?

It is one of the most destructive pests of fruit in the world, infesting the fruits of 253 species of plants, among them citrus and many other popular fruits. The females puncture a fruit to insert their eggs, and the maggots tunnel in the fruit. The "med-fly" is a native of South Africa that has spread to Europe, South and Central America, the islands of the Pacific, and Australia. It occurs in Hawaii but has not yet become established anywhere else in the United States. It has appeared in Florida and California several times but was always eradicated. The expense was great, but it was worth it in view of the damage this insect would do in our fruit growing areas. After the medfly appeared in Florida in 1929, it was eradicated within a year by destroying every fruit, both wild and cultivated, within the infected area—at a cost of over four million dollars.

Why do **yellowjacket wasps** show up at picnics in the fall but not in the summer?

There are several reasons. Yellowjacket workers are most numerous in the fall, and at that time the social structure of their colonies is disintegrating. The workers, faced with chaos at home, wander at loose ends. They are still hungry and search for food, but since nectar-producing flowers have become scarce, the wasps drop in at picnics to sip from sodas or other sweet drinks and to sample the vinegary dressing on salads.

CONTROLLING PESTS

What **methods of pest control** are there other than using insecticides?

Considering all insect pests, including those of humans, livestock, farms, and orchards, there are many ways to control pest insects besides using insecticides. Such methods are often more effective, less expensive, less dangerous, and friendlier to the environment. There are physical controls such as using traps or manipulating temperatures; genetic controls such as releasing sterile males to decrease a pest population; cultural controls such as rotating crops or using varieties of crop plants that are resistant to pest insects; biological controls such as introducing a disease, parasite, or predator of a pest; and even legal controls such as enforcing a quarantine to prevent the spread of a pest.

Is there **more to chemical control** than aiming a sprayer?

Chemical control, or using an insecticide, seems simple but has its complications. The insecticide must be applied in the right place and at the right time. You cannot, for example, kill corn earworms with an insecticide unless you put it in the right place (where the eggs are laid on the silks at the tips of the ears) and at the right time (before the eggs have hatched and the larvae have completed their short journey to safety beneath the husks). Insecticide applied elsewhere or at another time is wasted.

How can the **temperature be manipulated** to kill pest insects?

It can be raised to a lethally hot level or lowered to a lethally cold one. Some flour mills, for example, are equipped to raise the temperature of their buildings to above 125 degrees Fahrenheit for several hours on hot days. This is enough to kill caterpillars and beetles that feed on grain and flour. Lowering the temperature is also an

How are insect traps used?

They are occasionally used to destroy pests, but their main uses are as adjuncts to other forms of control, mainly chemical control. If well deployed, traps can tell us when an insect appears, how numerous it is, and where it is present. This is very useful information. It is pointless to apply an insecticide before an insect appears, and nothing is to be gained by trying to control a pest population that is so low that its damage in dollars and cents is less than the cost of applying the insecticide. Insect traps are simple and inexpensive, usually no more than a piece of cardboard covered with Tanglefoot or some other adhesive to which insects that land on the trap will stick. They are generally baited with a pheromone, usually a sex attractant. The traps are usually yellow or yellow-green, colors attractive to many insects, especially plant-feeding ones.

option in some cases. A person who had been in Africa noticed little piles of sawdust accumulating under some lovely wooden carvings that he had collected in Liberia. It was obvious that insects, almost certainly beetles, were destroying the carvings from within. What to do? When he took the carvings to a pest control firm, they—ever focused on chemical control—said that the carvings must be fumigated in a vacuum chamber so that the fumigant would penetrate the insect burrows in the wood. He then asked the advice of a clever entomologist, who suggested something far simpler that would cost next to nothing: keeping the carvings in a freezer for a few days. That killed the offending insects. Very few insects, certainly not species from tropical Africa, can survive a long exposure to the cold temperature in a household freezer.

How have **sterile males** been used to control an insect population?

The use of sterile males to eradicate the screwworm fly from all of North and Central America is the most spectacular solution to an insect problem that has ever been achieved. The screwworm, named for the screw-like ridges on the maggot's body, is quite likely the most horrifying of all the pest insects. The females lay their eggs on a wound, sometimes as small as a nick from barbed wire, and the maggots eat the healthy flesh at the edge of the wound, increasing the size of the wound and making it ever more attractive to egg-laying screwworm flies. The result is often the death of the animal. The maggots infest many different animals, commonly cattle and occasionally even people. At one time the only way to control this insect was to apply insecticidal ointments to the wounds, practically an impossibility with cattle that roam over range land. But Edward Knipling and Raymond Bushland of the U.S. Department of Agriculture came up with an imaginative solution to the problem.

Knowing that male screwworms mate as often as possible and that females mate only once, they thought that it should be possible to decrease or even eliminate a wild population of screwworms by releasing sterile males into its territory. But some questions had to be answered: How can the males be sterilized? The answer was to expose them to radioactive cobalt. Will females be sexually turned off by mating with a sterile male? The answer was yes. Then there were logistical problems: raising enough males and distributing them over a large area. They built factories in which they raised screwworms on offal from slaughter houses and used low-flying airplanes to distribute the sterile males. During the winter of 1958–1959 they released hundreds of millions of sterile males on 85,000 square miles of Southern Florida. (People weren't bothered by them because only 200 per square mile per week were released.) The result was fantastic! Screwworms were totally eradicated from Southern Florida. That freed the whole Southeast from this pest because each spring the screwworms moved north from their winter refuge in Southern Florida to occupy all of the Southeast. The screwworm has since been eradicated from all of the United States and Central America south to Panama, a project finally completed in the 1990s. The project was expensive but hugely profitable. The cost of eradicating the screwworm from Florida for all time was 10 million dollars. But in Florida alone the commercial loss to screwworms was 20 million dollars *each year.*

Why has the obvious **cultural control for European corn borers** been largely ineffective?

These insects, among the most destructive pests of corn, survive winter only as caterpillars in last year's corn stalks. The moths escape from the stalks in spring through little round holes that they had prepared for themselves when they were still caterpillars. The escape of the moths can be blocked by plowing down the stalks and covering them with soil before spring. In theory, this practice should largely eliminate the European corn borer problem. But there are several reasons why it did not work that way. When this insect, brought into North America with broom corn imported from Europe, arrived in Illinois in the 1940s, farmers did not plow down dead stalks if they planted oats after planting corn. Oats were seeded on ground covered with the litter of chopped corn stalks. Corn borers survived in these stalks. This difficulty disappeared when soybeans all but supplanted oats in the following decades. Corn stalks were plowed down before spring, but there were still more corn borers than would be expected. The reason was that large numbers of moths were emerging in spring from the cobs of whole ears of corn that had been stored in corn cribs over the winter. The moths easily escaped from the cribs, which had many openings for ventilation. Now there is a better method of harvesting corn: combines strip the kernels from the cob in the field, and the cob and every other part of the plant except the kernels is left behind in the field. Now that whole ears were no longer stored in corn cribs, plowing down stalks did the job—but not for long. Many farmers now plow as little as possible

European corn borer. (Photo by Edward S. Ross.)

in order to decrease the rate of soil erosion. Once again corn stalks are left on the surface of the soil, and European corn borers flourish. Minimum tillage is a good thing and is here to stay. Clean plowing as a cultural control for European corn borers is obviously a thing of the past.

What is the **cultural control** for corn rootworms?

Crop rotation, which has resulted in excellent control of these beetles for decades, works for several reasons. First, the tiny larvae are very limited in what they will eat, mainly just the roots of corn. Second, they have only one generation per year. Finally, they survive winter only as eggs in the soil, which the females lay only at the base of a living corn plant. Thus, if a field is planted in corn and soybeans in alternate years, the rootworms cannot survive; when the eggs hatch in spring, the tiny larvae find only the roots of soybeans and starve to death. But the rootworms flourish when crops are not rotated, when corn is planted in the same field where corn grew the previous year.

Have corn rootworms found ways of **surviving crop rotation**?

Yes, they have. So far they've managed this only in some areas, but their "resistance" to crop rotation is bound to spread throughout the corn growing regions of North

Are the leaves of cultivated soybeans hairy?

Always! The dense cover of hairs on a leaf blocks leafhoppers, very small but very destructive insects, from getting down to the surface of the leaf and sucking sap with their piercing-sucking mouthparts. But the same leafhoppers happily suck sap from leaves that have been shaved by an experimenter. In the midwest, soybean varieties with hairless leaves do very poorly, seldom growing to be more than eight inches tall, while hairy-leafed varieties in adjacent plots grow to a height of 36 inches or more.

America. Two species of corn rootworms, the northern and the western, have each evolved its own unique way of getting around crop rotation. The eggs of some northern corn rootworms now survive crop rotation by not hatching in the first spring of their lives—by remaining in the hibernation-like state of diapause until the second spring after they were laid. In other words, they sleep through the winter and the following summer when soybeans are in the field, and do not wake up until the second spring, when corn has once again been planted in that field. There was always a tiny fraction of northern corn rootworm eggs that remained in diapause for two winters. When corn and soybeans were rotated, some of these eggs survived to produce progeny that carried the gene for diapausing through a second winter. But none of the eggs that diapaused for only one winter survived to produce progeny. Natural selection for beetles that diapause through two winters was intense, and they now predominate in many corn growing areas. The western corn rootworm is just now evolving the behavior of laying its eggs in soybean fields, despite the facts that the egg-laying adult beetles do not survive on a diet of soybean leaves, and that the larvae do not feed on soybean roots. These eggs will hatch the following spring, and if soybeans and corn are rotated, the tiny, newly hatched western corn rootworm larvae will find the corn roots that they require.

Is there a cultural control for **Hessian flies**?

There is a simple and effective one for controlling this pest of winter wheat—the kind that makes up about 80 percent of the United States' wheat crop. Winter wheat is planted in fall and harvested early the following summer. Hessian fly larvae, the only destructive stage of this insect, are most injurious to young plants in the fall. These pests cannot be reached by insecticides because they feed on the stem as they hide behind the sheaths of the leaves that surround it. Hessian flies lay their eggs on wheat plants in late summer and early fall. Wheat sown after that period of egg laying will not be infested by this insect. A "fly-free date," after which it is safe to sow wheat, has been determined for most wheat-growing areas. This date is, of course, earlier in the

Orange infested by parasites. (Photo by Edward S. Ross.)

north than in the south. In Illinois, for example, the fly-free date is September 18 near the state's northern boundary, and is October 12 at its southern tip, about 370 miles away.

How did an American save the **French wine industry**?

Charles Valentine Riley, one of the greatest of the American economic entomologists, suggested to French wine growers a way of preventing infestations of the deadly grape *Phylloxera* that had been unintentionally introduced from its home in North America. This tiny relative of the aphids, which forms galls on the leaves and roots of grape vines, had destroyed almost a third of the vineyards in France by 1885. Riley suggested that French grapes be grafted onto American rootstocks, which are resistant to the *Phylloxera*. It worked! The French wine industry was saved, and the French government awarded Riley a gold medal.

How was a serious **pest of citrus fruits** controlled in Israel?

This invading relative of the scale insects, a mealybug, was first seen in Israel (then called Palestine) in 1938. By the next year the infestation was becoming catastrophic and threatened to annihilate the citrus industry in Israel. Insecticides proved to be useless, and the only alternative seemed to be biological control. After the mealybug was identified to species—no easy task—it was known to be of Japanese origin. An Israeli entomologist was sent to Japan to find and bring back to Israel natural enemies of the mealybug. Several parasites were brought to Israel and tested for their ability to control the mealybugs. The most successful of the parasites was released in the field in 1940 and soon had complete control of the mealybug, as it does to this day.

Have insects been used as **biological controls** for weeds?

There have been several cases of this, but the most spectacular is the use of a South American caterpillar to control prickly pear cactus in Australia. Cacti, which are

How can laws control insects?

In medieval Europe there were laws against pest insects. They were actually brought to trial and, if found guilty, they were put under an order of expulsion. If that didn't work, the pest insects were excommunicated from the church. No one has tried that in a long time, but we do have laws designed to keep insects out of an area. These quarantines have prevented many new pests from being brought into the country. You may have had first-hand experience with such a quarantine if you ever entered the United States from Central or South America. You were probably asked if you were bringing any fruits, vegetables, or other plants into the country. If you answered yes, they were probably confiscated. These confiscated fruits and vegetables are sometimes found to be infested with pest insects that do not—at least not yet—occur in the United States. A grade school teacher from Florida, for example, wanted to bring in a jar of coffee berries from South America. They were infested with Mediterranean fruit fly maggots that might have started an infestation that could have cost millions of dollars to eradicate.

strictly New World plants, were brought to Australia late in the 18th century. They soon escaped from cultivation and, free of their natural enemies, which had been left behind in North and South America, they began to spread widely. By 1925, a species of prickly pear cactus covered about 94,000 square miles of Australia, an area almost twelve times the size of New Jersey. All of this land was practically useless, and about half of it was so densely overgrown that it was literally impenetrable. Cactus-feeding insects from the New World were introduced in 1923 in an attempt to control the rampant prickly pears. It worked. By far, the most effective of these insects was the caterpillar of a moth aptly named *Cactoblastis*. By 1937, these insects had destroyed the last dense stand of prickly pears in Australia. To this day, the prickly pears, held in check mainly by *Cactoblastis,* grow only in scattered clumps as they do in the New World, and cattle, sheep, and kangaroos now live on once useless land.

Are there **laws** that control the use of insecticides?

Yes. These laws are expressed on the labels on insecticide containers. The labels state the contents of the container and specify the crops on which it may be used, the recommended rate of application, and how soon it is safe to harvest a crop to which the insecticide has been applied. Unfortunately, these laws are not always obeyed. For example, in 1984 growers in California illegally used an insecticide called aldicarb on watermelons. This resulted in eight deaths and 1,350 illnesses.

THE DOWNSIDE OF INSECTICIDES

Are insecticides a **mixed blessing**?

They certainly are. On the one hand, insecticides can be powerful tools for protecting people against insect-transmitted diseases and for reducing the loss of crop yield to insects. We have become dependent upon the modern synthetic organic insecticides and will probably become ever more dependent upon them as the human population grows out of control and agriculture races to keep up with the increasing demand for food—a race that must ultimately be lost unless we manage to curb runaway population growth. On the other hand, the unwise use of insecticides, unfortunately the general rule rather than the exception, has unwelcome side effects that are often very serious and sometimes catastrophic. Paradoxical as it may seem, the use of insecticides can aggravate insect problems. It may cause the population of the target insect to resurge above pretreatment levels, and it may elevate formerly innocuous insects to full pest status. The overuse of insecticides also accelerates the rate at which insects become resistant to them. Insecticides often have undesirable ecological effects such as polluting the environment and killing or even extirpating nontarget animals such as birds or pollinating insects. Insecticides can be hazardous to people, causing illness or even death. They are, after all, poisons, some of them among the most toxic of the known poisons. Insecticides may be having long-term chronic effects on people that have so far gone unnoticed. Some of them are known to cause cancer in rats.

What causes **resurgences of pests**?

They are usually caused by the very insecticides that are applied to control the pest. Insecticides are generally broad-spectrum poisons that kill not only the pest they are intended to control but also many other nontarget insects. Among the latter are parasites and predators that are natural enemies of the pest. Insect populations recover rapidly after the insecticide residue declines. However, the recovery of parasites and

Potato crop being sprayed with insecticide. (Photo by Edward S. Ross.)

predators must always lag behind the recovery of the insects that are their food. Consequently, the pest population, freed of its natural enemies, undergoes a resurgence, quickly rebounding to a high level that is often higher, and consequently more destructive, than it was before the insecticide was applied. Another application of insecticide may be necessary and sometimes several more as resurgence follows resurgence.

How do insecticides **create new pests**?

An insect that has not been numerous enough to do significant injury to a crop can undergo a population explosion after the application of an insecticide that does not kill it but does kill its natural enemies. The red-banded leaf roller, for example, almost never injured apples before synthetic organic insecticides were sprayed in orchards to control the codling moth, which, in its caterpillar stage, is the worm in the apple. The leaf rollers, naturally resistant to the insecticide used to control codling moths, underwent a population explosion because the insecticide did kill its natural enemies. Consequently, the application of yet another insecticide was required to control red-banded leaf rollers.

Is the **resistance of insects to insecticides** a serious problem?

It is, and it keeps getting worse. As of 1990, 500 species of insects and other pest arthropods had become resistant to one or more insecticides. Resistance to DDT, the first of the synthetic organic insecticides, began with the house fly. DDT, used widely by the military during World War II, was first released for civilian use in the United States in August of 1945. At first it resulted in miraculous control of house flies. The residue left after spraying the inner walls of barns seemed to kill all of the house flies, but actually a very tiny number of them did survive—individuals that happened to have an enzyme that converts DDT to a compound that is not toxic to insects. These few resistant flies were the sole parents of the next generation, and the gene for the enzyme spread rapidly. By 1946 it was apparent that house flies were becoming resistant to DDT, and by 1947 there were many house fly populations that could not be controlled with DDT.

What effect has resistance to insecticides had on **human malaria**?

Malaria was once considered to be the most serious disease of humans and is rapidly regaining that status. In 1955 the World Health Organization began a worldwide campaign to eradicate malaria by spraying the inner walls of homes with DDT, which left a residue that remained toxic for as long as six months and that was absorbed through the feet of the *Anopheles* mosquitoes that transmit malaria. For a time, the campaign was a great success, having eliminated malaria from 36 countries and reducing the number of cases in many others. But by 1986, 58 of the 60 important anopheline transmitters of malaria had become resistant to DDT and related insecticides. The eradication campaign failed because substitute insecticides were less effective and too costly to use. Worldwide, there are now 300 million to 500 million cases of malaria each year, and from 1.5 to 2.7 million deaths, most of them in Africa.

How serious have been the **consequences of resistance to insecticides** and the creation of new pests by insecticides?

In some cases they have been catastrophic. They were, for example, responsible for the demise of cotton growing in the Rio Grande Valley of Texas. In the beginning, the boll weevil, then the primary pest of cotton, was controlled by intensive insecticide applications. Resistance to these insecticides developed and other insecticides were substituted. Secondary pests, new pests created by the insecticides, became destructive, and yet other insecticides were applied to control them. The secondary pests soon became resistant to these insecticides. It finally got to the point that the cotton crop suffered heavy losses despite the fact that *18* applications of insecticides were used during the growing season. At that point, cotton growing was no longer profitable and it was abandoned in that region.

Why are **DDT and related insecticides** such pernicious environmental pollutants?

There are several reasons. First, DDT and related insecticides such as dieldrin, aldrin, and endrin are not readily biodegradable; they may persist in the soil for decades. Sec-

How dangerous are insecticides to people?

They can be very dangerous if used improperly. According to reasonable estimates, in the United States there are about 100,000 cases of insecticide poisoning and 150 deaths each year. The World Health Organization estimates that worldwide there are annually about 500,000 accidental poisonings and 20,000 deaths due to the use of insecticides.

ond, they accumulate in the fat of animals and become more concentrated as they pass up food chains. Third, they move all over the globe in air and water and are found hundreds of miles away from the nearest site of application. They have been found in fish caught far out at sea, and at one time 600,000 pounds of DDT fell on the glaciers on Greenland each year. Finally, these insecticides have serious or even catastrophic effects on birds and other wildlife. Bald eagles, peregrine falcons, ospreys, other hawks, and brown pelicans were totally or all but extirpated in many areas of North America. These insecticides have been banned from the United States and other developed countries, but they are still being used in many developing countries.

How did DDT affect **robins**?

It killed them. In many parts of the United States, DDT was sprayed on elm trees to kill the bark beetle that transmits the fungus that causes the Dutch elm disease, which was virtually eliminating white elms in many places. The DDT was applied at a rate that was thought to be too low to kill robins; nevertheless, dead and dying robins appeared in sprayed areas. Dead robins had large concentrations of DDT in their brains. They probably acquired some of it directly, but they acquired much of it indirectly through their food. Robins eat earthworms, and the earthworms in sprayed areas had concentrated in their body fat large quantities of DDT that they had ingested with the soil and fallen leaves from beneath the elms. The reduction of the robin population was disastrous. Robins that arrived in spring were all dead or gone by the end of June. Other birds were affected too. On the campus of Michigan State University, 49 of 77 formerly abundant bird species were greatly reduced in numbers or even eliminated.

Are insecticides concentrated in **food chains**?

They are—to a remarkable degree. An insecticide such as DDT or a related compound is stored in the body fat of animals, and is concentrated more and more as it passes up the food chain. Finally, the top predator in the food chain—an eagle, a bird-eating hawk, or a sea lion—acquires a very large dose that may be lethal or cause reproductive failures. This is exemplified by the food chain in Clear Lake in California. DDD, a compound related to DDT, was applied to the lake to control the pestiferous Clear Lake gnat. It was applied at the rate of 0.02 parts per million (ppm), enough to kill the aquatic larvae of the gnat but not enough to directly harm fish or birds. But the DDD was concentrated in the food chain to a level that killed bass and virtually wiped out the western grebes (fish-eating birds) that nested at the edges of the lake. The green algae in the lake, the base of the food chain, absorbed DDD from the water and concentrated it to about 10 ppm in their bodies. Herbivorous fish ate the algae and other plankton and accumulated 900 ppm in their bodies; fish-eating bass then ate the herbivorous fish and accumulated about 2,700 ppm of DDD. The grebes, which eat a mix of fish-eating and herbivorous fish, had about 2,130 ppm in the fat of their bodies.

How do insecticides interfere with **reproduction by birds**?

DDT and related insecticides interfere with the deposition of calcium in the egg shells of birds, causing the shells to be so thin that they break when a bird tries to incubate them. Comparing the thickness of the shells of recently laid eggs with the thickness of the shells of museum specimens laid before the advent of DDT showed that the shells of recently laid eggs were indeed abnormally thin. Many birds that are at or near the top of their food chain suffered severe population declines because of eggshell thinning, among them eagles, peregrine falcons, American kestrels, ospreys, and other hawks.

MORE INTERESTING INSECT INFO

Why do entomologists write **dragonfly as one word** and **house fly as two words**?

This is a convention that distinguishes between true flies—the two-winged members of the order Diptera—and insects that are flies in name only. Among the true flies are house flies, black flies, and horse flies. Damselflies, dragonflies, caddisflies, and scorpionflies, among others, are not members of the order Diptera.

Do entomologists **perform surgery** on insects?

Some do, most often insect physiologists—not to relieve the insect of some affliction, but as a way of finding out how an insect's body works. The surgery is done under a microscope and usually with fine instruments that the entomologist makes himself. Even the scissors that ophthalmologists use to operate on human eyes look huge when you put them next to an insect under the microscope. Microsurgery has been done on insects as tiny as fruit flies and mosquitoes. One researcher, for example, transplanted a gland from the body of a male mosquito into the body of a female mosquito (the female survived!) in order to demonstrate that the gland produces a pheromone that the male passes into the female during copulation—a pheromone that curbs her sexual appetite and thus assures that he, rather than some succeeding male, will be the father of her children. Sure enough, transplanted glands turned off the sexual behavior of females every bit as well as did copulating with a male.

Can insects be **resurrected after death**?

The answer to this question depends upon how you define death. Is a creature really dead if it can be resurrected? At least one insect, the larva of a midge, *Polypedilum,* that lives in Africa, can be resurrected from apparent death. The larvae can dry down to a water content of about eight percent, far below the usual of 75 percent or more, and about the

What is the world population of insects and how much do they weigh?

Very few people have ever taken on the virtually impossible task of estimating how many individual insects there are in the world and how much they weigh. In 1968, Brian Hocking, then a well-known Canadian entomologist, quoted the estimate, actually an educated guess, that the world population of insects is at any given moment about one quintillion individuals—a very big number, 1×10^{18}, or 1 followed by a string of 18 zeroes. Based on this estimate, Hocking calculated that the insects of the world weigh about 27 billion tons, 12 times the weight of the then-current human population of about three billion. In the 30 years since Hocking made his calculation, the human population has skyrocketed to about six billion, and, assuming that the insect population has remained about the same, the insects of the world now outweigh us by a factor of only six times. You may think that this is a good thing because each person will have to put up with only half as many insects. But is it really a good thing? If the human population continues to grow, there will eventually come a time when there aren't enough insects to support us by pollinating our crops, aerating our soil, and eliminating our waste.

same as the water content of a dry, well-seasoned piece of wood. In this condition they are shriveled and show no sign of life. But when dry larvae are rehydrated by immersing them in water, they swell up, become active, feed, and proceed with their lives. Dry larvae embedded in dried mud revived after 39 months, and a few larvae revived and survived temporarily after being kept dry for 10 years. *Polypedilum* larvae live in temporary pools that form in shallow hollows in sun-beaten rocks. Suspended animation allows them to survive even when their habitat dries up, which often happens. They can even survive being dipped in liquid helium (-454 degrees Fahrenheit) for 77 hours.

Why are **dead insects** almost always found lying on their backs?

The answer is simple. When an insect dies its legs curl up on its underside. The curled up legs are not a stable base, and, consequently, the dead body rolls over onto its back, which is usually flat and is a stable base.

Is it true that most of the as yet **undiscovered insects are threatened with extinction**?

Tropical forests, especially rain forests, are the only habitat of most of the insects in the world, including the great majority of the unknown species It is a sad fact that the

Who was Charles Valentine Riley, and how did he save the California citrus industry from ruin?

Riley, one of the first of the great American economic entomologists, became the state entomologist of Missouri in 1868 and was later director of the Division of Entomology of the United States Department of Agriculture. He had many claims to fame, but many think that the greatest was the control of the imported cottony cushion scale in California; accomplished by importing a scale-eating ladybird beetle from the cottony cushion scale's native home in Australia.

tropical forests of Asia, Africa, and Central and South America are disappearing at an alarming rate as they are cleared to serve as pastures or croplands. At the present rate of destruction, almost all of these forests will be gone by the year 2040, and millions of unknown species of plants, insects, and other animals will disappear with them.

What is the world's **most beautiful insect**?

There are so many outstandingly beautiful insects, particularly among the butterflies, moths, and beetles, that it is probably not possible to get general agreement on this question. But many would vote for the Madagascar Croecus moth, *Chrysiridia madagascariensis,* a large day-flying moth of the family Uraniidae with a wingspan of over three and a half inches. The hind wings have triple tails, and the unique structure of its scales produces an iridescent brilliance that is unsurpassed by any insect. The wings, bordered with brilliant white, are a shimmering black, interspersed with lustrous golden-green bands and areas of brilliantly iridescent blues, yellows, and purplish reds. (See color insert.)

What is the **longest insect** in the world?

According to the 1997 edition of the *Guinness Book of Records,* it is a walkingstick from Borneo. The body of a specimen in the British Museum of Natural History in London is 12.9 inches long. Its total length, including the legs, is 20 inches.

What is the **heaviest insect** in the world?

The goliath beetles of equatorial Africa are surely the bulkiest of the insects. Many of them are over four inches long, and according to *The Guinness Book of Records,* weigh close to a quarter of a pound, up to 3.5 ounces.

Walkingstick. (Photo by Edward S. Ross.)

What is the **smallest insect**?

This honor most likely belongs to the feather-winged beetles (family Ptiliidae), some of which are less than two hundredths of an inch long. They feed mainly on fungus and can be found in rotting wood and leaf litter.

Do insects **inhabit the seas**?

Very few insects have invaded the oceans and seas. There are oceanic midges (family Chironomidae) that live at depths down to 90 feet and may live in the canals in sponges. A few water striders skate on the ocean surface, often hundreds of miles from shore. They attach their eggs to floating mats of seaweed.

Why have **so few insects** invaded the marine environment?

The salinity of the water is probably not stopping them. After all, insects live in salt lakes that are much saltier than the seas. Brine flies, for example, flourish in the Great Salt Lake of Utah, which, at 22 percent salinity, is about 6.3 times as salty as the seas. The main reason why insects have not been successful in invading the oceans is probably that the crustaceans—an even more ancient group of arthropods—got there first and occupied the ecological niches that marine insects might have filled.

What insect takes the **longest time to complete its growth**?

It is probably the periodical cicada of the United States, which spends 17 years underground sucking sap from the roots of trees as it grows to full size. But under unusual circumstances, insects may live much longer. According to the *Guinness Book of Records,* an adult wood-boring beetle emerged from a timber in a house at least 47 years after the timber had been cut.

Do **birds** use insecticides?

Not exactly, but some periodically add to their nests fresh plant material that has insecticidal properties. Among these plants are wild carrot (Queen Anne's lace) and fleabane, whose ancient traditional name tells us that its insecticidal value has long been known. This behavior occurs mostly among birds that nest in cavities or reuse their nests in another year. They and their nestlings are more often plagued by fleas and parasitic mites, which survive the winter in their nests, than are birds that build a fresh nest each year. One researcher proved the value of insecticidal plants in an experiment with starling nests. From some nests he removed each day the fresh foliage that the birds had brought in; to other nests he added fresh carrot foliage each day. The results were spectacular! Nests protected by wild carrot foliage were infested with an average of 3,000 parasitic mites, but those not so protected were infested with an average of 80,000 parasitic mites.

What are **sloth moths**?

They are amazing insects that as adults live only in the hair of the two sloth species that live in South America. At one time it was assumed that they laid their eggs on the sloth, and that the caterpillars fed on the algae that grow on the sloth's hair. It was not until 1976 that it was discovered that the moth's life is actually much different. The moths do live and mate on sloths, but the larvae eat sloth dung. About once a week the sloths descend from the trees in which they live, hang from a vine by their front legs, and scoop out a cavity in the soil with their hind legs. They drop about a cupful of dung in the hole and cover it with leaf litter. Only then do the moths leave the sloth to lay their eggs on the dung. The caterpillars feed on the dung, and when they become adults, fly up into the tree canopy to look for a sloth.

What is **Spanishfly**?

It is the ground-up bodies of a certain blister beetle that, like all blister beetles, contains cantharadin, an extremely irritating substance that raises blisters on the skin. Spanishfly once had many medicinal uses and was considered to be an effective aphrodisiac. But don't try it: it is extremely toxic and can cause death at very low doses.

Periodical cicadas—nymph (bottom) and adult. (Illustration by James B. Nardi. Courtesy of Iowa State University Press.)

What is a **"tippling Tommy"**?

It is a small beetle that burrows in the wooden staves of wine or rum casks. Whether or not it gets inebriated on its unusual diet is not known.

Why do **mosquitoes** form swarms?

The swarm is a group of males hovering at a trysting place as they wait for females to show up. They dance up and down a bit but remain together by keeping a landmark below them in sight at all times, perhaps a rock, a signpost, or a plant at the edge of a pond. Females fly into the swarm but are immediately grabbed by a male who takes them out of the swarm to mate in the vegetation or some other concealed place.

What is a **woolybear**?

Woolybears, also known as woolyworms, are the large and very hairy caterpillars of tiger moths. They are often seen crawling across roads in autumn.

Can woolybears be used to **predict the weather**?

Some people think that they can, but this idea has no basis in fact. The color of a species banded with black and orange is said to predict the severity of the approaching winter. Folklore has it that the coming winter will be cold if the woolybear is darker than usual and has wider than usual dark bands.

Are some people more attractive to mosquitoes than others?

Keeping track of the number of times different people are bitten per unit of time has shown that mosquitos are definitely attracted to some people more than to others. This is almost certainly due to differences in personal body odors, but not much more than that is known.

Can you tell the **air temperature** from a cricket's chirp?

Yes. Since crickets are "cold blooded," the rate of their activities, including the rate at which they chirp, varies with the air temperature—the higher the temperature, the faster the rate. In some crickets, including the North American snowy tree cricket, the relationship between chirping rate and temperature is so predictable that it is possible to determine the air temperature from their calls. Adding forty to the number of chirps heard in 13 seconds gives a good estimate of the temperature in degrees Fahrenheit.

References

Abrahamson, W. G., Ed. *Plant-Animal Interactions.* McGraw-Hill, 1989.

Arnett, R. H. *American Insects: A Handbook of the Insects of America North of Mexico.* Van Nostrand Reinhold, 1985.

Askew, R. R. *Parasitic Insects.* American Elsevier, 1971.

Baker, R. R. and P. E. Dunn, Eds. *New Directions in Biological Control.* Alan R. Liss, 1990.

Barth, F. G. *Insects and Flowers.* Translated from the German by M. A. Biederman-Thorson. Princeton, 1985.

Bates, H. W. Contributions to an insect fauna of the Amazon Valley, Lepidoptera: Heliconidae. *Transactions of the Linnaean Society, Zoology,* 23: 95–566, 1862.

Bates, M. *The Natural History of Mosquitoes.* MacMillan, 1949.

Bell, W. J. and R. T. Cardé, Eds. *Chemical Ecology of Insects.* Sinauer, 1984.

Belt, T. *The Naturalist in Nicaragua.* Edward Bumpus, 1888.

Berenbaum, M. R. *Bugs in the System.* Addison-Wesley, 1995.

Blest, A.D. The function of eyespot patterns in the Lepidoptera. *Behaviour* 11: 209–256, 1957.

Blum, M. S. and N. A. Blum, Eds. *Sexual Selection and Reproductive Competition in Insects.* Academic, 1979.

Bodenheimer, R. S. *Insects as Human Food.* W. Junk, 1951.

Borror, D. J., C. A. Triplehorn and N. F. Johnson. *An Introduction to the Study of Insects,* 6th ed. Saunders, 1989.

Borror, D. J. and R. E. White. *A Field Guide to the Insects of America North of Mexico.* Houghton Mifflin, 1970.

Bristowe, W. S. *The World of Spiders.* Collins, 1976.

Brower, L. P. Ecological Chemistry. *Scientific American,* 220: 22–30, 1969.

Buck, J. and E. Buck. Mechanism of Rhythmic Synchronous Flashing of Fireflies. *Science* 159: 1319–1327, 1968.

Buxton, P. A. *The Natural History of Tse Tse Flies.* Lewis, 1955.

Carson, R. *Silent Spring.* Houghton Mifflin, 1962.

Chapman, J. A. Studies on summit-frequenting insects in western Montana. *Ecology,* 35: 41–49, 1954.

Colinvaux, P. A. *Why Big Fierce Animals Are So Rare: An Ecologist's Perspective.* Princeton, 1978.

Commonwealth Scientific and Industrial Research Organization. *The Insects of Australia,* Volumes I and II. Cornell, 1991.

Comstock, J. H. *An Introduction to Entomology.* Comstock Pub. Co., 1920.

Covell, D. V., Jr. *A Field Guide to the Moths of Eastern North America.* Houghton Mifflin.

Cowan, F. *Curious Facts in the History of Insects.* J. B. Lipincott, 1865.

Craig, J. B., Jr. Mosquitoes: female monogamy induced by male accessory gland substance. *Science,* 156: 1499–1501, 1967.

Craighead, F. C. *Insect Enemies of Eastern Forests.* U.S.D.A. Miscellaneous Publication no. 657, 1950.

Davidson, R. H. and W. F. Lyon. *Insect Pests,* 7th edition. Wiley, 1979.

DeBach, P., Ed. *Biological Control of Insect Pests and Weeds.* Reinhold, 1964.

DeBach, P. and D. Rosen. *Biological Control by Natural Enemies,* 2nd ed. Cambridge, 1991.

Dethier, V. G. *Crickets and Katydids, Concerts and Solos.* Harvard, 1992.

Eberhard, W. G. Horned Beetles. *Scientific American,* 242: 166–182, 1980.

Eberhard, W. G. *Sexual Selection and Animal Genitalia.* Harvard, 1985.

Edmunds, M. *Defence in Animals.* Longman, 1974.

Ehrlich, P. R. and A. H. Ehrlich. *How to Know the Butterflies.* Wm. C. Brown, 1961.

Evans, D. L. and J. O. Schmidt, Eds. *Insect Defenses.* SUNY Press, 1990.

Evans, H. E. *Life on a Little-Known Planet.* Dutton, 1968.

Farb, P. *The Insects.* Time Inc., 1962.

Farquharson, C. O. *Harpagomyia* and other Diptera fed by *Crematogaster* ants in S. Nigeria. *Transactions of the Entomological Society of London,* 1918: XXIX–XXXIX.

Feltwell, J. *The Story of Silk.* St. Martin's, 1990.

Fitzgerald, T. D. *The Tent Caterpillars.* Cornell, 1995.

Frisch, K. von. *The Dancing Bees.* Harcourt, Brace, and World, 1953.

Frisch, K. von. *The Dance Language and Orientation of Bees.* Translated from the German by L. E. Chadwick. Harvard, 1967.

Frisch, K. von. *Bees.* Cornell, 1971.

Gullan, P. J. and P. S. Cranston. *The Insects.* Chapman and Hall, 1994.

Hanski, I. and Y. Cambefort, Eds. *Dung Beetle Ecology.* Princeton, 1991.

Heinrich, B., Ed. *Insect Thermoregulation.* Wiley, 1981.

Heinrichs, E. A., Ed. *Plant Stress—Insect Interactions.* Wiley, 1988.

Helfer, J. R. *How to Know the Grasshoppers, Cockroaches and Their Allies.* W. C. Brown, 1972.

Hill, D. S. *Agricultural Insect Pests of Temperate Regions and Their Control.* Cambridge, 1987.

Hingston, R. W. G. *A Naturalist in the Guiana Forest.* Longmans, Green, 1932.

Hocking, B. *Six-Legged Science.* Schenkman, 1968.

Hölldobler, B. and E. O. Wilson. *The Ants.* Cambridge, MA, 1990.

Hölldobler, B. and E. O. Wilson. *Journey to the Ants.* Harvard, 1994.

Hubbell, S. *Broadsides from the Other Orders.* Random House, 1993.

Keen, F. P. *Insect Enemies of Western Forests.* U.S.D.A. Miscellaneous Publication no. 273, 1952.

Kettlewell, H. B. D. Darwin's missing evidence. *Scientific American* 200: 48–53, 1959.

Kogan, M., Ed. *Ecological Theory and Integrated Pest Management.* Wiley, 1986.

Linsenmaier, W. *Insects of the World.* Translated from the German by L. E. Chadwick. McGraw-Hill, 1972.

Mallis, A. *American Entomologists.* Rutgers, 1971.

Matthews, R. W. and J. R. Matthews. *Insect Behavior.* Wiley, 1978.

McGregor, S. E. *Insect Pollination of Cultivated Crop Plants.* U.S.D.A. Agricultural Handbook no. 496, 1976.

Metcalf, R. L. and W. H. Luckmann. *Introduction to Insect Pest Management,* 3rd edition. Wiley, 1994.

Metcalf, R. L. and R. A. Metcalf. *Destructive and Useful Insects,* 5th edition. McGraw-Hill, 1993.

Miller, J. R. and T. A. Miller, Eds. *Insect-Plant Interactions.* Springer-Verlag, 1986.

Morse, R. A. and T. Hooper, Eds. *The Illustrated Encyclopedia of Beekeeping.* E. P. Dutton, 1985.

Moss, A. M. Sphingidae of Para, Brazil. *Novitates Zoologicae* 27: 333–424, 1920.

Nardi, J. B. *Close Encounters with Insects and Spiders.* Iowa State University, 1988.

Newnham, A. The detailed resemblance of an Indian lepidopterous larva to the excrement of a bird. A similar result obtained in an entirely different way by a Malayan spider. *Transactions of the Entomological Society of London,* 192: XC–XCIV, 1924.

Oldroyd, H. *The Natural History of Flies.* Norton, 1966.

Opler, P. A. and G. O. Krizek. *Butterflies East of the Great Plains.* Johns Hopkins, 1984.

Opler, P. A. and V. Malikul. *Eastern Butterflies.* Houghton Mifflin, 1992.

Poinar, G. O., Jr. *Life in Amber.* Stanford, 1992.

Porter, G. S. *Moths of the Limberlost.* Doubleday, Page, 1912.

Richardson, R. H. *The Screwworm Problem.* University of Texas, 1978.

Roeder, K. D. *Nerve Cells and Insect Behavior.* Harvard, 1963.

Romoser, W. S. and J. G. Stoffolano, Jr. *The Science of Entomology.* McGraw-Hill, 1998.

Ross, H. H., C. A. Ross, and J. R. P. Ross. *A Textbook of Entomology,* 4th edition. Wiley, 1982.

Rothschild, M. *Dear Lord Rothschild.* Balaban, 1983.

Rothschild, M. and T. Clay. *Fleas, Flukes and Cuckoos.* Collins, 1952.

Rousch, R. T. and B. E. Tabashnik, Eds. *Pesticide Resistance in Arthropods.* Chapman and Hall, 1990.

Sandred, K. B. and J. Brewer. *Butterflies.* Harry N. Abrams, 1976.

Sargent, T. D. Background selections of geometrid and noctuid moths. *Science* 154: 1674–1675, 1966.

Schmidt, J. O. Hymenopteran venoms: striving toward the ultimate defense against vertebrates, in D. L. Evans and J. O. Schmidt, Eds. *Insect Defenses,* State University of New York Press, 1990.

Skaife, S. H. *Dwellers in Darkness.* Doubleday, 1961.

Smith, C. M. *Plant Resistance to Insects.* Wiley, 1989.

Smith, R. L. *Sperm Competition and the Evolution of Animal Mating Systems.* Academic Press, 1984.

Spencer, K. C., Ed. *Chemical Mediation of Coevolution.* Academic Press, 1988.

Stamp, N. E. and T. M. Casey, Eds. *Caterpillars.* Routledge, Chapman and Hall, 1993.

Stehr, F. W. *Immature Insects,* Volumes I and II. Kendall/Hunt, 1987.

Stokes, D. W. *A Guide to Nature in Winter.* Little, Brown, 1976.

Swan, L. A. and C. S. Papp. *The Common Insects of North America.* Harper and Row, 1972.

Thornhill, R. and J. Alcock. *The Evolution of Insect Mating Systems.* Harvard, 1983.

Tinbergen, N. *The Animal in Its World: Explorations of an Ethologist.* Vol. 1, Field Studies. Harvard, 1972.

Treat, A. E. *Mites of Moths and Butterflies.* Cornell, 1975.

Urquhart, E. A. *The Monarch Butterfly.* Toronto, 1960.

Usinger, R. L. *Monograph of the Cimicidae (Hemiptera-Heteoptera).* Entomological Society of America, 1966.

Uvarov, B. P. *Locusts and Grasshoppers.* Imperial Bureau of Entomology, 1928.

van Tyne, J. A cardinal's, Richmondena cardinalis, choice of food for adult and for young. *Auk* 68: 110, 1951.

Villiard, P. *Moths and How to Rear Them.* Funk and Wagnalls, 1969.

Waldbauer, G. P. *Insects through the Seasons.* Harvard, 1996.

Waldbauer, G. P. *The Birder's Bug Book.* Harvard, 1998.

Waldbauer, G. P. and S. Friedman. Self selection of optimal diets by insects. *Annual Review of Entomology* 36: 43–63, 1990.

Wargo, J. *Our Children's Toxic Legacy.* Yale University Press, 1996.

Waterhouse, D. F. The biological control of dung. *Scientific American,* 230: 100–107, 1974.

West, L. S. *The Housefly.* Comstock Publishing Company, 1951.

Wheeler, W. M. *Ants.* Columbia, 1910.

Wheeler, W. M. *Social Life among the Insects.* Harcourt, Brace, 1923.

Wickler, W. *Mimicry in Plants and Animals,* Translated from German by R. D. Martin. McGraw-Hill, 1968.

Wigglesworth, V. B. *The Life of Insects.* New American Library, 1964.

Wigglesworth, V. B. *The Principles of Insect Physiology,* 7th edition. Chapman and Hall, 1972.

Wilson, E. O. *The Insect Societies.* Harvard, 1971.

Wilson, E. O. *Sociobiology.* Harvard, 1975.

Wilson, E. O. *The Diversity of Life.* W. W. Norton, 1992.

Wilson, E. O. *Naturalist.* Warner Books, 1995.

Winston, M. L. *Killer Bees: The Africanized Honey Bee in the Americas.* Harvard, 1992.

Xerces Society. *Butterfly Gardening.* Sierra Club Books, 1990.

Zinsser, H. *Rats, Lice and History.* Little, Brown, 1935.

Index

B

C

E

F

G

H

I

J

K

L

M

N

O

Q

R

S

T

U